# JAMES MONROE

*Contested Boundaries*

DISCARD

UNIVERSITY PRESS OF FLORIDA

Florida A&M University, Tallahassee
Florida Atlantic University, Boca Raton
Florida Gulf Coast University, Ft. Myers
Florida International University, Miami
Florida State University, Tallahassee
New College of Florida, Sarasota
University of Central Florida, Orlando
University of Florida, Gainesville
University of North Florida, Jacksonville
University of South Florida, Tampa
University of West Florida, Pensacola

# JAMES MONROE

## A REPUBLICAN CHAMPION

BROOK POSTON

University Press of Florida
Gainesville · Tallahassee · Tampa · Boca Raton
Pensacola · Orlando · Miami · Jacksonville · Ft. Myers · Sarasota

Library of Congress Cataloging-in-Publication Data
Names: Poston, Brook Carl, author.
Title: James Monroe : a Republican champion / Brook Poston.
Other titles: Contested boundaries.
Description: Gainesville : University Press of Florida, 2019. | Series:
    Contested boundaries | Includes bibliographical references and index.
Identifiers: LCCN 2018018786 | ISBN 9780813056104 (cloth : alk. paper)
Subjects: LCSH: Monroe, James, 1758–1831. | United States—Politics and
    government—1817–1825. | Republicanism—United States—History.
Classification: LCC E372 .P68 2019 | DDC 973.5/4092 [B]—dc23
LC record available at https://lccn.loc.gov_2018018786

The University Press of Florida is the scholarly publishing agency for the State University System
of Florida, comprising Florida A&M University, Florida Atlantic University, Florida Gulf Coast
University, Florida International University, Florida State University, New College of Florida,
University of Central Florida, University of Florida, University of North Florida, University of
South Florida, and University of West Florida.

University Press of Florida
2046 NE Waldo Road
Suite 2100
Gainesville, FL 32609
http://upress.ufl.edu

To the memory of Helmut Proepper,
whose stories stoked my love of the past

# CONTENTS

# ACKNOWLEDGMENTS

I would like to thank the following people for their assistance in making this book a reality:

My wife, Kalen Poston. I don't have the time or space here to thank you enough for everything, but convincing me to leave the law and do something I loved led me to this. I could not have done any of this without you, and I might not even have tried.

My kids, Ben and Leah Poston. I love to write, but my favorite part is after I've finished a weekend afternoon alone at the office to come home and see the two of you to talk *Star Wars* with Ben and do silly voices with Leah.

The SFA History Department. Thank you for the support you've offered over the years, especially Steve Taaffe and Paul Sandul, who were kind enough to read this book in manuscript form, and to Mark Barringer, who as our department chair guided me through my first years as a college professor.

Dr. Gene Smith. Thank you for pushing me to finish my PhD, get a job, and get this book published. You've always been my greatest advocate in this profession.

Sue Poston, my mom and lifelong editor. Thank you for always listening.

Joe Poston, my dad. Thank you for introducing me to the *Lord of the Rings* books as a child, which were my gateway to real history.

Alex and Elise Poston, my brother and sister. Thank you for all the movie quotes, and the aforementioned silly voices.

My wife's parents, Frank and Beth Fisher, and my grandparents, Lloyd and June Poston and Helmut and Helen Proepper.

# INTRODUCTION

Our Revolution forms the most important epoch in the history of mankind.

JAMES MONROE

IN AUGUST 1794, a crowd of Parisians surrounded a young American diplomat on his way to the Tuileries Palace to address the French National Convention (the French legislature). The man working his way through the throng of French revolutionaries was future president of the United States James Monroe, the newly appointed American minister to the French Republic. The French mob had brought down Louis XVI, Marie Antoinette, and Maximilien Robespierre in recent months, but when they saw Monroe, they cheered him as a symbol of the revolutionary struggle. It was one of the most thrilling moments in Monroe's life. France had been the United States' key ally during the war against Great Britain a decade before, but more importantly for Monroe, it was a fellow republic. Beginning in 1789 the French had undertaken a revolution, overthrown their ancient monarchy, and declared themselves a republic, all while following in the footsteps of their American allies. When Monroe arrived at the palace and addressed the members of the National Convention, he assured them that the French and American republics would stand together against their common enemies.

But not all Americans agreed with Monroe. France was at war with much of monarchial Europe, including Great Britain, where Monroe's fellow American revolutionary John Jay was, at that moment, negotiating a treaty with the former mother country. Monroe's glowing praise of France horrified Jay and his fellow Federalists back in the United States. They feared that Monroe was implying that the United States would enter the conflict between France and Great Britain, despite President George Washington's Neutrality Proclamation of the year before.

Monroe knew his speech would cause strife, but he did not care. This was his opportunity to help spread the republican experiment abroad. If he had to irritate Jay and his "monarchist" friends, it was a price worth paying. Monroe believed that extending the boundaries of republicanism was among the most important causes in human history, and he hoped history would note the role he played in helping it spread to France.[1]

Unfortunately, few Americans remember Monroe's efforts in France. In fact, most Americans hardly remember him at all, certainly not the way they do Thomas Jefferson or George Washington. Monroe's famous contemporaries cast a massive shadow over his life, and even his death. Many students of history recall the peculiar circumstances surrounding the deaths of John Adams and Thomas Jefferson. After a half century as friends, correspondents, and rivals, the two revolutionaries both died exactly fifty years to the day of the signing of the Declaration of Independence. On that day, July 4, 1826, Adams famously uttered his last words, "Jefferson survives," not knowing that the "sage of Monticello" had died only hours earlier. Since then, Americans have marveled at the symmetry of these two American founders dying on the nation's fiftieth birthday. John Quincy Adams, then president and the eldest son of John Adams, spoke for many Americans when he called this coincidence a "mark" of the country's "divine favor." Conversely, almost no one remembers that Monroe died exactly five years later, on July 4, 1831, the fifty-fifth anniversary of the nation's birth. As they did during his life, Monroe's more illustrious colleagues overshadowed him in death.[2]

At first glance, it is unclear why Americans neglect Monroe. A brief introduction to his life reveals that this oft-forgotten American founder was always at the heart of the most important political events of the era. Indeed, his career holds up beside those of even the most decorated leaders in U.S. history. Monroe came of age during the American Revolution, when at eighteen years of age he fought with George Washington and received a wound at the Battle of Trenton on an icy Christmas night in

1776. He served in the Confederation Congress during the so-called critical period of the 1780s, and then opposed the Constitution at the Virginia Ratification Convention. During the nation's first elections under the new constitution, he waged a famous campaign against his friend James Madison for one of Virginia's seats in the House of Representatives.

Monroe went on to play a key role during the political struggles of the 1790s as a member of the growing Democratic-Republican opposition. Elected a senator from Virginia in 1791, he led the opposition to Alexander Hamilton's political program in the Senate, while Madison led the Republicans in the House. Immediately thereafter, from 1794 to 1797, he served as the U.S. minister to the French Republic, and, upon his return from Paris, won election as governor of Virginia in 1799. After Jefferson won the presidency in 1800, Monroe played a prominent role within the third president's administration, especially in foreign affairs. Jefferson first sent Monroe back to France to negotiate the purchase of the Louisiana Territory from Napoleon Bonaparte in 1803. Later, Monroe served as a diplomat in both Britain and Spain before returning home to become secretary of state in 1811 under President Madison. Monroe entered the cabinet as the fourth president's right-hand man just as the United States and Great Britain careened toward war. During the War of 1812, Monroe even headed the Departments of War and State simultaneously for a brief period.

In 1816, Monroe achieved the pinnacle of American political success when Americans elected him as their fifth president. Monroe's two-term presidency saw its share of successes. During his famous tour of New England, even his Federalist opponents greeted him warmly, and one newspaper called his administration the beginning of an "era of good feelings," with the apparent death of party strife.[3] Monroe's administration also acquired Florida, extended America's claim to a border on the Pacific, and helped broker the Missouri Compromise. Finally, after a near unanimous reelection he created the document that later became known as the Monroe Doctrine, undoubtedly his most famous accomplishment. The sheer breadth of Monroe's resume is nearly unmatched in American politics, yet history rarely remembers him as anything other than a bit player among the founders.

For most people it is enough if friends and family remember them fondly after they die, but for others a grander audience beckons. Politicians in particular usually hope that some great accomplishment during their careers will ensure their place in history. They want to leave a legacy. Most American presidents have considered their historical legacies while in office. Abraham Lincoln, often credited as the greatest U.S. president, was keenly aware that history would judge the way he handled the issue of slavery. A popular Lincoln anecdote illustrates the sixteenth president's concern for his legacy. On January 1, 1863, the Emancipation Proclamation sat on Lincoln's desk. The president twice picked up his pen and placed it back down without signing. In explanation, he turned to William Seward and told his secretary of state that he had been "shaking hands all morning." Lincoln knew that "if my name ever goes into history, it will be for this act, and my whole soul is in it. If my hand trembles when I sign the proclamation, all who examine the document after will say: 'he hesitated.'" Lincoln then took a moment and again picked up the pen, understanding that his decision to sign the Emancipation Proclamation would shape his legacy forever.[4]

Modern presidents are no different. George W. Bush recognized that he would be remembered, one way or another, for his response to the events of September 11, 2001. Though he faced staunch opposition and low approval numbers for his actions in Iraq and Afghanistan, Bush maintained that history would judge his actions less harshly than did his contemporary critics.[5] Barack Obama once told historian Doris Kearns Goodwin that he had "no desire to be one of those presidents who are just on the list." From the moment he entered office Obama knew that he did not want to be a "Millard Fillmore" or a "Franklin Pierce."[6] Obama was right to be concerned. When Millard Fillmore traveled to Oxford University in England the school offered the former president an honorary degree, but Fillmore declined, fearing that the students might ask, "Who's Fillmore? What's he done?"[7]

While most American presidents have fretted over their legacies, no group in history thought more about the way posterity would judge their actions than did the founders. Though often viewed as a secondary figure among his more famous contemporaries, Monroe cared deeply about the way history would judge his actions. This work examines Monroe's efforts to construct his historical legacy as a champion of American republicanism. In Monroe's mind, the American and French Revolutions had divided the world along a contested ideological boundary between monarchy and republicanism. He saw his legacy as intertwined with republicanism's boundaries. Whatever he could do to expand those boundaries would in turn secure his legacy.

Chapter 1 argues that Monroe saw American republicanism as unique, indeed superior to any form of government that had preceded it. In this, he was typical of his generation. The founders invented a new type of republicanism dedicated to liberty, and they believed that history would judge them on its success or failure. History would also judge each of them on what they had personally done to support the cause. For Monroe, this meant that he wanted not only for American republicanism to supplant monarchism, but also for history to remember his efforts in supporting the cause.

Where chapter 1 fits Monroe's republicanism within the context of the founding generation, chapter 2 focuses on his introduction to the American cause. Monroe's time as a soldier in the Continental Army, combined with his years apprenticed to Thomas Jefferson and his early political career, convinced him that the American Revolution was perhaps the most important cause in human history. During the war Monroe's fellow soldiers, chief among them George Washington, served as models for his own life. Upon the conclusion of his military service, Jefferson introduced Monroe to the intellectual side of the American cause. Jefferson instructed Monroe in the philosophy of American republicanism. Monroe dedicated his life to living up to the example of men like Washington and Jefferson by building his own legacy as a republican champion. It was also during this period that Monroe began his political career and decided to make his mark in the realm of foreign affairs, due in part to his experience as a member of the Confederation Congress. Monroe hoped to match his fellow revolutionaries' contributions to the cause by securing republicanism at home and helping to spread it around the globe.

Chapter 3 examines Monroe's first attempt to champion republicanism abroad. Monroe saw the French Revolution as a natural progression of the U.S. version. When the French embarked on their rebellion against Louis XVI, Monroe saw it as the beginning of a global movement toward republicanism. He saw the world increasingly divided along an ideological border between republicans and monarchists, and viewed France as the next battlefield in the conflict. President Washington, hoping to steer a middle course between pro-French Republicans and pro-British Federalists, chose Monroe to become his minister to France. Finding himself thrust into the greatest political controversy of the early republic, Monroe arrived in Paris during the summer of 1794, and spent three years there defending the French Republic from critics. Despite Washington's Neutrality Proclamation, Monroe publicly declared American allegiance to France and denounced the treaty John Jay negotiated with Britain as a betrayal of the cause. Monroe thought his primary role in France was to bring the two republics into accord by any means necessary, even at the expense of narrow U.S. foreign policy goals. Monroe believed that negotiating a permanent alliance between the two republics would secure his legacy as a republican champion. Instead, his actions infuriated the Federalists in power and led to Monroe's recall in 1797. For the rest of his life, Monroe believed that the United States had not done enough to support French republicanism during this critical period.

Chapter 4 looks at another defining period in Monroe's life, after his removal from France until his election as president in 1816. During this period, the contest over the republican-monarchial boundary shifted while Monroe's own personal ambitions evolved. With Napoleon's empire and monarchial Great Britain fighting for supremacy in Europe from 1800 to 1815, European republicanism was in decline. At the same time, Monroe's Republican Party had assumed power with Jefferson's election in 1800. These changes altered Monroe's strategy for both his career and for championing the republican cause. Monroe focused his efforts on securing republicanism in the United States while he ascended the ranks of the Republican Party. Monroe sought to acquire the power necessary to alter American foreign policy and cement his legacy as a republican champion. Jefferson sent Monroe to finalize the Louisiana Purchase in 1803, thus securing America's western border from Napoleon Bonaparte's growing ambition. Monroe's second stint in France, this time on Jefferson's behalf, produced far better results than did his first. Monroe manipulated the situation to ensure that he, rather than fellow diplomat Robert R. Livingston, received credit for negotiating the purchase and expanding the territorial reach of the American republic. After the purchase, Monroe tried unsuccessfully to secure a peace treaty with Britain to avoid the dangers another war with the mother country would pose to the republican cause, and perhaps even bring Britain closer to the republican side of the larger international contest against monarchy. When he returned to the United States, Monroe ran for president against his friend James Madison in 1808, because he believed that he better embodied the true principles of republicanism and could advance Jefferson's republican vision. During the campaign Monroe exhibited his growing political talents by taking the necessary steps to ensure that his relationship with Jefferson endured, thereby safeguarding his place within the Republican Party. This eventually facilitated Monroe's reconciliation with Madison and his eventual appointment as secretary of state in 1811.

Finally, during the War of 1812, Monroe helped lead the fight against Great Britain, while eliminating a potential rival for the presidency. American "victory" during the war preserved the republic from threats at home and abroad, and secured a final separation from Great Britain. For Monroe, the removal of Secretary of War John Armstrong ensured that Monroe would succeed Madison to the presidency in 1817. Throughout this period, Monroe worked to preserve American republicanism even as he developed a keen political sense that facilitated his road to the White House. During his presidency, Monroe used these skills to undertake a final act that he hoped would cement his legacy as a champion of the republican cause.

Once he achieved the pinnacle of American political success Monroe once again refocused on building his legacy by spreading republicanism abroad. Chapter 5 begins with a discussion of Monroe's acquisition of the Florida Territory and ends with his final attempt to secure his legacy through the creation of the Monroe Doctrine. During negotiations with Spain, Monroe used the full arsenal of his diplomatic and political skills to pave the way for U.S. acquisition of Florida and the signing of the Transcontinental Treaty, thereby greatly expanding the borders of the American republic. The doctrine was Monroe's message to the world that the United States supported the cause of republican revolution. Monroe took the opportunity to outline this new American position at a time when he believed the contest between monarchy and republicanism had reached a critical point. After Napoleon's defeat at Waterloo in 1815, several European monarchs created a "Holy Alliance," dedicated to quelling republican movements before another French-style revolution again drowned the continent in blood. Monroe saw this reactionary "concert of Europe" as a grave threat to the spread of republican ideals. Meanwhile, throughout Latin America, former Spanish colonies declared independence and formed their own republican governments. Rumors swirled that the Holy Allies might use military power to reestablish monarchial government in Latin America, just as they had done in Europe. Initially seeing the doctrine as a chance to use the British offer of cooperation as a way to build an alliance in support of republicanism around the globe, Monroe settled on supporting its spread to Latin America. Monroe saw the doctrine as his last, best chance to shape his legacy as a defender of the republican cause. He wanted his annual message of 1823 to be a signal to the world that Americans would support any people who hoped to throw off the shackles of monarchy and follow in the United States' footsteps by embracing the republican experiment.

For Monroe, the war between republicanism and monarchy was the greatest struggle of his time, and perhaps of all time. He wanted to make his mark on history, to stand beside Washington and Jefferson as one of the great heroes of this conflict. He was thus simultaneously engaged in two overlapping contests, one against old world monarchial forces desperate to stop republicanism's spread, the other against posterity (and his fellow republicans) for a prominent place in the history of that struggle. Throughout his life, Monroe hoped that helping to secure republicanism at home and expanding the boundaries of republican government abroad would be his legacy to the world, ensuring that succeeding generations would remember him as a republican champion.

# 1

*≻≻   ≺≺*

## The Celestial Cause

The best men ... choose one thing above all others—
everlasting fame among mortals.

HERACLITUS OF EPHESUS

Alas! That Heroes ever were made!
The Plague, and the Hero, are both of a trade
Yet the plague spares our goods which the Hero does not
So a plague take such Heroes and let their Fames rot!

BENJAMIN FRANKLIN

The great object is to promote the celestial cause of liberty.

JAMES MONROE

PRESIDENT JAMES MONROE was worried. Everything he had worked
for was unraveling. On the eve of his retirement in 1825 he could not
shake the feeling that his successors were poised to undo his generation's
accomplishments. Monroe agreed with Thomas Jefferson that the successes of the "generation of 1776" were being "thrown away by the unwise
and unworthy passions of their sons."[1] The symptoms of this problem
were clear to Monroe. His cabinet members were re-forming the political
factions he had personally tried so hard to destroy.[2] The political infighting was something Americans had not seen since the 1790s, and Monroe
feared that it would tear the nation apart. The president himself had nearly
come to blows with his treasury secretary, William H. Crawford, because
of the tension over the election of 1824. Further, slavery threatened to

divide the nation along regional lines, a prospect particularly terrifying to Monroe.[3] The Missouri Controversy, erupting as it did near the end of Monroe's first term in office, had, as Jefferson so eloquently put it, sounded as a "fire bell in the night" for Monroe and his mentor. As Monroe's presidency ended it was clear that the "era of good feelings" was over.[4]

In Monroe's mind the problem was simple. Americans were drifting away from the founders' political principles. Andrew Jackson and Martin Van Buren were forming the Democratic Party, effectively fracturing the consensus Monroe had helped build during the first three decades of the nineteenth century. As one of the founding Democratic-Republicans, the thought of his party splitting apart alarmed the last of the American founders. He and his fellow Republicans had worked so hard to save the country from the specter of Federalism that it would be a tragic irony for that harmony to collapse now that the opposition party was essentially extinct. Fortunately, Monroe thought that he might hold the key to getting the nation back on the right track. As his presidency neared its end, Monroe began writing a book that he hoped would help the nation rediscover its founding ideals.

This book, which Monroe titled *The People the Sovereigns*, has not received much attention from historians.[5] Monroe began work on the book in the last months of his presidency, though he had been wrestling with the ideas it contained for decades. Monroe worked on it until at least 1829, but he never finished the work, and it was not published until 1867, long after his death in 1831. *The People the Sovereigns* is a difficult read. Monroe's writing is often ponderous, and he provides few original thoughts on government.[6] This last apparent defect, however, was actually by design. Monroe was not attempting to outline his own unique political philosophy. Instead, as he explained in the opening sentence, his mind was turning toward "the principles of the system itself." Monroe's thoughts were fixed on the nation's "future progress," and he wanted this book to provide posterity with a clear picture of the founders' political philosophy. *The People the Sovereigns* was, therefore, not *his* ideology, but his generation's.[7]

Monroe believed that he was uniquely suited to reintroduce the nation's founding principles to the next generation. Monroe wanted them to understand the nature of the American republic. He believed that the founders had provided the perfect model for government, which future generations should strive to preserve. If Americans of the 1820s would return to these principles it would, Monroe believed, reverse the trend toward factionalism and possibly even halt the split of Jefferson's party. As he explained in the book's opening pages, Monroe had "witnessed our difficulties" at the republic's beginning, and knew that they had been "surmounted" by the "establishment of a new system of government." That new system of government was republicanism. The founders, Monroe explained, had created a historically unique American brand of republicanism built on liberty, and the revolution's success had depended on their dedication to that cause.[8]

For Monroe, the most critical thing about the American republic was its uniqueness. Monroe argued that the United States was unlike history's failed attempts at representative government. Monroe had this in mind when he chose a full title for his work: *The People the Sovereigns: Being a Comparison of the Government of the United States with Those of the Republics Which Have Existed Before, with the Causes of Their Decadence and Fall.* As he says in the opening pages, Monroe's aim was to "present in a clear light the difference in government between . . . the United States and those of other countries, ancient and modern." Monroe claimed that the "disastrous" problems other governments faced "do not exist . . . and are inapplicable" to the United States. Monroe spent most of his book outlining exactly how the founders had surpassed their republican predecessors.[9]

Monroe knew that many would see the American republic as simply following in the footsteps of the ancient Greeks and Romans, and there are several links between the United States and its ancient republican predecessors. The founders did make the somewhat peculiar decision to create a republic in a world surrounded by monarchies, and they certainly admired the classics. They read Cicero, Aristotle, and Plato voraciously, copied Roman architecture, and adopted classical pseudonyms when they waged their famous pamphlet wars.[10] In Monroe's mind, however, there was one fundamental difference between his republic and those that had come before. In the ancient, or classical, republics no separation existed between state and society. In other words, they were one and the same.[11] Politics, therefore, dominated life nearly to the exclusion of any other material interest, and in order to foster loyalty and civic pride the classical republics stressed political over personal liberty.[12] This meant that in ancient Greece and Rome, as Aristotle pointed out, "the state is by nature clearly prior to the individual."[13] In a classical republic citizens had no rights other than those granted by the state, and it was here where Monroe thought they diverged from the United States. Monroe and his contemporaries were fundamentally opposed to the ancient republicans on the relationship between politics and society.[14] They did not envision an all-encompassing role for the state in the American republic. Monroe and the American founders viewed government and society as distinct entities, and because of this fundamental difference they rejected classical republicanism as a basis for their government.[15]

Monroe spent a lot of time in *The People the Sovereigns* explaining the founders' reasons for rejecting classical republicanism. The ancient republics had made the mistake of "wedding" ultimate sovereignty with the state, and had therefore provided "no checks whatever on the government." Monroe saw this as "despotic."[16] A sovereign government could not effectively be held in check. Instead, its powers would expand indefinitely. There was, therefore, nothing to stop the ancient republican governments from descending into tyranny. The founders, according to Monroe, solved this problem by building a state where sovereignty remained outside the government, with the people.

Monroe highlighted the false comparisons between the United States and history's failed republics. Lamenting the "gloomy spectacle" the ancients offered to students of history, Monroe couched his distaste for classical republics in this very divide over government and society. Comparing the ancient Greeks' government to the American version, Monroe saw a wide chasm. In fact, they had so little in common that Monroe considered it impossible for anyone to compare the government of the United States with its ancient counterparts without "being forcibly struck" by the vast differences between the two "in all those circumstances which are most important." Monroe even dismissed the comparisons to Athens, the most liberal of the ancient city-states, because "so numerous and vital were its defects" that no one could draw any "unfavorable" comparisons "to our system."[17]

Monroe knew he was not alone in pursuing this line of thinking. *The People the Sovereigns* was designed to show his successors something that the founders had often expressed: that their government should not be compared to the ancient republics. Americans of the founding era on either side of the political divide often expressed disdain for classical republican-ism. Federalist leader Alexander Hamilton shuddered at the example set by the ancients in *Federalist* no. 9, "It is impossible to read the history of the petty republics of Greece and Italy without feeling sensations of horror and disgust." In fact, throughout the *Federalist Papers*, Hamilton blamed the ancients for saddling republics with their poor reputation in the late eighteenth century.[18] Similarly, Thomas Jefferson, Hamilton's archrival and Monroe's mentor, shared their dislike for ancient republicanism. He scorned Plato's political theories, marveling that the world had held Plato's "nonsense" in such high regard for so many centuries. Jefferson rejected Plato's republic ruled by philosopher kings dedicated to the public good, expressing his great relief that "platonic republicanism had not obtained the same favor as platonic Christianity."[19]

Benjamin Rush, the famous physician of the founding era, is a great ex-ample of the founders' most extreme rejection of the ancients. He thought that the United States had no need to consult the great Roman writers. Instead, "Shakespeare, Milton, Thomas, Pope, Hume[,] . . . and a dozen others more than fill their places." Rush wanted to eliminate the classical education that he and most of the founders had received. As he put it, hopefully half in jest, "were every Greek and Latin book (The New Testa-ment excluded) consumed in a bonfire the world would be wiser and bet-ter for it."[20] He then added, "Delenda, delenda est lingua Romana" (The Latin language must be destroyed, yes destroyed!) in an ironic homage to Cato the Elder's famous phrase "Delenda est Carthago."[21] Monroe's with-ering criticism of the ancients was just the first stage in explaining the unique nature of the American republic to posterity.

Unlike their ancient counterparts, Monroe and the founders believed they had successfully divided sovereignty from government, but the trick now was to ensure that government remained in check. For them, one of the greatest threats to republican government was individual political am-bition. Both the American republic and its classical forebears tried to find a mechanism to channel this impulse in a positive direction. The ancients adopted the concept of fame for the purpose of harnessing these selfish instincts. But just as they rejected the ancients' method of conflating the state and society, Monroe and the founders also adopted a different way of coping with human ambition. Before turning to the American republic's method of channeling man's self-centered urges it is necessary to first look at how the ancient republicans dealt with this troublesome issue.

The desire to stand out politically presented a problem for the ancient republics. These selfish passions could threaten the preeminence of the state, and the ancients realized that these desires could not be simply switched off. Thus, they placed great emphasis on the idea of fame. What they called "fame" resembles something close to public honor. Fame could be achieved only by "great men," such as statesmen or generals. Only those who undertook action that set them apart and lifted them above their fellow men could achieve it. The lust for fame goaded these men to become a force in history—indeed to "make" history by imposing their will on events.[22] Fame thus provided an outlet for these potentially destructive desires by giving ambitious men a conduit through which they could satisfy their selfish instincts.[23] The ancients wanted to harness man's self-interested desires to benefit the state rather than undermine it. Fame, therefore, emerged as a cornerstone of classical republican ideology, and its importance to the ancient world can be seen in the works of philosophers from both Greece and Rome.

Greek scholars often focused on fame. The pre-Socratic philosopher Heraclitus of Ephesus put it simply, "The best men . . . choose one thing above all others—*everlasting fame among mortals.*"[24] According to the Greek philosopher Xenophon, the "lust" for fame arose only in the greatest men, who sought to ensure their immortality. Plato went even further on this point in the *Symposium:* "I am persuaded that all men do all things, and the better they are the more they do them, in the hope of the glorious fame of immortal virtue." While many classical philosophers recognized fame as a driving force within the Greek world, others put it to more practical use.[25]

Fame held a fascination for more than just ancient philosophers. In the greatest of the ancient world's epics, Homer chose fame as a major theme for the *Iliad.* Fame, perhaps more than any other desire, drove Achilles to fight the Trojans. During the long siege of Troy, Achilles considered abandoning the war entirely. Achilles's mother told him that his life and memory hung on his decision. She told her son that he had two possible fates. He could either leave the fighting to enjoy a happy and long life back in Greece and forfeit any glory. Or he could stay, fight, and live forever in immortal fame. Achilles knew that the war would claim his life, but he willingly faced his death for the chance at immortality. Homer used Achilles's decision to highlight the power the lust for fame and glory could have on the Greeks.[26] What made fame most useful to the ancients, however, was not simply that certain men hoped to set themselves apart, but that it contributed something tangible to the community. Classical republics tied the winning of fame to service to the state, and in no place was this more apparent than in ancient Rome.

As they did so much else, the Romans appropriated the Greeks' love of fame, but they harnessed it to a degree hitherto unknown. While discussing the death of a soldier during the Punic Wars, the ancient historian Polybius illustrated how the Romans dressed mourners in death masks of the soldier's family, highlighting their service to the republic. Polybius explained that this guaranteed that "the *fame* of those who have performed any noble deed is never allowed to die." This would inspire young Roman men to serve the state unflinchingly in the hope of obtaining "the glory which awaits the brave." By glorifying death in the service of the republic, the Romans indoctrinated succeeding generations into believing that the honor associated with sacrificing oneself for Rome outweighed life itself. This mindset endured from Polybius's day to the republic's end.[27]

Perhaps the best example of fame's importance to the Romans can be seen through the life and works of Cicero. Throughout his long and remarkable life, Cicero played the part of both philosopher and statesman. He, therefore, offers keen insight as a man who considered fame from a theoretical level and actually achieved it in the political world. Cicero very nearly repeated Plato's thoughts on fame from three centuries earlier: "We are motivated by a keen desire for praise, and the better a man is the more he is inspired by glory."[28] He explained fame's importance to his fellow Romans in *The Republic*, claiming that the strength of the Roman republic came in part because of their ancestors' "eagerness for glory." In fact, fame offered sustenance for great men, and helped provide the mortar upon which the republic had been built, by tying past, present, and future generations to Rome. As the "New Man" from Arpinum put it, "the leading men of a state must be fed on glory."[29]

The ancients understood fame as a means for convincing individuals to subordinate their lives and achievements to the good of the polity. For the greatest of the Greeks and Romans this would result in lasting fame and a measure of immortality. But was this true for James Monroe and the rest of the American founders nearly two thousand years later? He knew full well that while the ancients fully endorsed the role fame would play in their governments, the founders were not convinced that the lust for fame could play a wholly positive role in their new republic. As a result, when Monroe outlined the American republic's guiding principles in *The People the Sovereigns* he, like his fellow revolutionaries, rejected fame.[30]

## The Founders and Fame

Monroe did not trust men who lusted after fame. As far back as the 1780s, during the Virginia ratification convention, Monroe ranked the lust for personal glory among the greatest of human calamities. "The causes of half the wars that have thinned the ranks of mankind," he explained in a speech, "are caprice, folly, and ambition." He went on to explain that these traits belonged only to a select group, "where the passions of one, or of a few individuals, direct the fate of the rest of the community."[31] As he wrote *The People the Sovereigns* several decades later, Monroe knew that most of his contemporaries had been equally uneasy with the role of fame in their republic.

Fame did not enjoy the same reverence during the founding as it did during the classical era. Indeed, the founders came to fear fame. While they admired certain qualities of antiquity's "great men," they also dreaded the havoc they could wreak. They occasionally praised men like Cicero and the younger Cato, but they also feared the rise of their own Julius Caesar. The founders believed that those driven by the lust for fame could as easily become tyrants as heroes. Indeed, even the most "famous" of the American founders condemned fame.[32]

Benjamin Franklin provides unique perspective on the subject of fame because he alone among the founders achieved a significant measure of it before the revolution. By 1776, when other American revolutionaries found themselves thrust onto the world stage, Franklin was already a celebrated figure on both sides of the Atlantic. Despite his own celebrity, Franklin feared and distrusted the role the lust for fame played in society.

In fact, he held a particular distaste for history's so-called heroes. Consider the following poem from *Poor Richard's Almanac*:

Alas! That Heroes ever were made!
The Plague, and the Hero, are both of a trade
Yet the plague spares our goods which the Hero does not
So a plague take such Heroes and let their *Fames* rot.

These lines sum up Franklin's view of those who sought fame. He made the same point in plainer language: "There are 3 great destroyers of mankind: plague, famine, and Hero. Plagues and Famine destroy your persons only, and leave your goods to your Heirs; but Hero when he comes, takes life and goods together; his business and glory it is to destroy men and the works of man." Franklin compared the "great men" of history with the greatest evils faced by mankind. He recognized that fame-seekers could destroy the fragile republic the founders were building.[33] Other founders shared Franklin's distrust of fame. In *The Age of Reason*, Thomas Paine called the *Iliad* "a book of false glory, tending to inspire immoral and mischievous notions of honor." Achilles may have been a fine example for the ancients, but he was no role model for a modern republican.[34]

This is not to say that the founders rejected political ambition, or ignored the judgment of history. They were every bit as ambitious as any classical republican, and they knew that history would ultimately judge their actions. But they nevertheless feared what the drive for fame could push a man to do. John Adams is an excellent example. Early in his life Adams saw little chance for achievement and advancement in colonial Massachusetts, and he worried that he would forever remain an "obscure fellow."[35] But, even at this early age, he recognized the dangers associated with the lust for recognition and glory. In his study of history, Adams wrote in 1761, he had discovered that most of the world's evils had spawned from so-called great heroes, whose "unquenchable thirst for superiority and power" drove them to seek after fame. A consummate student of history, Adams saw fame as a historically destructive force, tending to cause mischief for the rest of society.[36] In *The People the Sovereigns* Monroe agreed with Franklin and Adams, explaining that while ancient leaders had displayed great talents, most were of a "military character." He no doubt had someone like Julius Caesar in mind when he wrote this passage. Monroe wanted future generations to know that he and his contemporaries had rejected this kind of fame, where the dominance of men like Caesar had forever reduced the people to "a state of degradation and oppression." Instead, he and the founders had done their best to guard against the rise of this kind of tyrant.[37]

Perhaps the most troubling thought to the founders was the fear that some of their number might pursue fame with the same reckless abandon that the ancients had, thereby endangering their fledgling republic. For Monroe, and indeed for several of the most prominent members of the founding generation, Alexander Hamilton was thought to be a prime candidate for this kind of rash ambition. An illustrative example of this can be found in a well-known anecdote from the tumultuous 1790s. In an 1811 letter to Benjamin Rush, Thomas Jefferson, by then retired, relayed his version of a conversation with archrival Alexander Hamilton twenty years before. The year was 1791 as Hamilton and Jefferson were emerging as the leaders of the two major political factions within the new nation.[38] At that time the Federalists and Republicans had not yet become political parties, but Secretary of the Treasury Hamilton and Secretary of State Jefferson were discovering that they had very different visions for the future of the country.

Jefferson kept portraits of three men in his lodgings, and while attending a dinner there one evening, Hamilton asked his rival who they were. Jefferson replied that they were John Locke, Francis Bacon, and Isaac Newton, who made up Jefferson's "trinity" of the greatest men in human history. Hamilton, according to Jefferson, scoffed at this notion and boldly declared that Julius Caesar was the greatest man in history.[39] In his seminal essay arguing that fame drove the founders as much as it had the ancients, historian Douglass Adair claims that this story's significance lies not in the fact that Jefferson came away from the meeting convinced that Hamilton sought even then to overthrow the American republic, but in that it underscores that both men sought fame. Both Hamilton and Jefferson, according to Adair, applied the same standard of fame. Where they differed was only in the type of glory they admired. Hamilton identified with statesmen and soldiers while Jefferson admired men of science and reason. Each man therefore chose a famous figure upon which to pattern their lives, based on their own particular interests. Thus, according to Adair, fame ruled Hamilton and Jefferson alike.[40]

The gap Jefferson saw between himself and Hamilton, however, was far greater than a simple difference in the type of fame each man hoped to acquire. Consider Jefferson's choices for his great trinity. He did not select either an ancient role model or a political one, despite his own largely politics-dominated life. Instead, he chose perhaps the three most iconic figures of science and reason in the modern era. More importantly, it is critical to remember that Jefferson *did* suspect that Hamilton wanted to overthrow the American republic. Jefferson was writing twenty years after this alleged discussion took place, and was trying to prove to Rush that he, a modern republican, venerated modern thinkers, scientists, and philosophers, while his archenemy Hamilton, a tyrant in waiting, saw Caesar as his model. Jefferson was effectively making the case, retroactively, for his creation of an oppositional party to prevent Hamilton's ultimate takeover.

Jefferson feared that Hamilton harbored the same kind of reckless ambition that drove all the great classical heroes, Caesar most of all. Caesar had, after all, overthrown the Roman Republic. If Hamilton identified with a man like Caesar it would be natural for Jefferson to fear that the secretary of the treasury might have "Caesarian" designs on the American republic. Jefferson dreaded what the lust for fame might push Hamilton to do. If the treasury secretary used Caesar as his political role model it would mean disaster for the republic. Hamilton's actions throughout the 1790s only confirmed Jefferson's fears as his rival consolidated federal power, pushed for war against a fellow republic in France, and eventually placed himself at the head of an American army. Jefferson firmly believed that Hamilton's philosophy was built on "principles adverse to liberty, and was calculated to undermine and demolish the republic."[41]

Hamilton's opponents often mentioned his Caesar-like ambition. John Adams had his fair share of disagreements with Jefferson, but he agreed with the Virginia Republican when it came to Hamilton, whom Adams called "ambitious as Caesar." He warned his wife that Hamilton's "thirst for Fame is insatiable. I have ever kept my eye on him."[42] Hamilton represented a threat to Adams and Jefferson precisely because they thought he thirsted for the classical version of fame. What is perhaps most telling about the pervasiveness of the fear of fame in the founding era however is that Jefferson was almost certainly wrong about Hamilton. Despite Jefferson and Adams's fears, Hamilton did not admire Caesar, and he did not even fully embrace the classical idea of fame. He saw liberty as the primary object of government, and recognized that "a fondness for power is implanted, in most men, and it is natural to abuse it, when acquired." Hamilton particularly feared a certain kind of man who might seek fame and power through demagoguery. "Of those men who have overturned the liberties of republics," Hamilton warned, "the greatest number have begun their career by paying an obsequious court to the people, commencing demagogues and ending tyrants." Despite their many differences the founders almost universally believed that the quest for fame and glory could prove deadly to the nation they were building.[43]

Sharing what he saw as Jefferson's distrust of the arch-Federalist's naked ambition for classical fame, Monroe also quarreled with Hamilton, nearly fighting a duel with him in 1797. Monroe spent his career trying to keep men like Hamilton from damaging the republic in their quest for fame. But though Monroe and the founders feared the carnage the lust for fame might wreck, they obviously did not lack ambition. Monroe, in particular, spent nearly all of his adult life in public office of one kind or another. What distinguished his ambition from Hamilton's, or for that matter Caesar's, lust for fame?

Monroe had long envisioned a special role for statesmen like himself within the American republic. As early as 1791 Monroe explained that he and other like-minded "high publick [sic] servants" had to maintain their virtue. This alone would protect the republic from those enemies who sought to undermine it.[44] Monroe believed he could do this by dedicating his life to the creation of a republic built on liberty. Any political figure who did not dedicate himself to this cause meanwhile was suspect. Monroe thus saw Hamilton's thirst for power combined with his refusal to truly commit to American republicanism as a threat every bit as great as the ancient tyrants.

Throughout his life, Monroe believed it was up to him and the other "friends of free government" to protect the republic from its enemies. Only their constant vigilance had kept the republic from falling into tyranny.[45] Building a modern republic dedicated to liberty was a way for the founders to secure their legacies. If they accomplished this task, posterity would forever remember them as champions of the American republic. They would stand not simply with the ancient leaders of the past, but far above them. Men like Jefferson and Monroe could therefore spend nearly their whole lives in public office because they saw themselves as dedicated to creating this new American republic. For Monroe, the founders' "exertions in favor of liberty" were unmatched in the annals of history. Their efforts would give them more than simple classical fame, but would ultimately secure their legacies as champions of a new kind of republicanism: American.[46]

## MODERN REPUBLICAN LEGACY

The founders replaced fame by focusing almost single-mindedly on this new form of republicanism. Monroe wrote *The People the Sovereigns* to prove to his successors that their republic was unique in human history not because of its adherence to classical republicanism, but because the founders adopted liberty as the foundation for their government. Monroe believed that their "liberal" republic was of vital historical significance, and that the future of human freedom itself depended upon their experiment. This was the cause upon which he and his colleagues had dedicated all their efforts, and it came with an understanding that its success or failure would ultimately shape their historical legacies.

Monroe had long believed in the unique nature of the American republic. In a speech to the Virginia Ratification Convention in 1788 he explained his belief that "the American states exhibit at present a new and interesting spectacle to the eyes of mankind." As such, the classical republics could not provide a roadmap for the founders.[47] Their republic represented a complete break with the past. Thomas Paine's famous line from *Common Sense* says it best: "We have it in our power to begin the world over again."[48] Monroe and the other founders did not see a model for their new government in the pages of history. Again, it was not just the radical Paine who took this position. One of Monroe's closest confidants, James Madison, a far more moderate voice among the American founders than Paine, claimed that one of the very things that made the U.S. experiment worthwhile was that, while they studied the past, they had not suffered from a "blind veneration" for the ancients. Instead, the founders had used their own "good sense" and taken lessons from "their own experience." Monroe shared this sentiment with his longtime friend and colleague.[49]

The founders decided upon liberty as the foundation for their new government. In an essay on the new U.S. constitution, Monroe explained that he knew of "no analogy between the present case and any to be found in the annals of mankind." In the United States "men are equal" and their government had been created to serve "the common good." This new republic had been created by "enlightened minds" to protect liberty.[50] Such a thing was unprecedented. It had no counterpart in either ancient or modern times. After all, as Madison commented, in Europe "charters of liberty have been granted by power. America has set the example . . . of charters of power granted by liberty."[51] In the American republic liberty preceded and superseded government, and thus its importance to Monroe and his generation was almost immeasurable.

In *The People the Sovereigns* Monroe called liberty the "celestial cause" of his life.[52] Comparing the United States to the nations of Europe, Monroe is thought to have told his daughter, "Our country may be likened to a new house. We lack many things, but we possess the most precious of all—liberty!"[53] For Monroe, a government based on liberty had one goal: ensuring man's rights. Individual rights were sacred. A government could not deprive individuals of their natural, pre-political rights. In the American republic, unlike its classical counterparts, rights were derived not from the state but from God and nature. If a government impinged on the rights of its citizens it lost its legitimacy.

For Monroe, a government based on liberty was not merely unique; it was also perhaps the most important political accomplishment in human history. In *The People the Sovereigns* he wrote that "it has been often affirmed that our Revolution forms the most important epoch in the history of mankind."[54] Monroe was absolutely correct. The founders constantly stressed the importance of their republican experiment. George Washington, Thomas Paine, and Benjamin Franklin all called the American struggle "the cause of all mankind."[55] The United States represented a test case for this new kind of republicanism. If a republic based on liberty collapsed, the earth would revert to the tyranny of old world monarchy. If a government built on liberty succeeded, however, the world would be forever changed. This meant that, as John Adams eloquently put it, "objects of the most stupendous magnitude, and measure in which the lives and liberties of millions yet unborn are intimately interested, are now before us." The freedom of mankind literally depended on the success of the American republic.[56] Monroe wanted future generations to understand this fundamental fact. The founders, he explained, had created a government "better calculated to secure to the people the blessings of liberty, and under circumstances more favorable to success, than any which the world ever knew before."[57]

Monroe and the founders therefore had not sought fame in the classical sense through service to the state, but through the creation of a new kind of state altogether, one dedicated to liberty, and Monroe hoped that *The People the Sovereigns* would convince Americans of the 1820s to return to these founding principles. With that in mind he sent the half-finished manuscript to his son-in-law George Hay in 1829. Hay bluntly told the former president that he did not think the book would resonate with the younger generation. Instead, Hay suggested that Monroe write a history of his times. Rather than take offense, Monroe took this to heart and immediately began work on his autobiography. If the founders' political philosophy did not inspire the public, perhaps the tale of one man's dedication to the cause might. After all, his whole life had been devoted to defending the ideas he had outlined in *The People the Sovereigns*.[58]

While *The People the Sovereigns* was, in part, a reaction to the split of the Republican Party in the 1820s, Monroe had expressed these ideas consistently throughout his life. It was the culmination of Monroe's republicanism. He had made republicanism the guiding light of his life. At every major point in his career Monroe had expressed the same kinds of ideas that animated *The People the Sovereigns*. In 1788, during the debate over ratification Monroe explained that freedom had found "an asylum" in the United States that it could have found "nowhere else."[59] A decade later, during the French Revolution, he chafed at those who pointed to the ancients as proof that republics were more "turbulent" than other forms of government. These republics, he protested, had been governments of "men" rather than of principles, and thus had no relevance to American republicanism. The founders had created a more enlightened government, built on uniquely American principles, which had effectively avoided the causes of such "turbulence."[60] In 1806 while serving the republican cause as the American minister to Great Britain, Monroe told a friend that "the causes which have produced the overthrow of other republics do not apply" to the United States.[61] Even after Monroe reached the pinnacle of American politics he continued to express his confidence in the American republic.

When Monroe became president in 1817, he touched on the republican theme in his inaugural address. From the "revolution to the present day," he explained, the American system had operated under what "may emphatically be called self-government." The results for the American people had been nothing short of miraculous. Despite the great difficulties they faced, American citizens were "happy" and the country remained "prosperous." This, according to Monroe, owed to the "excellence of our institutions." American republicanism "contains within it no cause of discord" and "protects every citizen in the full enjoyment of his rights."[62] Four years in the presidency did nothing to dampen Monroe's belief in the importance and uniqueness of the American cause. In his second inaugural address in 1821 Monroe marveled that the United States had "shunned all the defects" that eventually "destroyed the ancient republics." Next, Monroe discussed the "defects" of these ancient republics, including their "distinct orders," the existence of a "nobility," and the problems inherent in being governed by a single assembly. All of these, he explained, contributed to the "perpetual conflict between the orders" found in other republics. This invariably led to "the overthrow of the government and the ruin of the state." Meanwhile, "in this great nation," Monroe claimed, "there is but one order, that of the people." The people elected representatives to operate the government in a "free, enlightened and efficient" manner. Thus the good sense of the American people had avoided the defects that brought down so many other republics. If Americans remained true to their principles, Monroe said, he had no doubt "our system [would] attain the high degree of perfection of which human institutions are capable."[63] Monroe even finished the Annual Message of 1823, where he created the Monroe Doctrine, with a comment on "the vast improvement" Americans had made in "elevating the character and in protecting the rights of the nation as well as individuals." As he had explained before, Americans owed this to "the excellence of our institutions," and Monroe hoped that Americans would continue "to adopt every measure which may be necessary to perpetuate them."[64]

As Monroe prepared to leave the presidency in 1824 he expressed similar thoughts in his last annual message to Congress. Continuing on a now well-worn theme he explained that "our institutions," unique as they were, marked "an important epoch in the history of the civilized world." Their continued success made the U.S. government "the happiest which the world ever knew." Monroe then turned to his own role in preserving these great institutions. He thanked the country for recognizing his long service, and for entrusting the presidency to him. Everything depended upon preserving American institutions in their "utmost purity." Throughout his career he had done everything he could to "preserve" the American republic and all its "blessings," in order to "hand them down to the latest posterity."[65] Monroe had always been mindful of his role in defending American republicanism. In 1811 he said to a friend, "My support of the republican cause . . . commenced at a very early period, and has been continued in every situation in which I have been placed. The same principles will animate and guide me through life."[66] As president, he said to another correspondent, "The effort of my whole life has been in support of the republican cause, and it will continue to be the object of my future exertions." As he sat to write his autobiography in 1829 Monroe decided it was time to remind Americans of his lifelong sacrifice for the cause.[67]

Whether it was his criticism of the Constitution in 1788, his defense of the French Revolution in the 1790s, his adherence to Jeffersonian principles in the first decade of the nineteenth century, his defense of the American republic during the War of 1812, his inaugural addresses, or even the Monroe Doctrine, Monroe had dedicated his life to the cause. After failing to ignite even his future son-in-law's interest in the founders' ideas with The People the Sovereigns, Monroe hoped that the tale of his personal dedication to American republicanism might help succeeding generations renew their own devotion to the cause.

As he began work on his autobiography Monroe thought the best way to instruct future generations was to use his own career as a model for future Americans. Monroe believed that the founders should be viewed by succeeding generations as "a school of practical instruction" in the "science of government" of which "history has furnished no equal example." Their model for running a government would instill "on the youthful mind those sound moral and political principles on which the success of our system depends."[68] Throughout his retirement Monroe was concerned about the future of American republicanism. When George Hay showed no interest in *The People the Sovereigns*, it was natural for Monroe to write his memoirs. He viewed his entire life as the perfect vehicle to coax Americans back to the republican path from which they had strayed. He firmly believed that posterity would judge him on his republican credentials. By that point Monroe saw himself as a champion of this "celestial cause," and hoped that posterity would agree. In fact, Monroe hoped that his service to the cause would ensure his place in history. His public life was ultimately a quest to leave his legacy as a champion of the republican cause, and the tale had begun long ago, on an icy Christmas night in 1776 on the Delaware River.

## Conclusions

When the retired Monroe sat down to pen *The People the Sovereigns* and his *Autobiography* the prospect of his political successors abandoning American republicanism was fresh in his mind. But the cause had inspired Monroe throughout his entire political career. He had fought for this cause against both foreign monarchies and even his own countrymen, like Alexander Hamilton, whom he saw as a man as obsessed with fame as Julius Caesar. Monroe saw his own career quite differently. To his mind fame-seekers like Hamilton and Caesar had done irreparable damage to republican forms of government throughout history. Monroe believed that his own ambitions had been directed in a more productive way, toward championing a new kind of republicanism.

Monroe saw American republicanism as having successfully divorced government from national sovereignty. The people rather than the government itself maintained ultimate sovereignty. Monroe therefore saw the people's liberty as sacrosanct, and to be preserved at almost any cost. As a result of this singular achievement in government, Monroe saw the United States as distinct from both modern European monarchies and the ancient republics. In order to ensure this government survived, Monroe believed, this new republic's leaders could not simply focus on their own fame, but had to channel their efforts to ensure that government did not encroach on the people's liberty. Unlike the ancient seekers-after-fame, the future of human liberty itself depended on their championing the cause.

Thus Monroe saw both *The People the Sovereigns* and his *Autobiography* as an opportunity to remind succeeding generations that the founders' dedication to the cause had ensured its success.

Monroe also wrote these books for another purpose. He wanted to stoke the people's memory of his personal commitment to republicanism. He recognized that if history remembered him at all it would be for his service to the cause. Throughout his life Monroe was not content to serve American republicanism in obscurity. He wanted to be remembered as one of its greatest champions. In this Monroe was in some ways as ambitious as Hamilton, if not Caesar, but he differentiated himself by his adherence to liberty. Monroe justified his own ambitions as a way to champion the cause. Yet Monroe's conceptions of republicanism did not spring into existence fully formed. They developed as he embarked on a military career during the Revolutionary War, and then a career as a statesman-politician in the 1780s. His education in republicanism eventually convinced Monroe that the best way he could both support the cause and build his own legacy was in the realm of diplomacy. Specifically, Monroe became fascinated with championing republicanism through various means, including securing and expanding American territorial borders, preserving the American republic from monarchial threat, and spreading republicanism to other nations around the globe.

# 2

## REPUBLICAN APPRENTICE

What I am at present ... or whatever I may be in the future
has greatly arisen from your friendship.
JAMES MONROE TO THOMAS JEFFERSON, 1780

MOST AMERICANS RECOGNIZE Emanuel Leutze's famous painting *Washington Crossing the Delaware*. This 1850 work shows a towering George Washington proudly standing in a longboat, leading a band of American soldiers across the icy Delaware River to a glorious Christmas victory over the Hessians at the Battle of Trenton in 1776. Fewer people realize that the man holding the American flag standing beside the general is meant to be a young James Monroe, at the time an eighteen-year-old lieutenant in the Continental Army, who suffered a bullet wound during the battle. Leutze's painting, which has since become one of the most iconic images of the American Revolution, was actually made in response to the European revolutions of 1848. Though Leutze's portrayal of the battle itself is apocryphal, Monroe would have agreed that he captured the spirit of the American Revolution. After all, Monroe believed that the revolution was the most important event in human history.[1]

James Monroe became closely associated with the American cause at an early age. He was born in 1758, and few records from his early life exist. In 1766, he watched as his father, Spence, joined the Virginian resistance to the Stamp Act.[2] Spence Monroe died in 1774, and James came under the protection of his uncle Joseph Jones, a prominent member of the Virginia gentry. Jones, a representative in the House of Burgesses, later served on the Committee of Public Safety that governed Virginia during the war. Jones was Monroe's first mentor, and with the loss of his father became the dominant influence during Monroe's formative years. Many years later, Monroe said of his uncle that "few men possessed in a higher degree the confidence and esteem of his fellow citizens, or merited it more, for soundness of intellect, perfect integrity, and devotion to his country."[3]

Jones brought his nephew with him to Williamsburg, then the Virginia capital, and enrolled him at the College of William and Mary in 1774. While at school, Monroe, still only sixteen, witnessed Virginia's colonial leadership move toward open rebellion against Great Britain.[4] Many Virginia leaders saw the British response to the Boston Tea Party, specifically the closing of the Port of Boston and the other "Intolerable Acts" as they were called in America, as a violation of the colonies' rights. As reports of events in Massachusetts came to Williamsburg in 1774, the Virginia leadership called for a day of fasting and prayer in order to, as Thomas Jefferson put it, "turn the king and Parliament to moderation and justice."[5] In response, Virginia governor John Murray, the Fourth Earl of Dunmore, dissolved the House of Burgesses. The members of the Virginia assembly refused to disband, and declared that the measures aimed at Massachusetts constituted an attack on all the colonies, thus pledging solidarity with the New Englanders.[6]

Events in Williamsburg made quite an impression on the teenaged Monroe. Like many students at William and Mary, he became actively involved in the rebellion. He took part in a raid on the governor's mansion during the summer of 1775. Upon learning of the governor's refusal to turn over a cache of weapons, a group of two dozen men, of whom Monroe was the youngest, stormed the governor's "palace" on June 24, 1775. They met no resistance and confiscated 230 muskets, 301 swords, and 18 pistols, and from that point on the revolution dominated Monroe's life.[7]

Whether through his father's lingering influence, his uncle's patronage, or his time in Williamsburg, Monroe reacted strongly to what he saw as British tyranny. As Virginia and the other colonies moved toward war, Monroe found he could not sit idle. During the spring of 1776, after only two years at William and Mary, he abandoned his schooling to join the Continental Army. Training for several months in Williamsburg, Monroe

departed to join George Washington's forces in New York as a lieutenant in the newly created Third Virginia regiment. Monroe arrived in New
York in September just before the British invaded Manhattan Island. He
saw action in a number of engagements during the fall and early winter
of 1776, but it was at Trenton on Christmas night where Monroe actually
shed blood for the cause.[8]

The Battle of Trenton occurred when General Washington, after weeks
of retreating from the British in the early winter of 1776, decided to strike
back. A detachment of fifteen hundred Hessian mercenaries occupied the
New Jersey town of Trenton. Washington's troops re-crossed the Delaware River on the night of December 25 in preparation for a counterstrike.
Monroe's own exploits at the Battle of Trenton were only slightly less dra-
matic than the famous scene in Leutze's painting. On this "tempestuous"
Christmas night Lieutenant Monroe accompanied a unit of fifty men
through "a heavy fall of snow" toward the Hessians.[9] Along this frigid road
Monroe's company met Dr. John Riker, who initially berated the soldiers
for occupying the path near his home. When he discovered that they were
American patriots, the doctor insisted on accompanying them because,
as he told Monroe, "I know something is to be done and I am going with
you. I am a doctor and I may help some poor fellow." That "poor fellow"
eventually turned out to be none other than Monroe himself.[10]

The American cause in large part depended upon the coming battle.
Losses at Long Island and White Plains, and the capture of Forts Washington and Lee, put the war effort in jeopardy. American morale desperately needed a victory. These were, as Thomas Paine wrote, "the times that
try men's souls."[11] Years later, Monroe echoed Paine's dire assessment. The
army's setbacks had, he believed, "put fairly at issue with the nation the
great question whether they [the American people] were competent and
resolved to support their independence."[12] On that day, Monroe showed
that he would not, as he put it, "sink under the pressure."

Monroe and his commanding officer, Captain William Washington, a
relative of the commanding general, led the advanced guard. As the attack
began William Washington, Monroe, and their men surged forward and
captured the enemy cannon just before the Hessians opened fire.[13] During the assault, Captain Washington suffered a wound and Monroe assumed command. In his memoirs, James Wilkinson, the nefarious future

commanding general of the U.S. Army, remarked that "these particular acts of gallantry have never been noticed and yet they could not have been too highly appreciated."[14] Victory at Trenton did not come cheap for Monroe. "Shot down by a musket ball which passed through [his] breast and shoulder," he would have died but for the actions of Dr. Riker, who "took up an artery," and saved his life.[15] Although the eighteen-year-old officer survived the battle, the wound troubled him for the rest of his life and served as a constant reminder of the cause.[16]

This marked the high point of Monroe's military service. Upon recovering from the wound, he returned to Virginia and during the next few months attempted, without success, to recruit men for the war effort.[17] Monroe then served as an aide-de-camp to William Alexander (the heir to a Scottish earldom who was known to his contemporaries by the honorific Lord Stirling). Monroe served with some distinction at the Battle of Monmouth Courthouse and spent the winter of 1777–78 at Valley Forge before returning to Virginia in early 1779 with a commission as a colonel in the militia and orders to recruit a regiment to command. Again, his recruitment efforts failed. While the rest of Monroe's military career paled in comparison to the excitement of his exploits at Trenton, it did reinforce his dedication to the cause. His interaction with the men who led the revolutionary struggle made a significant impression on the young officer.[18]

Monroe was awestruck by his fellow revolutionaries, who served as models for his career. As a staff officer for Lord Stirling, Monroe met men like Alexander Hamilton, John Marshall, and even the young French general the Marquis de Lafayette. In his autobiography, Monroe explained how he had become acquainted with both the officers and their aides, and came to admire their "talents." He believed that his own exploits during the war were unworthy of notice when compared with those of these men. "In the great events of which I have spoken Mr. Monroe, being a mere youth, counted for nothing in comparison with those distinguished citizens who had the direction of public affairs." The most "distinguished" of these citizens was George Washington, who left a particularly strong impression on the young Monroe.[19]

Though Thomas Jefferson ultimately became the dominant influence in Monroe's political life, Washington also served as an important role model. Monroe patterned his philosophy after Jefferson's, but during his career he also strove to emulate Washington's style of leadership. In his autobiography, Monroe commented on the impression Washington made on him during the war. He marveled at the commanding general's "firm," "dignified," even "exalted" attitude in the face of nearly insurmountable difficulties. He had "never seen" that level of dedication "in any other person." Monroe called Washington a perfect example of "integrity" and "fortitude." Most importantly, he praised Washington's tireless "devotion to the rights and liberties of his country." In this, the general was a republican the likes of which "neither Rome nor Greece have exhibited the equal." As the American republic's greatest champion Washington was, for Monroe, perhaps the greatest man in history.[20]

Washington is the one founder who might be said to have embodied the classical ideal of fame. Indeed, the terms used to praise him smack of classical republicanism. The revolution made him, like Cicero two thousand years earlier, "father of his country." His countrymen also called him the "American Cincinnatus," after the Roman farmer who was plucked from his farm to serve as dictator and promptly returned to the plow after defeating Rome's enemies. Yet even for Washington, simple fame was not the goal. He dedicated his career to preserving the American republic, making him a perfect model for Monroe.

George Washington demonstrated time and again that he understood his legacy. At the end of the Revolutionary War, Colonel Lewis Nicola urged Washington to seize power and proclaim himself king. Washington denounced the idea. Affirming his dedication to republicanism, Washington informed Nicola that he had presented his schemes to the worst possible person. He urged Nicola that if he had "any regard for your country, for yourself, or for posterity" to refrain from suggesting such a thing ever again.[21]

Two hundred years of stable American republicanism blinds modern Americans as to how critical, and indeed groundbreaking, such a decision was. When King George III learned that Washington planned to give away his power, he replied that doing so would make the former general the "greatest man in the world."[22] Washington understood that the greatest question of the age was liberty, and the ability of a republic to protect it. According to the first president it was the duty of every American "to bear in mind that his conduct will not only affect himself, his country, and his immediate posterity; but that its influence may be co-extensive with the world, and stamp political happiness or misery on ages yet unborn."[23] In Washington's letter surrendering his command of the Continental Army, he described himself and the rest of the founding generation as "actors on a most conspicuous theatre." He believed that the United States had been granted a better chance "for political happiness than any other nation has ever been favored with." He hoped that his actions and the remarks he made concerning the experiment would "be the *Legacy* of one who has ardently wished on all occasions to be useful to his country."[24] Washington recognized that by turning down the kingship and subordinating himself to civilian government, he took a major step toward proving that a republic dedicated to liberty could survive. In the process, Washington secured his own legacy as a champion of modern republicanism.

Washington's contemporaries praised his dedication to republicanism. The Marquis de Lafayette, one of Monroe's close friends, summed up the relationship between the general and the American cause: "Never did one man live whom the soldier, statesman, patriot, and philosopher could equally admire." More importantly the Revolution's success would "immortalize its Glorious Chief."[25] One observer nicely outlined the difference in how the founding generation viewed the kind of fame the ancients possessed with the republican legacy of a man like Washington: "How much stronger and bolder the claims of Washington to immortality! In the impulses of mad and selfish ambition [Caesar and Alexander] acquired fame by wading to the conquest of the world through seas of blood." Washington was different. For his countrymen he "stood forth, the pure and virtuous champion of their rights."[26] Lafayette agreed, calling his old friend the "Savior of his country, Benefactor of mankind, the Protecting angel of Liberty."[27] His aide, David Cobb, gave Washington the greatest praise imaginable when he wrote that "the United States are indebted for their republican form of government solely to the firm and determined republicanism of General Washington." Only through championing the American cause did Washington secure his legacy, and his example was not lost on Monroe.[28]

Monroe witnessed Washington's exploits firsthand. During a retreat from the British, Monroe saw Washington "at the head of a small band, or rather in its rear for he was always near the enemy, and his countenance and manner made an impression . . . which time can never efface."[29] Throughout his career, Monroe tried to at least approach Washington's exploits. Washington made such an imprint on Monroe that he even followed Washington's example during his own presidency. Monroe built a geographically and politically diverse cabinet just as Washington had done. He also, again like Washington, took a series of presidential tours designed to unite the country after a divisive war. But while men like Washington provided a model of behavior for the young patriot, others did not live up to Monroe's lofty expectations.[30]

As the Revolutionary War continued, Monroe began to question his fellow Americans' dedication to the cause. He criticized those whom he thought were shirking their duty in the struggle. He lamented that many of his fellow countrymen sat at home, "retired from the war & neglecting the cause." He raged when he saw how many of his fellow countrymen were giving "themselves up to domestic repose," rather than serving the cause. Like most Americans, Monroe recognized the right of men to enjoy their private lives and concluded, "Tis true that these men in a moral point of view do no injury." Still, Monroe believed that with "the perpetual freedom and Independence of an extensive Continent at stake, something more is required from good Citizens than barely to avoid moral evil." It infuriated him that the "best" men shirked their duty by refusing to support the cause that had nearly taken his life. This was especially true considering many of these "stay-at-homes" had led the country into the war in the first place. He felt the sting greater on his return home when he compared his own wartime service with the lack of resolve exhibited by his fellow Virginians. Monroe's inability to recruit troops for the war effort in particular frustrated the young colonel, and he was appalled that most of the men refused to defend the country without some kind of bounty.[31]

It appeared to Monroe that many Americans had abandoned the cause. In a letter to his company's commanding officer, Captain John Thornton, Monroe proclaimed, "The principles on which the war is carried on now is intirely [sic] different from what it was at first." This represented both an ideological and a personal affront to Monroe. His fellow Virginians' lack of motivation for the cause irritated him, and their cowardice deprived him of his much coveted field command. Yet Monroe's failure to secure such a post eventually turned out to be a blessing after he found himself apprenticed to Thomas Jefferson.[32]

When his military career ended in frustration in 1780, Monroe was still only twenty-two years old. He had witnessed his home state, led in part by his uncle, rebel against the mother country. He had achieved some measure of notoriety on the battlefield, having been wounded in service to his country. Yet up to this point Monroe did not fully grasp the ideas upon which the revolution stood. In many respects, Monroe fought for the American cause before truly understanding it. Prior to his apprenticeship to Jefferson, there is little evidence from Monroe's surviving correspondence that he understood the nature of the founders' republicanism. Before his association with Jefferson, Monroe described the "spirit" of the war in an almost militaristic fashion; highlighting classical republican characteristics such as honor and self-sacrifice. In the same letter complaining of his fellow Americans' lack of resolve for the fight, Monroe told John Thornton that "patriotism, publick [sic] spirit and disinterestedness have almost vanished and honor and virtue are empty names." Under Jefferson, Monroe learned that the revolution they were waging ultimately hinged upon modern principles.[33]

Thomas Jefferson's impact on Monroe's life was profound. Jefferson emerged as the guiding influence in the younger Virginian's political career. While it is probably too much to say that Monroe came to his mentor as a political tabula rasa, Jefferson did help mold his new apprentice into a modern republican. According to Monroe, his time at William and Mary had only laid "a good foundation" for his education. Jefferson built upon that groundwork by schooling Monroe in the liberal republican philosophy upon which the republic stood.[34]

Monroe may have met Jefferson in Williamsburg before the war but their close association did not begin until after Monroe left the army. After failing to recruit a regiment in Virginia, Monroe decided to put military life behind him.[35] In 1779 his uncle Joseph Jones provided Monroe with a letter of introduction to Jefferson, then serving as governor of Virginia in Williamsburg. Jones told his nephew that he "would do well to cultivate his [Jefferson's] friendship," because, as he put it, "while you continue to deserve his esteem he will not withdraw his countenance."[36] Jefferson, who adopted a number of protégés during his career, took to the young colonel immediately. He eased the professional soldier back into civilian life by permitting Monroe to study law under his watchful eye. While working with Jefferson, Monroe also reenrolled in the College of William and Mary to finish his formal education.[37]

Monroe's apprenticeship began after "a variety of disappointments with respect to the prospects of [his] private fortune" had "nearly destroyed [him]." Monroe was frustrated that his military career had stalled, and feared that his chances for advancement were slim. Monroe credited Jefferson with his salvation, telling the older man in 1780 that had they not met Monroe would have "retired from society with a resolution never to have entered on the stage again." Monroe recognized almost immediately how important his apprenticeship to Jefferson would be for his career. In fact, Monroe went as far as to tell Jefferson, "Whatever I am at present in the opinion of others or whatever I may be in future has greatly arose [sic] from your friendship." In Monroe's mind, it was Jefferson who set him down his chosen career path.[38]

Monroe's devotion to Jefferson is clear throughout his autobiography. In a book otherwise devoid of personal sentiment, an obvious fondness and attachment to Jefferson emerges.[39] While discussing his early years studying with Jefferson, Monroe gushed over the opportunity to read law under this "enlightened and distinguished patriot."[40] Monroe strove to prove himself to his mentor, assuring Jefferson that his "kindness and attention" had made the "proper impression." He remained forever grateful to Jefferson for his tutelage, of which Monroe told Jefferson, "[It] really put me under such obligations to you that I fear I shall hardly ever have it in my power to repay."[41]

One particular incident shows how important Jefferson had become in Monroe's life. When the Virginia capital moved from Williamsburg to Richmond, Jefferson asked his protégé to accompany him and continue his apprenticeship. Following Jefferson meant leaving William and Mary and foregoing the opportunity to study under one of Virginia's preeminent legal minds, George Wythe, who had recently taken a position as the college's professor of law. In many ways Monroe's decision to follow Jefferson spoke to his own preference for the future. Had Monroe decided to stay at William and Mary, he likely would have focused primarily on the law and may have become a country attorney largely forgotten by history. But following Jefferson meant pursuing an entirely different kind of career. Though Monroe was ostensibly "reading law" under Jefferson, his apprenticeship was designed to prepare him for more than the Virginia bar. Jefferson introduced Monroe to the Enlightenment.[42]

The hope men like Jefferson had for their revolution was tied up with the spirit of the age in which they lived. George Washington, who was among the least formally educated of the founders, understood that "the foundation" of the United States "was not laid in the gloomy age of Ignorance and Superstition, but at an Epocha [sic] when the rights of mankind were better understood and more clearly defined, than at any former period." This "epocha" was the Enlightenment.[43]

Historian Peter Gay, one of the foremost authorities on the Enlightenment era, provides this excellent summation of the age and those who lived through it:

> The men of the Enlightenment united on a vastly ambitious program, a program of secularism, humanity, cosmopolitanism, and freedom, above all, freedom in its many forms—freedom from arbitrary power, freedom of speech, freedom of trade, freedom to realize one's talents, freedom of aesthetic response, freedom, in a word, of moral man to make his own way in the world.[44]

Enlightenment-era thinkers believed that the movement represented a break with the past, and this idea went a long way toward shaping the founders' philosophy.[45] They believed that reason, observation, and science could unlock the secrets of the world. This was the age of Benjamin Franklin, his kite and key—Isaac Newton and his apple. Science and reason, the founders believed, were rapidly replacing superstition. Further, the universal principles of nature could be discovered through observation and experiment.

Enlightenment thinkers believed that reason had virtually no limitation, and this held true for political theory as well as scientific. Just as Newton and Franklin had unlocked the secrets of gravity and electricity, the founders believed, they could uncover the science behind government, or, to paraphrase David Hume, reduce politics to a science. They pored over the histories of the ancient republics to discover how and why they failed. They read diligently from Locke, Hume, and Montesquieu to find the theory behind government, and it was this world through which Jefferson guided Monroe.[46]

Monroe embarked on a course of study that taught him the revolution's core Enlightenment-inspired principles. Though often dismissed as a practical politician uninterested in political theory, Monroe was fascinated by the intellectual work Jefferson offered. He had been exposed to Enlightenment thinking at William and Mary, through his association with the Williamsburg Masonic Lodge, and through his friendships with French officers like Lafayette and Pierre DuPonceau at Valley Forge, but it was Jefferson who helped him understand the revolution's underlying principles.[47]

Monroe took to this kind of teaching immediately precisely because it led him to the kind of career he envisioned for himself. He told Jefferson that although he would be happy to practice law, he wanted to, as he said, "prosecute my studies on the most liberal plan to qualify myself for any business I might chance to engage in." The law would be Monroe's nominal business, but he recognized that his true calling lay elsewhere. The work Jefferson assigned Monroe was designed to prepare his new apprentice for a career of championing the American cause.[48]

Because they were often separated during the early 1780s, Jefferson's mentorship of Monroe came primarily through assigning the younger man a reading list. Two documents provide evidence as to the kind of workload Jefferson provided. The first is a list of books Jefferson assigned another protégé a decade before Monroe began his apprenticeship. In 1771 Jefferson sent Robert Skipwith a list of books outlining the works he thought would help any young aspiring politician. The second document is another list of works Jefferson sold to Monroe in 1784. In the list provided to Skipwith, Jefferson included works from various scholars, including old legal standards such as Coke and Blackstone. But he also suggested others, less obviously useful for a future lawyer. He wanted to provide his students with a well-rounded education. He advised Skipwith to read the great political works of John Locke, Algernon Sidney, and Montesquieu. He assigned works of history, choosing David Hume as the best of the modern historians and Livy and Plutarch as the best of the ancient scholars.

Jefferson also recommended works like Georges Buffon and Benjamin Franklin in the sciences, and even John Milton and Joseph Addison under the heading "Fine Arts." Jefferson defended his inclusion of works of fiction from critics who argued that "nothing can be useful but the learned lumber of Greek and Roman reading." Jefferson wanted his pupils to understand much more than simple legal doctrine. He hoped to mold his students into well-rounded Enlightenment thinkers like himself.[49]

Jefferson sold a similar set of works to Monroe in 1784 before the former departed for Paris as the new American minister to France. Jefferson conveyed these books to Monroe after the younger man's formal apprenticeship had ended, by which time Monroe, presumably, was already familiar with the books Jefferson had assigned to Skipwith a decade earlier. This second set of works leaned toward the more radically liberal side of the Enlightenment of the late eighteenth century. It included writers such as Helvetius, whose "On Mind" was considered heretical and atheistic by the 1780s French government. Jefferson also added works by the Prussian nobleman Anacharsis Cloots, an advocate of a "cult of reason," who once declared himself a "public enemy of Jesus Christ." He included a book by Gabriel Mably, a former French official turned rabid republican, and Denis Diderot, the famous author of the *Encyclopedia*, which for many at the time was the living embodiment of the Enlightenment's spirit.[50]

Monroe spent long hours with the works Jefferson assigned. In his memoirs he wrote that he was "devoted to his studies," pursuing them with "utmost zeal and perseverance."[51] He also took steps to advertise the fact that he had been studying with Jefferson. In a note to George Washington thanking him for a previous letter of recommendation, Monroe described the amount of time he spent on his education. "Upon relinquiching [sic] my military pursuits," Monroe told his former commanding general, he was "returning to those studies in which I had been engaged previously to my joining the army." The work Jefferson assigned was so all consuming, Monroe explained, that "till of late I have been literally a recluse."[52] With the war winding down, Monroe told his former commander Lord Stirling, "Being fond of study I submitted the direction of my time & plan to my friend Mr. Jefferson, one of our wisest and most virtuous Republicans." His use of the word republican was no idle choice.[53]

In addition to exposing Monroe to the great writers of the Enlighten-ment, Jefferson also instructed Monroe on the principles of republicanism. Jefferson's teachings were designed to help the former soldier understand the political principles upon which the revolution was fought. Monroe thought himself lucky to work under of one of the great champions of re-publicanism and hoped to become one of its defenders in his own right. It is hard to say exactly how much of Monroe's political philosophy directly resulted from his apprenticeship to Thomas Jefferson. What is clear is that in 1791 Monroe told Jefferson, "upon political subjects we perfectly agree." Throughout their careers, Monroe and Jefferson maintained similar politi-cal ideologies, and the fundamental concept on which they agreed was the importance of safeguarding liberty. This was the one philosophical point above all others that Jefferson tried to instill within his protégé.[54]

Jefferson's dedication to liberty provided the framework for his political philosophy.[55] In 1791 he informed Archibald Stuart that he "would rather be exposed to the inconveniences attending too much liberty than those attending too small a degree of it."[56] For a man whose political ideas con-stantly shifted and evolved, his dedication to liberty and individual rights remained remarkably constant. Jefferson called the revolutionary struggle the "holy cause of freedom." He believed that the goal of government was to provide (white) men with the freedom to live their lives for themselves rather than the state, and that anything less was slavery.[57]

Jefferson took pains to instill this philosophy within his protégé. In 1782, just as Monroe began his own political career as a member of the Virginia legislature, Jefferson refused an appointment to the same body. Monroe attempted to coax Jefferson back to public life by appealing to his sense of duty. He reminded Jefferson that it was a "fundamental maxim of republican government" to serve the country in times of need, and that he should accept the position out of deference to the people.[58] Jefferson, ever the teacher, took the opportunity to explain the principles of liberty to his young pupil, "If we are made in some degree for others, yet in a greater degree are we made for ourselves. It were [sic] contrary to feeling and indeed ridiculous to suppose a man had less right in himself than one of his neighbors." The very thought was abhorrent to Jefferson's dedication to liberty. "This would be slavery & not that liberty which the bill of rights has made inviolable."[59] Further, he explained, "nothing could so completely divest us of that liberty as the establishment of the opinion that the state has a perpetual right to the services of all its members."[60] Liberty took precedence over any duty to the community. The kind of sacrifice to the state found in classical republicanism had no place in Jefferson's philosophy. Instead, he adhered to the American version of republicanism with its protection of liberty, the best example of which, Jefferson believed, could be found in the writings of John Locke.

Locke had a tremendous influence on both Monroe and his mentor.[61] Monroe embraced Locke, whose "work was written with great ability." From Locke, Monroe absorbed the same principles that shaped his mentor's philosophy. The most important being the "support which he gives to the general cause of liberty." Monroe believed that "there is no difference of sentiment on these points with us. All our governments are founded on that principle."[62] Monroe credited Locke with tracing "the origin of government to its true source, the consent of the people and equal rights to all." Thus, Locke, "in all that he advances in favor of the rights of the people[,] . . . is unquestionably correct." According to Monroe, the true value of "Mr. Locke's work may, therefore, be viewed in the light in which I have placed it[:] . . . as exhibiting a true picture of the nature of government." Locke encapsulated Enlightenment-era thinking on government, and Monroe believed that the United States had put his theories into "practical and successful operation since the Declaration of our Independence." What made the American Revolution successful, in Monroe's mind, was that the United States had successfully crafted a government built on Locke's ideas.[63]

Jefferson and Monroe agreed that preserving Lockean liberty should be government's primary function. Jefferson explained that "the equal rights of man, and the happiness of every individual, are now acknowledged to be the only legitimate objects of government." Monroe believed that the people's rights could be protected only if they created a government "founded on just principles." The founders' greatest achievement was succeeding in "having discovered the only device by which these rights can be secured, to wit: government by the people, acting not in person, but by representatives chosen by themselves"—in other words, republicanism.[64] According to Jefferson, republicanism served as "the only form of government which is not eternally at open or secret war with the rights of mankind." Jefferson's dedication to republican government convinced him to abandon his own private lifestyle, leaving the comforts of Monticello for the world of politics.[65]

Jefferson also taught Monroe that the founders' dedication to republicanism would shape their historical legacy. Perhaps the best example of Jefferson's cultivation of his legacy was the way he highlighted his role in writing the Declaration of Independence. It was the first thing he chose for his tombstone:

> Here was buried
> Thomas Jefferson
> Author
> of the Declaration of Independence,
> of
> the Statute of Virginia
> for Religious Freedom and
> Father of the University
> of Virginia[66]

He wanted posterity to remember, above all, his part in creating the American republic. This, he believed, would secure his legacy. Jefferson's inclusion of the Declaration on his epitaph was the last in a series of small battles he had waged to highlight his role in creating the document. Federalists like John Marshall had tried to diminish Jefferson's role as primary author of the Declaration. In his autobiography Jefferson responded by including his first draft of the Declaration, along with the changes made by Congress.[67] Jefferson's final words on the subject of the Declaration give great insight into how he hoped to be remembered by succeeding generations. In 1826 Jefferson was invited to the fiftieth anniversary celebration of the Declaration in Washington, DC. Far too sick to attend, Jefferson penned what historian Merrill Peterson calls his "last opportunity to embellish a legend." Jefferson wanted the anniversary of his famous Declaration to be the symbol for this new age: "Let the annual return of this day forever refresh our recollection of these rights and an undiminished devotion to them." This is how Jefferson hoped to be remembered—as a champion of the republican cause—and he tried to instill these same ideas in Monroe during his mentorship of the younger Virginian.[68]

Under Jefferson's tutelage, Monroe adopted the founders' goal of building a government based on liberty. And, like Jefferson, Monroe believed that the best way for him to make his mark on history was to dedicate his life to championing this cause. As Monroe wrote Jefferson, "My plan of life is now fixed, has a certain object for its view."[69] Monroe did not hope simply to achieve power and fame on his own, though of course he had ambition to spare. Neither did he adhere to the classical republican ideal of sacrificing himself to the state. Monroe believed that his task was to ensure that government itself did not become tyrannical. In 1791 Monroe told Jefferson that they shared "the reprobation of all measures that may be calculated to elevate the government above the people." They distrusted political measures that invested the government with additional power. Monroe and Jefferson also agreed on the role statesmen should play within the new republic. Monroe thought it was up to public servants like himself to keep the government from descending into tyranny.[70]

The role of the statesman then was crucial to this new experiment, and it was the part Monroe envisioned for himself. "Government is a trust created by compact," he explained, "in which those who discharge its duties have no rights or interests of their own, but are mere agents employed for the people."[71] Thus, during his lifelong dedication to politics and service in government he worked, somewhat counterintuitively, to ensure that the very government he served did not grow so powerful as to threaten liberty. Monroe believed, and said so in *The People the Sovereigns*, that "as power proceeds from the people it must be made subservient to their purposes." The only way to achieve this was for "those who exercise" political power to consistently "feel their responsibility to their constituents in every measure which they adopt."[72] Years later Monroe made a point to assure the public that he understood his role as president in his first inaugural address. The president, like "every officer in every department," derived his authority from the people, and Monroe assured them that he would remain "responsible to them for his conduct."[73] Monroe and Jefferson, as agents of the people, endeavored to protect republican government from those who wanted to transform it into despotism. As a result, Monroe saw his career as part of a struggle between the defenders of republican liberty and its many enemies.

Monroe's distaste for monarchy ran deep. In *The People the Sovereigns* he called "the doctrine of divine or paternal right . . . to the sovereign power of the state . . . utterly absurd." It "belonged to the dark ages." The Enlightenment had proven that "all men are by nature equally free." It was the monarchial form of government that had "subverted" man's "natural rights."[74] In this, he agreed with his mentor. As Jefferson penned in his first inaugural, "sometimes it is said that man cannot be trusted with the government of himself. Can he, then, be trusted with the government of others? Or have we found angels in the form of kings to govern him?" For Monroe and Jefferson, the threat came from foreign rulers and would-be monarchists within the United States.[75]

As Monroe's apprenticeship concluded and his political career began, he concluded that not all Americans held to the same principles as he and Jefferson. Certainly, Monroe explained, "no one suspected" that Washington wanted "to promote the establishment of Monarchy," but "of the political principles, however, of some other of our Revolutionary patriots . . . a different sentiment was entertained." Even some of his revolutionary brethren had abandoned their republican principles. According to Monroe, "they did not confide in a government founded exclusively on the sovereignty of the people." Further, "they considered the experiment" in republican government "as sure to fail." In Monroe's mind the Federalists, whom he considered nothing less than American monarchists, wanted to overthrow the system the revolution had put into effect. They "looked forward to its failing as leading to a change more favorable to their political views and principles."[76] Monroe argued that many in what would become the Federalist Party, most prominently Alexander Hamilton and Monroe's own personal political nemesis, John Jay, did not adhere to the principles of republicanism. They wanted what Monroe called "consolidation" of federal power, which would eventually "lead to monarchy and to despotism."[77] Monroe believed that Hamilton and the Federalists advocated for the expansion of federal power to pave the way for a monarchical system to replace the republic in fact if not in name.[78] Thus, Monroe saw his fight against monarchy as a war against both the kings and queens of Europe and their allies within the United States, who hoped to align the nation economically and politically with Great Britain.[79] For much of Monroe's career, American foreign policy provided the primary battlefield in his war against these foreign and domestic monarchists.

Monroe himself wrote in his autobiography, "Our relations with foreign powers even at this early period became an object of the highest importance."[80] Foreign policy dominated the political discourse for a number of reasons. As a former colony of Great Britain, America's relationship with the former mother country remained a source of contention. The United States had also secured independence largely through French aid, and remained tied to that nation through treaties dating back to 1778. The United States also remained relatively weak compared to nations like Great Britain and France. Finally, with so little power invested in it domestically, the federal government's overriding sphere of operation was in directing the nation's foreign affairs. It was in this realm therefore where Monroe hoped to champion American republicanism. Monroe became, for all intents and purposes, a foreign policy specialist, and his autobiography reflects this. Of the book's seven finished chapters, six relate directly to U.S. foreign affairs.[81]

The first time Monroe played an important role in American foreign policy came when he found himself elected to the Confederation Congress in 1783. Beginning in 1785, John Jay undertook negotiations with the Spanish government. As Congress's secretary of foreign affairs, Jay agreed to surrender American access to the Mississippi for twenty-five to thirty years in order to secure trade concessions from Spain. This infuriated westerners, who viewed the free navigation of the river as critical to their economic survival. Monroe had undertaken several tours of the western portions of the United States during the 1780s and took it upon himself to defend the interests of westerners in Congress. He worked diligently drumming up opposition to the treaty. For Monroe, maintaining access to the Mississippi was crucial to securing the American republic. He argued, "If we entered into engagements to the contrary, we separate . . . all those westward of the mountains from the federal government." If that were to happen, Monroe warned, the west might be thrown "into the hands . . . of a foreign power." The young congressman became so anxious over the treaty that he even suggested the negotiations be taken out of Jay's hands entirely.[82]

For Monroe, there were several elements at play in his reaction to the proposed treaty. The Jay-Gardoqui negotiations were one of the first incidents in U.S. history to reveal stark regional differences. Those in the Northeast saw a commercial agreement with Spain as easily worth the price of access to the Mississippi for the West. They also had no fear of limiting westward expansion; indeed Monroe thought part of Jay's scheme was designed to prevent expansion in order to promote population growth in the Northeast. Monroe saw access to the Mississippi as critical to the continued expansion of the American republic to the west. He also viewed Spain as the weakest of the European powers and could not understand what he saw as Jay's prostrating the nation's interest to the Spanish monarchy. Eventually Monroe and his political allies in the Confederation Congress succeeded in convincing Jay and others that the resistance was too great to proceed and the treaty was scrapped. Nevertheless, the events surrounding it helped shape Monroe's attitude in two important ways.[83]

First, from this point forward, Monroe remained interested in western frontier issues, and particularly in securing the American border from monarchial threats, whether from Spain, France, or Great Britain. Second, on a more personal level, Monroe never trusted Jay after 1786. He saw him as an intriguer, far too enamored of currying favor with various monarchial courtiers like Gardoqui. Jay had already shown himself to many revolutionaries as too accommodating to Britain on the issue of forts and debt after the war. Monroe's distrust of Jay would come to a head during the 1790s when the two found themselves on opposite sides of the French Revolution. Monroe's early foreign policy experiences, combined with his Revolutionary War background and apprenticeship to Thomas Jefferson, helped form the beginnings of his republican diplomacy, which ultimately became focused on championing republicanism both at home and abroad.

Monroe's interest in foreign affairs and the spread of republicanism continued undiminished after France undertook their own revolution in 1789. Monroe saw it as the next theater in the war between republicanism and monarchy. He believed that the French were following in America's footsteps, and that support for the French Revolution was required of any good American republican. He saw the Revolution in France as an opportunity to champion the cause abroad and help begin the process of spreading American-style republicanism around the world.

## CONCLUSIONS

The 1770s and 1780s were perhaps the most important years in forming Monroe's republican ideology. They instilled within the young Virginia statesman a burning desire to leave his own mark on American republicanism, to build a legacy as a champion of the cause. From his youthful beginnings watching his father's protests against the Stamp Act to his relationship with his uncle Joseph Jones and his brief stint at William and Mary, Monroe became sufficiently dedicated to the cause to join the Continental Army. His relationships with revolutionary veterans during the war, and especially his apprenticeship to Thomas Jefferson, shaped Monroe's republican ideology. Monroe adopted a largely Jeffersonian view of republican liberty, and saw Jefferson as one of the movement's greatest champions. For the rest of his life, he saw Jefferson as a model upon which to view his own career. Jefferson's influence also helped convince Monroe to make politics and statesmanship his calling.

Monroe did not see the republican movement as limited to the United States' shores. He viewed foreign policy issues as just as critical as domestic concerns. To Monroe's way of thinking the United States needed to champion republicanism both at home and abroad. Championing the cause took a number of related but distinct forms throughout the rest of Monroe's career. First, he wanted to ensure that the U.S. republic itself remained secure from its most powerful monarchial enemies, particularly Great Britain with its allies in the Federalist Party. Monroe also saw opportunities to advance the republican cause by extending the United States' boundaries at the expense of weaker nations such as Spain. But perhaps most importantly, Monroe saw it as his duty to try to spread republicanism to other nations, to support their attempts to follow the American example. This would create natural allies for the United States, who, as one of the world's few republics, needed friends. Though it was not part of Monroe's vision to spread republicanism through military means, Monroe did think that American moral support for nascent republicanism could prove decisive in the contest for the hearts and minds of the people. As a result, Monroe saw national security concerns in the context of this wider struggle. To him, the United States' interest and the republican cause were linked. Monroe saw a world divided between monarchists and republicans, with each side competing to spread their ideas. The front lines in this contest between the two competing ideologies could be on actual battlefields (as he experienced at Trenton), in the halls of Congress, on the western frontier, or, as he was about to discover, on the streets of Paris.

# 3

-->-->    <--<--

# UNNECESSARY ÉCLAT

Cultivate the French Republic with zeal, but without any unnecessary éclat.

SECRETARY OF STATE EDMUND RANDOLPH
TO U.S. MINISTER TO FRANCE JAMES MONROE, 1794

THE *AMITY* SAILED INTO Philadelphia harbor on June 27, 1797.
On shore, Thomas Jefferson, Albert Gallatin, and Aaron Burr stood
waiting for the ship to dock. Aboard ship were James Monroe, his wife
Elizabeth, and their ten-year-old daughter Eliza, who had spent the past
three years in France. Before the Monroe family disembarked, the republican delegation boarded the vessel to greet them. Most immediately, they
wanted a firsthand account of Monroe's time in France, but there were
greater issues at stake. By June of 1797 John Adams had been elected as the
second president of the United States. Jefferson, meanwhile, was his vice
president and the nominal leader of the nascent Democratic-Republican
Party. The Swiss financier-diplomat Gallatin and the New York lawyer-
politician Burr were likewise two of the most prominent figures within
the growing oppositional movement to Adams's administration. The Federalists had accused Monroe of showing too much enthusiasm for the
French Republic in its struggle against monarchial England, and he had
been summarily dismissed from his post as minister to France. The three
Democratic-Republicans' decision to meet Monroe upon his return home
was meant as a show of support for both him and the French cause. At that
moment, Monroe was a symbol for the controversy upon which the entire
American political world revolved: the French Revolution.[1]

The revolution that began in Paris at the Bastille on July 14, 1789, dominated the American political landscape throughout the 1790s. After the execution of Louis XVI in 1793, Britain and France made war upon one another with only occasional lapses until Napoleon's final defeat at the Battle of Waterloo in 1815. Throughout this period the United States found itself caught between the world's two great powers.[2] Initially most Americans cheered the outbreak of revolution in France, seeing it as the natural extension of the American Revolution. Federalists and Republicans alike enjoyed the legitimacy it seemed to grant their own republican experiment. In October of 1789 John Fenno's *Gazette of the United States*, which later emerged as the mouthpiece of the Federalist Party and a harsh critic of the Revolution, initially called the French uprising "one of the most glorious objects that can arrest the attention of mankind."[3] As the violence in France increased, however, many Americans, especially Federalists like Alexander Hamilton and John Jay, questioned whether the two revolutions truly shared a common nature. Meanwhile, men like Monroe and his fellow Democratic-Republicans continued to see it as fulfilling the dream of spreading republicanism to Europe. As a result, the French Revolution became the crucial issue that ultimately divided the nation into two opposing political camps.[4]

It was fitting for Thomas Jefferson to meet his former protégé in 1797 when Monroe arrived in Philadelphia after his unceremonious removal as the U.S. minister to France. After all, Monroe's actions while in Paris came largely as a result of his adherence to a Jeffersonian interpretation of the French Revolution. Jefferson himself had watched the opening stages of the Revolution as the minister to France during the late 1780s, reporting on the world-shattering events gripping Paris to his former protégé. Jefferson, as he did in so much else, helped shape Monroe's view of the French Revolution. In August of 1788, almost a year before the fall of the Bastille, Jefferson described the opening moments of the great drama to Monroe. He depicted the Revolution as a contest with "the authority of the crown on one part & that of the parliament on the other." Jefferson described the French uprising as a fight between monarchial forces and republican revolutionaries, and with the government, "yielding up daily one right after another to the nation," he foresaw a rapid republican victory.[5]

Jefferson saw the French Revolution as a close cousin to the American version. The new French provincial assemblies, he explained, served as, "perfect representations of the nation and stand somewhat in the place of our state assemblies." He looked forward to the next year with optimism, believing that the Estates General, called for the first time since 1614, would create a "bill of rights" and a "national assembly" in the image of the institutions of the United States. Jefferson predicted that after centuries of suffering under a cruel monarchy, the French would soon be in possession of a "tolerably free constitution." He added, ironically as it turned out, that France stood to achieve all this "without its having cost them a drop of blood."[6] Jefferson used similar terms to describe the Revolution to other correspondents. To John Adams he marveled that in only a few short months the French people had "gained as much ground" as England did "during all her civil wars under the Stuarts."[7] In January of 1789 Jefferson told the Welsh philosopher Richard Price that "the American war seems to have first awakened" France "from the sleep of despotism."[8] In March, he told John Jay that the movement was proceeding "without encountering anything which deserves to be called a difficulty."[9]

Jefferson presented an even more sanguine picture of the Revolution's future. Only weeks after the fall of the Bastille he told a correspondent that he would "agree to be stoned as a false prophet if all does not go well in this country." France's revolution formed "but the first chapter of the history of European liberty."[10] It would mark the beginning of a European movement toward American-style republicanism. Jefferson left Paris just after the fall of the Bastille. When he arrived back in the United States he carried with him a firm belief that Americans were duty-bound to support the French cause.[11]

Jefferson returned home to assume his post as secretary of state in 1789 while his protégé Monroe found himself elected to the U.S. Senate in 1790. Relying on his mentor's reports, Monroe championed the French cause throughout the early part of the decade. Writing under the pen-name of Aratus in 1791, Monroe defended the Revolution from its growing number of critics.[12] He scoffed at those who treated the Revolution as a disease they feared the United States might catch. Like his mentor, Monroe connected events in France to America's own revolution. He explained that Americans, three thousand miles removed from King George III, had experienced the tyranny of monarchy only from a distance and only in its least oppressive form whereas "in France it was at its height and at home." In Monroe's mind France was now the front line in the war between monarchial forces and the champions of republicanism. He argued that, like their American brothers, the French people were justified in rising up to secure their rights. Monroe insisted that "whoever owns the principles of one revolution, must cherish those of the other." Further, Monroe attacked anyone who did not agree with this assessment, claiming that those who denied this truth were "blinded by prejudice." For Monroe, the two revolutions could not be separated.[13]

During the next few months Monroe penned two more essays. He warned Americans that the future of republicanism depended upon a French victory. For centuries the failure of free governments around the world "shielded despotism behind a wall of impregnable strength." Now the forces of "truth and reason" had a chance to destroy the "dark cloud" of absolutism. But if Americans failed to adequately support the French cause, the "light" of free government would be "extinguished forever." Monroe told his countrymen, "As a friend of humanity I rejoice in the French Revolution, but as a citizen of America the gratification is greatly heightened," because with the creation of these two new republics, he said, "a fair experiment will be made . . . whether mankind are [sic] capable of self-government." If the French and American revolutions ended in failure it would destroy republicanism forever. Americans, therefore, as the original "authors of a great revolution," owed it to themselves to aid this new revolution. Although the fates of both governments seemed to Monroe to be "intimately linked," other former revolutionaries did not share his rosy portrayal of events.[14]

During the years following the fall of the Bastille in 1789, when Jefferson watched its opening stages until Monroe's own posting as minister to the new French Republic in 1794, the French Revolution bitterly divided Americans. Those who supported it began to refer to themselves as Republicans or Democratic-Republicans while those who opposed it were called Federalists. By March 1793, after word had reached the United States of King Louis XVI's execution and the outbreak of war between

France and Britain, the two budding political parties stood at odds on what American policy should be in regard to the two warring nations.[15]

As secretary of state and the nominal leader of the Republican Party, Jefferson agreed with the Federalists that the United States should distance itself from the actual fighting between Britain and France. Yet he and his Republican allies hoped to delay an actual declaration of neutrality so the United States might coax Britain into granting concessions to her former colonies. Also, unlike his Federalist opponents, he remained committed to the 1778 Treaty of Alliance with France. When President Washington did eventually issue his neutrality proclamation in 1793, Jefferson and Monroe objected to its tone because they believed it favored Britain, and did not properly reflect the country's support for the French revolutionary struggle. While they did not advocate direct action, they also thought it improper to declare American neutrality in a contest between monarchy and republicanism.[16]

With tension mounting, the two parties vehemently contested President Washington's choices for diplomatic posts to the two belligerent superpowers. Washington, over objections from the Republican camp, appointed Gouverneur Morris as American minister to France in early 1792. Morris, who detested the Revolution, eventually proved a poor choice for the post.[17] Washington then sought a diplomat to travel to Great Britain to come to terms over unresolved issues from the Revolutionary War. Initially, rumors swirled that Hamilton himself might be chosen for the post, before Washington eventually settled on the Federalist-leaning Chief Justice of the Supreme Court John Jay as his new envoy extraordinary to the British Empire.[18]

Republican outcry over Jay's appointment, and criticism of Morris's mission in France, where he predictably alienated the French Jacobin leadership who eventually demanded his recall, convinced Washington to send a Republican supporter of the Revolution to Paris as his next minister to France. He turned to James Monroe. A more circumspect, or less ambitious, politician might have declined the appointment. In fact, a number of more prominent men did turn the post down, including James Madison and Robert R. Livingston. Monroe himself expressed some surprise and even a bit of unease at accepting the job. He was right to be cautious.

Jefferson had already left the cabinet by the time of his appointment, and with Hamilton acting as the primary power behind the scenes a pro-French Democratic-Republican would be placed in a difficult position. Monroe ultimately accepted the post for two reasons. First, the new secretary of state and fellow Virginian Edmund Randolph assured him that President Washington "was resolved to send a republican character" to represent American interests in France. According to Randolph, Washington had chosen Monroe for the post precisely because of his strong support of the Revolution. The secretary of state assured Monroe that his appointment was made in order to prove to France that the United States remained its staunch friend. Washington calculated that sending someone sympathetic to the French cause would act as a counterweight to Jay's presence in London. Monroe's second reason for accepting the job, however, was more personal.[19]

In considering his decision, Monroe came to believe that only a republican could bridge the divide between the two nations. He told Jefferson that there was "no sacrifice I would not be willing to make for the sake of France and her cause."[20] Monroe also believed that if he could successfully forge a lasting alliance between the two fledgling republics it would help shape his historical legacy.[21] He told Jefferson prior to his departure that "French historians will record the conduct of this country toward theirs." Future generations would no doubt remember the names of those Americans who aided the cause. He believed that "those who shall take any part which the world & posterity may not approve . . . will be handed down in their proper colours [sic]."[22] Monroe desperately wanted to be remembered in the proper "color." He hoped to secure a grand republican alliance to stand united against the monarchies of Europe. This was Monroe's first chance to build a legacy by helping expand the boundaries of republicanism to France. A French-American alliance against the British monarchy would, in his mind, go a long way toward securing worldwide republicanism. Monroe's zeal for the cause convinced him to accept the post, and it also helped shape his actions while in Paris.

While Monroe understood that he officially represented the interests of the U.S. government, he thought he owed a greater duty to the republican cause. The new minister to France believed that the United States' narrowly defined national security goals were of less importance than his higher calling to forge a union between the two republics. To help secure this alliance, Monroe portrayed the French Revolution as a close cousin of its American forebear in his reports to the secretary of state. As he studied the situation in Paris upon his arrival, Monroe became convinced that the Revolution's violence did not accurately reflect its true principles. Monroe reached France a mere five days after the execution of French leader Maximilien Robespierre, the major architect of the "Terror." Alternatively nicknamed "The Incorruptible" by his supporters and the *dictateur sanguinaire* (bloodthirsty dictator) by his enemies, Robespierre had, for the past year, ruled France with an iron fist. The Thermidorian Reaction,[23] a revolt against the Jacobins, executed Robespierre on July 28, though only after he and his comrades had sent thousands to the guillotine.[24]

Monroe felt no sympathy for Robespierre. He told Secretary of State Randolph that "The Incorruptible" bore sole responsibility for the recent bloodshed. Robespierre, in Monroe's estimation, "amassed in his hands all the powers of the government." Before his fall he had stood nearly "omnipotent" within the French Committee of Public Safety, which then ruled France. Most importantly, it was Robespierre's "spirit" that directed "the unceasing operation of the guillotine" that horrified so many Americans. Monroe was trying to defend the course the Revolution had taken by using Robespierre as a scapegoat for its excesses.[25]

Monroe knew his audience well. Americans strongly distrusted executive tyranny, and he assured them that none of antiquity's great tyrants could match Robespierre, whose "acts of cruelty and oppression are perhaps without parallel in the annals of history." Monroe focused exclusively on this "bloody and merciless tyrant" in order to defend the Revolution from its detractors in America. Monroe told Randolph that Robespierre "aimed at despotic powers," and ultimately hoped to "establish himself on the throne of the Capets." He depicted Robespierre as a power-hungry aspiring monarch antithetical to true republicanism. Such imagery resonated with Americans. Doubtless, Monroe hoped to evoke memories of George III, or even thoughts of the cruelty wrought by ancient tyrants like Lucius Cornelius Sulla, Gaius Marius, and Julius Caesar, all of whom ultimately played a role in overthrowing the Roman Republic and were well known to American leaders. A single power-hungry tyrant could easily, and most plausibly, be blamed for the Revolution's descent into brutality.[26]

Monroe continued in this theme. He knew that Federalists and Republicans alike feared that the chaos within France might give rise to a Caesar-like figure using the military to crush the budding republic. Monroe believed the soldiers themselves would prevent such a disaster. He dismissed the idea of the French army participating in a "March on Rome." Showing a high regard for the typical French soldier, Monroe believed that the "spirit of the age" imbued the French revolutionary warriors with a zeal that precluded such a calamity. He even claimed that Robespierre's rise and fall actually demonstrated the Revolution's continued ideological purity. Robespierre had been dedicated to the Revolution's principles during his rise to power, but the "moment doubts were entertained" concerning his commitment to the movement "his influence began to decline." The Revolution itself, Monroe argued, remained pure. Though tyrants like Robespierre, Danton, and Brissot had risen in the ranks, once their actions clashed with the Revolution's principles, they were quickly deposed, and subsequently guillotined. Monroe assured his fellow countrymen that the French people themselves would eliminate any who betrayed the revolutionary cause.[27]

Monroe never lost faith in French republicanism. In February 1795, Monroe informed Robert R. Livingston, a New York Republican, of the various treason trials for the fallen Jacobins. Monroe assured Livingston that with the Jacobins gone "tranquility prevail[ed]" within the National Convention and dismissed fears that the famine striking France might derail the Revolution. The "patience and fortitude of the people" were such that they could "surmount much greater difficulties than are like to threaten them."[28] In fact, he repeated this refrain several weeks later to Randolph, again stressing Paris's "tranquility," marveling that the French people faced such "internal convulsions" yet still remained staunch supporters of the Revolution.[29]

According to Monroe, the French people stood prepared to support the Revolution indefinitely. Even with the constant problems facing them, Monroe claimed to have "neither seen nor heard any symptom of discontent showing itself among the people at large." Monroe informed Randolph that he had never seen a people so apparently "content." He had personally witnessed celebrations of French military victories. He had also seen citizens willingly hand over money, supplies, and even their own sons for the war effort against the other European monarchies. These were not the "symptoms" of a people weary of republicanism and willing to reject it. The revolutionaries, Monroe assured his superiors, refused to "turn aside from the great object of revolution." They would not "countenance in any individual, schemes of usurpation."[30]

With Robespierre's downfall, Monroe assured his fellow Americans, the Revolution would stabilize itself and transition from the tyranny of the Jacobin terror into a sister constitutional republic. Monroe asked Randolph rhetorically, "Is there any hope that the vicious operation of the guillotine may be hereafter suspended?" In answer to his own question, Monroe explained that with Robespierre gone the entire country "appear[ed] to enjoy perfect tranquility." Monroe often used the word tranquility to sum up the new French republic. He knew that it would be much easier for his Federalist superiors to support a stable France than one wracked by chaos. Monroe desperately wanted to show Federalist doubters that the Revolution's violence to this point would not continue unabated forever. He even fancifully dismissed the Terror itself as a monarchial conspiracy. Robespierre and his allies were, he claimed, "probably in the pay of foreign powers & employed to perpetrate those atrocities merely to make the revolution odious & thus oppose it." If the Revolution was entering a period of calm, as Monroe assured his superiors it was, it meant that they were moving closer to American republicanism.[31]

Whether to friends such as Madison and Jefferson, or in his official correspondence to the secretary of state and the president, Monroe continually stressed the Revolution's steady progress toward an American-style republic. In January of 1795, Monroe informed Edmund Randolph that Robespierre's excesses showed every sign of healing.[32] The culmination of Monroe's triumphant reports came when the French National Convention finally, after two failed attempts, created a new constitution in 1795. Monroe reveled in the achievement, telling the new secretary of state Timothy Pickering that this new French Constitution "resembled in many respects what we see daily acted on our side of the Atlantic." Monroe saw the constitution as the French finally achieving American republicanism.[33]

Though his evaluation of the Revolution was excessively optimistic, Monroe genuinely believed most of the reports he sent back to the United States. He was not simply downplaying the Revolution's violence to score political points. Monroe saw the Revolution as "essentially moderate" and the violence as only an interruption. The true Revolution was, in Monroe's mind, the quest for freedom from monarchial rule in favor of republican government. Monroe could, with intellectual honesty, omit anything that did not fit the model of a revolution toward American republicanism. This mindset also helped Monroe justify his quest to bring these two republics together by any means necessary, even if that meant sacrificing narrower American interests.[34]

As he portrayed the Revolution in glowing terms to his American colleagues, Monroe also tried to convince the French that the United States would continue to support their cause. Here he found himself in a difficult position. Robespierre's fall had thrown the French government into chaos. Meanwhile, Franco-American relations had been strained to the point of breaking. Gouverneur Morris's recall, combined with the U.S. declaration of neutrality, contributed to the frosty reception Monroe received when he provided his papers to the Committee of Public Safety, which directed foreign policy for the French within the National Convention. After waiting in vain for the committee to recognize his credentials as the new minister, Monroe took drastic measures, taking his case to the entire National Convention.[35] He sent a letter to Philippe Merlin de Douai, president of the French National Convention, on August 13, 1794, requesting recognition as a representative of a "Sister Republic." Monroe believed that only a grand gesture of solidarity would heal relations between the two nations. The French Convention agreed to Monroe's request and he addressed them the next day.[36]

A crowd surrounded Monroe as he made his way to the hall of the French National Convention on August 17, 1794, shouting, "Long live the United States of America, our brave brothers." The Parisian mob cheered him as a symbol of their American revolutionary predecessors. Monroe positioned himself at the dais, standing before the seven-hundred-member Convention, and affirmed the two nations' connection. "Republics should approach near to each other," he began as a translator related his words in French. "The French and American republics in particular should stand side by side." After all, their "governments are similar," built upon "the equal and inalienable rights of man." He assured the French that just as America once endured her own "day of oppression," and emerged from it "in the enjoyment of peace, liberty and independence," so too would France.[37]

Monroe ended his speech with reference to the role he hoped to play in this great drama: "I pursue the dictates of my own heart in wishing the liberty and happiness of the French nation." Further, he vowed to do "everything in [his] power to preserve and perpetuate the harmony so happily subsisting at present between the two Republics" and thus "merit the approbation of both." This, Monroe believed, was the most important cause to which he could possibly devote his energies: "I shall deem it the happiest event of my life, and return with a consolation, which those who mean well and have served the cause of liberty alone can feel." Monroe also presented declarations from both houses of Congress wishing the French people well, and he personally expressed President Washington's own fond wishes for the cause.[38] Even as he took these measures, Monroe recognized that some in the United States might not appreciate his actions. Some, he knew, would have preferred that he had "smuggled" Congress's statements of support for the French Republic under the cover of darkness.[39]

Knowing his actions would be criticized by many Federalists, Monroe preemptively wrote to the secretary of state explaining the positive reaction his address had received from the French people.[40] Monroe was right to fear the response his speech would elicit back home. When the text of Monroe's remarks reached Philadelphia it irritated both the Washington administration and Federalists everywhere. In December of 1794 Randolph admonished Monroe that in future he should behave in a more "circumspect" manner. He reminded Monroe of his duty to present the administration's policy to the French government, rather than his own views on the Revolution. Randolph feared the British reaction to such a public display of support for France, warning Monroe that "the extreme glow" of his address exceeded the parameters of his instructions. He urged Monroe to use caution when making public speeches. He wanted Monroe to walk a tight diplomatic line by cultivating the "French Republic with zeal, but without any unnecessary éclat."[41]

The administration's reaction contrasted sharply with the encouragement Monroe received from his supporters. James Madison told Monroe that though his speech had been "grating" to many in the Federalist camp, his fellow Republicans heartily approved his actions.[42] Kentucky senator John Brown told Monroe that his address to the convention "has been read with enthusiasm and approbation by every friend to the Rights of Man, as breathing the genuine sentiments of republicanism and as expressing the sense of nineteen twentieths of the citizens of the Union."[43] This was no doubt an exaggeration, but the support Monroe received from his political allies relieved some of the sting from the administration's rebuke. Monroe felt vindicated by the backing he received from these "true" republicans. Further, his successes in the diplomatic realm convinced Monroe that this was the best course to improving relations with France.

When Monroe learned of the administration's reprimand in February of 1795 he responded by reminding Randolph that relations between the two countries had been seriously strained when he arrived. The treaty of 1778 had been violated, American commerce harassed, and the previous minister removed. "Connections between the two countries," Monroe argued, "hung, as it were, by a thread." In fact, the Committee of Public Safety had initially distrusted Monroe's very presence in France, fearing that he might have been appointed merely to provide political cover to Jay's mission to Great Britain. Monroe believed that without strong measures the relationship between the two republics might collapse. It was his duty, therefore, to assure the French that the United States supported their revolution in order to reestablish amicable relations. Furthermore, Monroe argued, his plan had worked. With the bulk of the French people and the National Convention on his side, the Committee of Public Safety had relented and accepted his ministerial credentials. He had also gained significant concessions from the French, including their agreement to discontinue the seizure of American ships. All of this, Monroe thought, had been worth ruffling a few feathers in the Federalist camp and in Great Britain. Monroe did not yet fully grasp how strongly some in the Washington administration opposed his appointment.[44]

While Monroe experienced some difficulties from the administration following his early outpouring of support for the French cause, it was the completion of Jay's Treaty that placed his mission in serious jeopardy. Jay finalized a treaty of amity and commerce with Britain during the fall of 1794, and Democratic-Republicans saw the agreement as a betrayal of France. For Monroe, however, it was more personal. From the beginning, the Washington administration knew Jay's mission to Britain might arouse suspicion in France. Before his departure, Secretary of State Randolph instructed Monroe to assure France that Jay did not have authorization to make any agreement with the British that imperiled America's relationship with France. He told Monroe that Jay was "positively forbidden to weaken the engagements between this country and France." Hoping to "remove all jealousy with respect to Mr. Jay's mission in London," Randolph assured Monroe that its goals included only obtaining "immediate compensation for our plundered property, and the restitution of the posts." In other words, securing reimbursement for property lost during the Revolutionary War and the return of America's western frontier forts still in British hands. Jay's mission, the administration insisted, did not signal a decision to forfeit the U.S. relationship with France in exchange for a closer connection to England.[45]

While this may have been strictly true, Randolph and the administration misled Monroe when it came to Jay's mission in London. In addition to authorizing the goals Monroe understood, the administration also cleared Jay to negotiate a commercial treaty with Britain. Monroe was not informed of these instructions.[46] Randolph told Monroe, "You know how Mr. Jay is restricted," and even went on to lament the chances of Jay coming home with any concessions from the British. "I must acknowledge to you," he told Monroe in September of 1794, "that notwithstanding all the pompous expectations," the prospects for compensation for merchants from the revolutionary war were "illusory." He even told Monroe that it was "indispensable" that he keep the French "in good humor" because Randolph did not "entertain the distant hope of the surrender of the Western Posts." The administration kept Monroe in the dark regarding Jay's instructions because only someone believed to be a friend to the revolution could mollify both the French government and the growing pro-French faction in the United States. The United States desperately needed to keep the French happy in the event that Jay failed to secure a treaty. They feared Monroe would refuse the appointment if he knew the full terms of Jay's instructions, which would scuttle any chance of repairing the relationship with France.[47]

Rumors of the Jay Treaty's contents reached Monroe in late 1794, but he told the French to put no stock in them: "I cannot believe that an

American minister would ever forget the connections between the United States and France."[48] Monroe immediately wrote to Jay for an update, and the minister to Great Britain informed Monroe that the treaty did not infringe on any U.S. commitment to France, but he did not immediately send its contents to Paris.[49] The rumors, mostly from the British press, put Monroe in a difficult position. The French government felt a growing "uneasiness" concerning Jay's mission, which Monroe tried to alleviate by consistently repeating Randolph's assurance that Jay possessed only restricted powers to treat with the British. The French government asked Monroe to "communicate to us the treaty in question as soon as possible." Only by doing so could Monroe dispel these reports. The French reiterated that they would view any commercial treaty between the United States and Great Britain as damaging to Franco-American relations.[50] As the rumors persisted, the French feared that Jay's Treaty included "an alliance" between the United States and Great Britain both "offensive and defensive." According to Monroe, it began to elicit a "kind of horror" from the French government. As a result, Monroe told the French that he would acquire a copy of the treaty and show them the contents as soon as possible.[51]

Monroe formally asked Jay for a copy of the treaty in January of 1795. He, perhaps foolishly, told the pro-British Jay that "nothing will satisfy this government [France] but a copy of the instrument itself."[52] Jay refused. Though he originally promised to send Monroe a copy, Jay now agreed to do so only "in the most perfect confidence." He did not believe it proper to send an unratified treaty to a foreign government, "however friendly." Jay was, of course, in the right in terms of diplomatic protocol. A foreign nation had no right to inspect a proposed treaty between two other powers. It would make the United States appear supplicant to French interests. But diplomatic protocol did not overly concern Monroe, who believed that a closer alliance with France could only enhance American prestige, and strengthen the republican cause. He believed that his efforts had held together the fragile Franco-American alliance, and that Jay's treaty would undo all his work. If it meant breaking diplomatic protocol to keep the two republics in accord, it was a price worth paying.[53]

Monroe refused to accept the contents of the treaty under Jay's stipulation. Monroe thought it incumbent upon him to communicate the treaty to the French per his promise. Jay, therefore, again refused to send him a copy of the treaty. When the French heard nothing from Monroe, they suspected that the contents of Jay's agreement were as harmful to France as initially feared. After all, Monroe wrote to Randolph explaining the French mindset, "if the treaty was not injurious to France, why was it withheld from her?"[54] Monroe finally received a basic outline of the treaty in March of 1795, which, true to his word, he passed on to the Committee of Public Safety.[55]

Monroe was appalled by the treaty. He thought that the one saving grace was that it would mark an important moment in "the history of our country." To Monroe, the treaty laid bare the Federalists' true colors by shedding light on the "views of its author and his political associates." He believed that Jay had sacrificed the interests of both the country and the republican cause in order to preserve a relationship with monarchial Great Britain. Meanwhile, the treaty convinced France that the United States planned to "abandon this republic for a connection with England."[56]

After learning the full contents of the treaty, Monroe realized that Jay's instructions had been kept secret from him, and that he would be unlikely to receive help in repudiating the agreement from the administration. He therefore looked to his fellow Republicans for support. He hoped that his allies in the United States could defeat the treaty in Congress. In a letter circulated to Republican leaders John Beckley, Aaron Burr, George Logan, and, of course, Thomas Jefferson, Monroe explained that Jay's Treaty risked destroying everything he had accomplished during his ministerial tenure. The treaty had "operated like a stroke of thunder and produced upon all France amazement." He saw it as nothing less than a betrayal of republicanism.[57]

By now Monroe's position as minister was in serious jeopardy. Two developments eventually sealed his recall from France. First, after the creation of the French Constitution of 1795, the Committee of Public Safety gave way to a new multiperson executive known as the Directory. In response to Jay's Treaty, the French Directory adopted the old Jacobin policy of directing the same kind of harsh measures against the United States that Monroe had done so much to reverse during his time as minister. Meanwhile, back in the United States, Secretary of State Edmund

Randolph was replaced by Timothy Pickering. Randolph, a moderate, actually supported a strong relationship with France and personally opposed Jay's Treaty. Pickering was a different animal entirely. An arch-Federalist, the New Englander was also a well-known Anglophile.[58]

Monroe learned of the Directory's new policy in February of 1796. The new French government, Monroe reported to Pickering, "considered the alliance between us as ceasing to exist, from the moment the [Jay] Treaty was ratified."[59] Monroe tried to convince the Directory to reconsider. He warned that only France's monarchial enemies would benefit from a split between the two republics, and assured them that despite the treaty France still had many friends in the United States. If France broke off relations now, many Americans would turn against her cause. Their mutual enemies would seize upon such a measure and use it against them. Remarkably, and rather inappropriately, he even told the French that if "left to ourselves everything will I think be satisfactorily arranged, and perhaps in the course of the present year," a thinly veiled hint that Jefferson's potential election as president in November 1796 could overturn Jay's Treaty and reverse its ill effects. Unfortunately for Monroe, his Federalist rivals had already set in motion his recall from Paris.[60]

Almost from the moment he assumed control of the State Department, Timothy Pickering decided that keeping a Francophile like Monroe as minister to France threatened both national security and the Federalist Party itself. Pickering seized on Monroe's unsuccessful replies to French complaints of the Jay Treaty as a pretext for dismissing him.[61] Upon learning of Monroe's recall, France officially suspended relations with the United States. Monroe, meanwhile, did not blame them. On the contrary, upon receiving his notice of removal, Monroe once again addressed the French government. He reflected on having borne "witness to a revolution in my own country. I was deeply penetrated with its principles which are the same with those of your revolution." Monroe felt as though he had "partaken with you in all the perilous and trying situations in which you have been placed." The French were poised to enter a "dawn of prosperity," and Monroe had tried to preserve a "close union and perfect harmony between our two nations." His entire ministry had been dedicated to "promot[ing] this object." Monroe left his position in December 1796 and arrived back in the United States in late June of 1797.[62]

The administration's conduct at the end of his ministry enraged Monroe.[63] Privately, he lashed out at President Washington, acerbically deriding the tone of his famous farewell address as akin to those of historical monarchs who "practiced ingratitude in their transactions with other great powers." Washington went further though in making such thanklessness a "publick virtue." He continued with a typical anti-Federalist tirade: "Where these men will plunge our affairs God only knows, but such a collection of vain, superficial blunderers, to say no worse of them, were never I think before placed at the head of any respectable State."[64]

Later, as the United States undertook an undeclared naval war with France during John Adams's administration, Monroe lamented that as the "despots of Europe united against France . . . our administration actually favored the despots." It made sense, Monroe wrote in 1798, that the kings of Europe had gone to war with France. With "Reason, philosophy and commerce" sapping the "foundations of the old feudal system," there was too much at stake for the European monarchs to simply allow the French Revolution to continue unopposed. The republican cause presented a growing threat to these monarchs. If the Revolution succeeded in France, it was only a matter of time until "not a tyrant in the world would be left to oppress mankind."[65] They could not allow the republican "infection" to spread. Further, because the French Revolution "emanated" from America it was logical to assume that if the monarchies were successful in defeating France they would soon set their sights on the United States. This meant that Americans had a role to play in the crisis whether the Federalists wanted to admit it or not. Thus, in Monroe's mind the Federalists had damaged "national honor and interest." Perhaps more importantly, they had also squandered a golden opportunity.[66]

Monroe made several private notes to himself about this lost chance. As the war raged between France and her enemies the United States was situated near colonies vital to all of the combatants. Monroe believed that Washington's administration should have used this position as a weapon in their negotiations with the monarchists. If the United States found itself in difficulty with any European power, they could simply "cut the thread which bound the two hemispheres together." In a final remarkable comment that hints at the doctrine he would create a quarter-century later, Monroe wrote that he foresaw the "complete emancipation" of the

Western Hemisphere, though he admitted that "perhaps the period for so great a revolution has not yet arrived."[67]

Monroe was not content to keep his criticism of the Federalists private. In 1797 Monroe published an account of his ministry criticizing the conduct of the Washington administration, titled *A View of the Conduct of the Executive, in the Foreign Affairs of the United States, Connected with the Mission to the French Republic, during the Years 1794, 1795, 1796*. In it, Monroe laid out his entire three-year ministry in a sixty-four-page narrative, complete with accompanying correspondence. According to Monroe, the United States had enjoyed a standing with France "so advantageous . . . so easy to preserve! And yet all these advantages have been thrown away." The administration instead sought to "plunge us into a war with our ancient ally, and on the side of the kings of Europe contending against her for the subversion of liberty!" The Federalists, Monroe claimed, hoped to bring the United States in line with England and had in the process thrown "our national honor . . . in the dust."[68]

All this might easily have been avoided. If the administration had simply "stood well with France . . . we might have preserved our ancient renown . . . and even appeared as a defender of liberty" without the necessity of going to war. This last is a critical point. Monroe primarily wanted to lend ideological support for republicanism in France. He did not envision U.S. military intervention in the French Revolution. A strong statement of support from the United States would have thrown the moral weight of the United States, the beacon of republicanism, behind the French cause. By failing to do so the United States had squandered an opportunity that would haunt it for ages to come. Monroe predicted that it would take many years "to raise us to the high ground from which we have fallen." Over the next two decades Monroe's "éclat" for the republican cause merged with a growing political savvy that helped him win the presidency, and take the first steps toward retaking the "high ground" the United States had surrendered in France.[69]

## Conclusions

Monroe's stint in France was a critical period in Monroe's life for several reasons. Though Federalists saw his behavior as disgraceful, Monroe's profile within the Democratic-Republican opposition was greatly enhanced by his time in Paris, as evidenced by his election as governor of Virginia in December of 1799. More importantly, though, Monroe's ministry proved and indeed solidified his dedication to the republican cause. Monroe knew his actions were likely to irritate men like Jay and Pickering, if not more moderate figures such as Randolph and Washington. He viewed the risks as worthwhile to spread republicanism abroad by forging a bond between the French and American republics. Monroe ultimately came to view his time in France as a lost opportunity, and this helped shape his republican diplomacy and his political career.

While in Paris Monroe initially succeeded in repairing what he saw as the damage done by his Francophobic predecessor Gouverneur Morris, but Jay's agreement with the British government undid all his work. It was perhaps nothing less than he expected coming from Jay, whom he had distrusted for at least a decade. The treaty nevertheless dealt a harsh blow to Monroe. He hoped that Jay's agreement would force moderates like Washington to the republican side. He also tried to limit the treaty's damage by agreeing to share its contents with the French government, criticizing it openly, and even hinting to French officials that Jefferson would rescind the agreement if he were elected in 1796. After the administration approved the treaty, Monroe believed that he had been misled by his Federalist superiors, whom he began to suspect shared Jay's dangerous fondness for monarchy. Monroe's support from Republicans like Jefferson, Madison, and Albert Gallatin meanwhile convinced him that his actions had been justified. This prompted Monroe to turn his righteous indignation at George Washington, a significant step for a man who idolized the first president for most of his career.

Of course, Monroe's disappointment was doubly frustrating because he also saw his ministry as a missed chance to build his own personal legacy as a champion to the cause, to be remembered as the man who had built a lasting alliance between the world's foremost republics. After Monroe was recalled from France, he remained on the lookout for other opportunities to build his legacy. Monroe's passion for republicanism endured even as both world and domestic politics shifted, forcing him to alter his own immediate goals for championing the cause. Over the next two decades Monroe focused on securing republicanism at home, while making his way up the American political ladder. Monroe's experience in France never left him, however, and it played a powerful role in shaping his republican diplomacy throughout the rest of his career.

# 4

→> <-←

## JAMES MONROE

### TRAITOR

I have always been a Republican.
JAMES MONROE, 1810

James Monroe: Traitor.
JOHN RANDOLPH OF ROANOKE, 1811

Monroe has furnished unequivocal evidence that his lust for power is insatiable.
JOHN ARMSTRONG JR., 1816

IDEALISTS ARE RARELY SUCCESSFUL in politics, and Monroe was no exception. His enthusiasm for the republican cause continued unabated when he returned from France, as he clashed with his Federalist opponents. He nearly fought a duel with Alexander Hamilton in 1797 over the Maria Reynolds affair, and even considered challenging President John Adams over the latter's criticism of his actions in France. Then Jefferson was elected in 1800 and, as a key member of the new president's inner circle, Monroe found himself in an altogether different position.[1] Over the next decade and a half Monroe evolved into a shrewd political operator. In many ways he became the most astute politician of the Virginia dynasty. Monroe developed keen political survival skills in his rise to the presidency, but he also never lost the idealism of his youth. While Monroe's talents grew, his immediate goals for the republican cause underwent a similar transformation. As the Republican Party asserted increasing dominance in the United States, and republicanism in Europe wilted under the tyrannical thumb of Napoleon Bonaparte, Monroe saw opportunities for spreading the cause abroad increasingly scarce. Instead, he focused on securing republicanism at home, expanding its boundaries across the continent, and ensuring his own political future. His growing political skills, combined with his continued commitment to securing the American republic at home, helped him climb the Democratic-Republican hierarchy all the way to the presidency in 1817. By that time the political situation had shifted once again, giving Monroe an opportunity to cement his legacy as a champion of republicanism.

Three critical moments illustrate Monroe's efforts to both secure American republicanism and climb the American political hierarchy. First, with the Republican Party in the ascendancy after the election of 1800, Jefferson sent Monroe back to France to negotiate what eventually became the Louisiana Purchase in 1803. Monroe's second stint in France, this time on Jefferson's behalf, produced far better results than did his first sojourn. The Purchase secured the United States' western border and helped spread republicanism across the continent. Monroe also manipulated the Purchase's aftermath to ensure that he, and not Minister to France Robert R. Livingston, received credit for finalizing the negotiations with France. The second incident occurred in 1808 when Monroe returned from Europe to run for president against his friend James Madison. Monroe fell out with Madison, and to a lesser extent Jefferson, because he thought their policy concerning Great Britain was flawed. Monroe saw an opportunity to bring the British closer to the side of republicanism with the Monroe-Pinkney Treaty. The treaty was ultimately discarded by President Jefferson and Secretary of State Madison, and the humiliation over this rebuke convinced Monroe to vindicate his actions by running for president against Madison in 1808. Yet even as he challenged Madison for the presidency, Monroe cunningly took the necessary steps to ensure his standing within the Republican Party by maintaining his close relationship with Thomas Jefferson. This eventually facilitated his return to the Republican hierarchy, and helped him secure a position within Madison's cabinet in 1811. Finally, during the War of 1812 Monroe, by then serving beside President Madison as secretary of state, helped lead the United States to war in order to secure republican government from the threat of monarchial Great Britain. As he fought the war Monroe eliminated a potential rival for the presidency in Secretary of War John Armstrong, a man Monroe saw as wholly unfit for the office, due to his anti-republican tendencies. Thus, by war's end Monroe had helped secure American republicanism as well as his own path to the presidency.

## LOUISIANA

The fate of the republican experiment in Europe looked increasingly uncertain in the years following Monroe's stint in revolutionary France. While the future of republicanism looked bright in the United States with Jefferson's election in 1800, the promise Republicans beheld in the French Revolution faded as Napoleon Bonaparte assumed power as First Consul in November of 1799 with the coup of 18 Brumaire (November 9). Napoleon's ascension disabused many Republicans of the notion that France's revolution mirrored the American version.[2]

As a result of this change in French fortunes, panic ensued in 1801 when word circulated throughout the United States that Napoleon had forced the Spanish to retrocede the Louisiana Territory to France. Americans, Republicans included, viewed French occupation of Louisiana as a grave threat to the young country. Jefferson nicely summed up the crisis when he claimed to Robert R. Livingston, minister to France, that "nothing since the Revolution has produced more uneasy sensations through the body of the nation."[3]

French control of Louisiana presented a host of fears for the country. Spain, with its crumbling empire, made for an ideal neighbor while France, then the world's preeminent military power, presented a much greater potential threat to American interests. To complicate matters, French interest in the Western Hemisphere appeared ascendant. As the Louisiana crisis unfolded, Napoleon sent his brother-in-law, General Charles Leclerc, to the French colony of St. Domingue (present-day Haiti) in 1801 to crush a slave rebellion. It appeared that Napoleon aimed at re-creating a vast French empire in the New World. A renewed French Louisiana would also prevent the kind of westward expansion that Republicans envisioned for the country. Historian James E. Lewis argues that the major reason Americans feared French occupation of Louisiana was not the threat of French troops somehow appearing on the Mississippi, but the prospect of disunion. American leaders feared that new states west of the Appalachians might form separate nations independent of the United States. With a rival power controlling the Mississippi and with it the trade of these nations, they might look to the French for support in remaining independent from the United States. Even Jefferson, the prototypical arch-Anglophobe, asserted that French control of Louisiana would force the United States to "marry" the British fleet.[4]

The crisis intensified in October of 1802 when the Spanish intendant at New Orleans suspended the right of deposit, preventing American boats on the Mississippi from unloading their cargo in New Orleans. This effectively cut off the entire American West from the global economy. Jefferson wrote that this news created an extreme "agitation in the public mind." He faced public pressure as "every eye in the United States was now fixed on the affairs of Louisiana." The public, particularly westerners, clamored for Jefferson to take action. The president planned to diffuse the situation by purchasing the city of New Orleans. This would, hopefully, alleviate westerners' fears by ensuring that their goods reached the open market. With the port of New Orleans closed, and Robert R. Livingston achieving little headway in reaching an agreement with Napoleon, Jefferson decided the crisis warranted more drastic measures. As Washington had a decade before, Jefferson turned to James Monroe.[5]

In January of 1803 Jefferson appointed Monroe as envoy extraordinary to France for the express purpose of acquiring New Orleans to secure access to the Mississippi. Monroe was an obvious choice to send to France. Personally loyal to Jefferson and politically bound to the Republican Party, he maintained many of his former connections in France and was well liked in that country due to his unerring support for their revolution. He also had a reputation as one of the few American political figures who advocated westerners' interests.

As discussed in chapter 2, Monroe had earned this reputation as a champion of the American West while serving in the Confederation Congress during the 1780s controversy over the Jay-Gardoqui Treaty. Two decades later, Jefferson believed that the "strong proofs of the interests he took in the free navigation of that river [the Mississippi]" made Monroe a perfect candidate for the mission to France in 1803. Jefferson told Monroe that "no other man can be found" who possessed all the attributes necessary to pull off the bargain.[6] In his letter conferring the appointment, Jefferson told Monroe that the very future of the nation itself depended upon his mission.

Jefferson asked his former apprentice to travel back to France to help secure American access to the Mississippi. The mission was another legacy-building opportunity for Monroe. Jefferson explained the stakes when he asked his friend to take the position. "On the event of this mission," Jefferson warned, "depends [sic] the future destinies of this republic." If the purchase failed Jefferson feared that "war cannot be distant." He also knew enough about his former apprentice to appeal to his sense of duty, while hinting at the recognition success would bring Monroe. He urged his former apprentice to remember that he was one of the few men "born for the public," destined to serve "the human race on a broad scale."[7]

Seeing this as a chance to advance both the republican cause and his own career, Monroe quickly accepted the position in France. He was eager to aid Jefferson's administration in this crisis. Most important though was the chance to help secure republicanism in the United States. As he made ready to leave Monroe had a clear idea of the stakes involved in his mission. Determined to head off the French threat, Monroe assured his mentor that he would "never suffer France or any other power to tamper with our interior." The Louisiana Purchase ultimately helped spread republicanism across much of the continent, but initially Monroe was more concerned about securing the cause in the United States. He believed that if his mission were a success, the "union [would] be consolidated, republican principles confirmed, and a fair prospect of permanent peace and happiness presented to our country." It would secure the cause in the United States for decades to come and effectively confirm the principles upon which Jefferson, Monroe, and the Republican Party stood throughout the 1790s. The consequences of failure on the other hand were almost too dire to consider. It might "result in a war" with France, or, just as troubling, "restore the federal party to power." In any scenario, Monroe believed that should he fail to come home with a favorable resolution the "result might be fatal" to the new republic.[8]

After Monroe arrived in France in April of 1803 a breakthrough in the long-stalled negotiations between Livingston and his French diplomatic counterparts occurred almost immediately. Two years of frustrating negotiations had prompted Livingston to lament, only a few months before, that he "saw little use for a minister here." Then suddenly and seemingly out of nowhere the French finally offered to negotiate.[9] When news arrived in Paris of Monroe's arrival at the port city of Le Havre, the wily French foreign minister Maurice de Talleyrand almost casually asked Livingston whether the Americans wanted to buy the entire Louisiana Territory. Livingston, who had authority only to buy New Orleans, hesitated and missed a chance to seal the bargain before Monroe could take part. Once Monroe arrived in Paris, Livingston, fearing his new negotiating partner would swoop in and take credit, tried to exclude him from the subsequent talks.[10] Tension between the two diplomats mounted because Livingston feared his efforts would be overshadowed by Monroe's arrival. He worried that Monroe would take the glory for the Purchase, credit Livingston believed he himself deserved. After all, he had spent two years in France before Monroe arrived. Now it appeared that the new envoy would reap the rewards of Livingston's hard work. What ensued was a petty squabble between the two men over recognition for the Purchase.

Most historians of the Purchase agree that Livingston began the battle over credit for acquiring Louisiana. In *Negotiating the Louisiana Purchase*, Robert Brecher takes this view. In his biography of Livingston, Historian George Dangerfield accuses Livingston of doctoring the official record to deprive Monroe of recognition. Monroe's own biographer, Harry Ammon, asserts that "in this unseemly contest for glory Livingston bears a large share of the blame." Ammon absolves Monroe of almost any culpability, claiming that "Monroe merely asserted that the treaty was a joint work in which administration policy had played a decisive role." Dangerfield, meanwhile, waxes eloquent on Monroe's character, calling him "transparently a good man." This portrayal of Monroe underestimates his rather deft handling of the affair. Monroe managed to appear magnanimous by deferring personal acclaim for the Purchase while portraying the "facts," as he called them, in such a way that assumed credit for himself without appearing self-aggrandizing.[11]

Immediately upon his arrival in Paris, Monroe's friend and fellow Virginian Fulwar Skipwith told him of Livingston's plan to sideline him. Monroe told Madison that Livingston feared his appearance would take "from [Livingston] the credit of having brought everything to a proper conclusion." Written only a few days after he arrived in Paris, this missive set the tone for Monroe's part in the debate over the question of credit. He warned the secretary of state that Livingston planned to argue that he had "accomplished what was wished for without my aid." Monroe cautioned Madison that Livingston would try to assume all the acclaim for the Purchase. Meanwhile, Monroe crafted his own version of the negotiations.[12]

Monroe wisely credited the administration for their policy in sending him to France. He argued that his arrival in France on April 8, known in Paris on the following day, led to Napoleon's offer of April 10 to sell all of Louisiana. In couching the question of credit in this manner, Monroe scored points with his superiors by praising the "wise and firm and moderate measures" of the administration. On the surface, Monroe humbly downplayed his own direct role in the negotiations, admitting that the offer "was not the effect of any management of mine." It was simply the administration's choice to send him that ultimately induced the French to sell.[13]

While never directly pointing to his own part in the negotiations, Monroe nevertheless made indirect statements designed to highlight his role. If the negotiations failed, Monroe pointed out, "all responsibility would have been on the government and myself," rather than Livingston. Further, he praised Jefferson's motives in nominating him, and the president's "belief that I would bring the affair promptly to an issue." Monroe implied that his arrival in France persuaded Napoleon's government to sell the territory. Monroe explained that his familiarity with those in the French government, combined with his well-known advocacy for American access to the Mississippi, went a long way toward convincing the French that the administration took the crisis seriously. Both the French and Jefferson knew that Monroe would bring "invariable zeal to promote the object of the cession." Monroe implied that the administration's "wise measures" made the difference. Their wisest measure of course was sending Monroe. "If my mission produced any effect it was owing altogether to the motive which induced the President to nominate me." It was a clever line for Monroe to take. It heaped praise on his superiors while implying that his very presence in Paris had prompted the French to sell.[14]

Monroe also made indirect jabs at Livingston. First, he informed Madison of Livingston's attempt to preclude Monroe from the negotiations.

He then explained that during the early negotiations, when Monroe did not think it proper for him to participate before his official introduction to the emperor, Livingston had met with the French minister of finance, Francois Barbe-Marbois. Monroe claimed to have coached Livingston on how to behave with the French finance minister. Monroe told Madison of his fear that Livingston would appear too bold and eager in his negotiations, cautioning the minister to "hear and not to speak," presumably until Monroe could provide further instructions. Monroe wanted Madison to recognize that, while he had not been present at these early talks, he had directed Livingston throughout the negotiations.[15]

Monroe even went so far as to subtly undermine Livingston's future political career. In November 1803, exactly a year before the presidential election, Monroe learned that Livingston hoped to replace Aaron Burr as the Republicans' vice presidential candidate. Livingston planned to return home in the spring of 1804 to capitalize on his reputation from the Purchase and make his case for inclusion on the ticket. Monroe informed Madison of Livingston's plans, and suggested that the administration request Livingston stay at his post for another year. This, Monroe believed, would flatter Livingston and tempt him to remain. Monroe did not want his colleague returning to the United States, trumpeting himself as the sole negotiator of the Louisiana Purchase, while Monroe remained in Europe unable to respond. Ultimately, Monroe's campaign for credit succeeded. Livingston's political career all but ended after France. His hopes for the presidency, if ever he had any, were dashed when Jefferson selected George Clinton as his vice president. Afterward, he left politics entirely. Monroe, meanwhile, became Jefferson's "man" in Europe. During the next half decade Monroe shuttled from one European capital to another negotiating on behalf of Jefferson and the United States.[16]

Secretary of State Madison nicely summed up the effect the Purchase had for both the American republic and Monroe's career when he wrote that "the bargain will be regarded on the whole as highly advantageous."[17] Monroe went much further in his assessment of the Purchase's impact. He believed that it would put the United States forever "beyond the reach" of Europe. It would secure everything "essential to the sovereignty of our country" and the "peace, prosperity and happiness of our people."[18] For Monroe, the Purchase would strengthen the "bond of our union" while effectively separating the United States from the "European world." He went as far as to say that the acquisition of the Louisiana Territory provided the United States with "real and substantial independence."[19] Monroe's second mission to France had helped secure the western border of the United States and American access to the Mississippi. No longer would the United States have to fear monarchial threats on their western border, and no longer would westerners be dependent on a foreign power for access to the Mississippi River. It was, in his mind, a major victory for the republican cause. Just as importantly, it put him well on his way to capturing high political office. Before he did so however, his political skills would be tested again, this time against James Madison.

## THE MONROE-PINKNEY TREATY AND THE ELECTION OF 1808

One of Monroe's many correspondents understood exactly how important the Purchase was to his legacy. John Randolph of Roanoke wrote to Monroe in the fall of 1803 praising Monroe's acquisition of Louisiana. Randolph, a Virginia congressman, told Monroe that his "name and character" would be forever linked to the Purchase, which was "destined to form a new aera [sic] in our annals."[20] Randolph's letter marks the beginning of a transition in Monroe's career. The Louisiana Purchase made Monroe a celebrated figure within the Republican Party, but the kind words from Randolph also foreshadowed what became a difficult part of Monroe's life as he split with Jefferson's administration over foreign policy questions.

Monroe did not return home after his success in France. Instead, he stayed in Europe until 1807. When he finally returned to the United States, he challenged Madison for the presidency. Few people today remember that James Monroe ran for president in 1808, mostly because he lost badly. Monroe received only 3,408 votes, all in the state of Virginia. Instead, Madison succeeded Jefferson as America's fourth president. Nevertheless, the campaign of 1808 caused a complete break between Monroe and Madison. In fact, from 1808 to 1810 they neither spoke nor exchanged a letter. Yet in 1811, Madison made Monroe his secretary of state and effectively the heir apparent to the Republican Party and the presidency.[21]

Before delving deeper into this incident it is critical to understand Monroe's relationship with Madison. Monroe always saw Thomas Jefferson alone as the head of the Republican Party. To Monroe's thinking, it was his former mentor who led Republicans through the crises of the 1790s, and to victory in 1800. Madison, like Monroe, was merely one of Jefferson's chief lieutenants. To Monroe, Madison was therefore not necessarily the automatic choice to become the next president. Indeed, Monroe saw himself as a better candidate to carry on the republican legacy when Jefferson retired in 1808.[22]

Jefferson introduced Monroe to Madison just before assuming the position as American minister to France in 1785. As such Jefferson became the tie that bound Monroe to Madison during the first years of their relationship. It is also important to note that Monroe never thought of Madison as a mentor. Madison was merely a colleague and Jefferson's political ally. This is not to say that Madison and Monroe did not have a good relationship; they became friends and collaborators in their own right. The key point is that Monroe did not defer to Madison as he did to Jefferson. Traces of this can be seen throughout Monroe's autobiography. While Jefferson, as we saw in chapter 2, has a prominent place in Monroe's narrative, Madison hardly gains notice. Madison does not seem to hold any particular place of honor during Monroe's early years. Monroe did not, for instance, comment on his first meeting with Madison. Instead, Monroe portrays him as just another Virginia politician, and as such quarrels between the two men, while rare, played a part in their association. Monroe's occasionally contentious relationship with Madison can be traced as far back as 1789.

During the first election under the new federal constitution, Madison and Monroe became rivals in a contest for a seat in the House of Representatives. Madison's role in creating and ratifying the Constitution has since made him a celebrated figure, but not everyone in Virginia supported him. Rabid antifederalist Patrick Henry only grudgingly accepted the establishment of a more powerful federal government. To keep it in check he determined to fill Congress with as many Virginia antifederalists as possible. When Madison chose to run for the House of Representatives, Henry turned to Monroe as a suitable alternative.[23] Henry and the antifederalists questioned Madison's republican credentials. He had, after all, helped create a strong central government at the Constitutional Convention and had coauthored the *Federalist Papers*. Some questioned whether he remained too enamored of federal power to be truly dedicated to the republican cause. Madison and Monroe remained cordial throughout the election process, traveling throughout the district while speaking to various audiences on key issues. They made these journeys together and even shared lodgings during the campaign. This type of campaign was common before the partisan feelings of the 1790s split the political system into two rival factions. Madison eventually won the election and the two men resumed their friendship. Nevertheless, many of the same issues, both political and personal, that had divided the two men in 1789 still lingered in 1803.[24]

Though he respected and admired Madison, Monroe did not see him as an unassailable pillar of republicanism like Jefferson. Monroe thought of himself as a more natural heir to the republican leadership. Monroe saw his republicanism as similar to Jefferson's, while Madison had supported a strong federal government in the past and had appeared to do the same during Jefferson's presidency. Furthermore, while many still viewed Madison as the heir apparent to the party's leadership, a distinct faction within the Republican ranks distrusted him and favored Monroe.

This faction, known as the "Old Republicans," made up the radical wing of the Republican Party and purported to uphold the true principles of republicanism.[25] A significant portion of these malcontents resided in Virginia, including leaders such as John Randolph of Roanoke and John Taylor of Caroline. They held Madison responsible for what they saw as the administration's centralizing tendencies. They distrusted federal power, advocated states' rights, and saw Madison's political philosophy as too similar to that of the Federalists. Monroe's natural republican leanings made him sympathetic to the Old Republican faction, and with his national reputation he offered a credible alternative to Madison for president.[26]

Initially, Monroe refused to listen to the Old Republicans' advances, but as differences between him and the administration mounted, he became more receptive. With pressure mounting from Randolph and Taylor, Monroe gradually came to believe that the administration was pushing him aside in favor of Madison. When Monroe eventually decided to run for president, it was to illustrate his importance within the Republican Party, and prove that he commanded a significant personal following. What better way to appear as a champion of republicanism than to represent the most dedicated members of the Republican Party? At the same time, Monroe knew that challenging Madison presented a significant risk to his political future, so he took steps to ensure that his run for the presidency in 1808 did not cost him his career.[27]

Problems between Madison and Monroe began with basic disagreements over the direction of American foreign policy. After his time in France, Monroe traveled to Spain in 1803 in an effort to obtain West Florida as part of the Louisiana Purchase. He began to question the administration's decision-making when they ignored his advice concerning Spanish-American relations. Monroe proposed an aggressive policy against Spain.[28] He suggested to Madison that the United States ought to occupy Texas to force the Spanish to cede Florida.[29] Monroe then urged the administration to take possession of Florida itself in 1805.[30] Though Jefferson and Madison occasionally made veiled threats to the Spanish government they had no intention of carrying out any action to force Spain into a settlement. Spain ultimately proved unwilling to part with Florida, and in Monroe's mind the blame for his failure to complete the negotiations was a result of the administration's refusal to listen to his advice. Monroe continued to see Florida as critical to securing the republic's southern border, but as we will see in chapter 5, he would have to wait until his presidency to finalize the acquisition of the territory.

When the administration disregarded his counsel on Florida it was the first of a series of disagreements that persuaded Monroe that they no longer trusted his judgment.[31] The Spanish incident also taught Monroe a valuable lesson on the state of American power in Europe. While he had enjoyed great success in acquiring Louisiana from France, he had been lucky. Monroe knew full well that it was the French military disaster in Haiti, combined with the rumblings of a renewed war with Great Britain, that had convinced Napoleon to sell the territory. In the future, the United States could not depend on such favorable circumstances. Monroe feared that in America's "present feeble state" the "whole system" was at risk. If the U.S. leadership did not take action the public would lose faith with them and eventually the "manly spirit which characterizes us will most probably disappear." In other words, American republicanism required a strong diplomatic hand to ensure its success at home.[32]

Monroe consistently urged Jefferson and Madison to take a hard line when dealing with European nations during this period. He wanted Jefferson's administration to adopt an "attitude of menace" toward foreign governments. Otherwise, he assured the president, "all will insult us, encroach our rights, and plunder us, if they can do it with impunity."[33] After his disappointment in Spain, Monroe traveled to London to complete a new treaty with Britain. His second stint in France in 1803 had more than made up for his disappointments during the French Revolution, and now he traveled to Great Britain to complete a new treaty with the British to hopefully repair the damage done in 1795 by his old nemesis, John Jay.

Jefferson's administration hoped to duplicate their success during the Louisiana negotiations by sending a second diplomat to aid Monroe in Britain. Monroe wanted the administration to allow him to negotiate the treaty alone, arguing that the arrival of a new envoy would undermine his position with the British ministry. This line of reasoning provided Monroe with political cover. More importantly, Monroe feared that he would not be credited for his hard work in laying the foundation for a treaty (just as had happened to Livingston in France). His successor would "take the ground at a moment of calm, under auspices more favorable," and would only be "concluding a bargain after the opinion of both parties has in some measure been made up." Again, as in Spain, Jefferson and Madison ignored his advice. The administration sent Maryland Republican William Pinkney as a special envoy to Great Britain. Monroe interpreted Pinkney's appointment as a sign that his voice carried little weight with his friends in Washington. As historian Harry Ammon explains in his biography of the fifth president, Monroe tended to view relatively commonplace disagreements as personal attacks on his professional abilities. Transatlantic communications, notoriously slow during this era, also played a role in the problems between Monroe and his superiors in Washington. An ocean away, Monroe could not meet face-to-face with his colleagues to receive an explanation for their actions. Monroe could not understand why, after he had been part of the Republican leadership during its rise to prominence during the 1790s, Madison and Jefferson suddenly no longer heeded his counsel.[34]

John Randolph supplied Monroe with an answer. Indeed, he and the other Old Republicans helped turn Monroe against Madison. They began courting Monroe as early as 1804, well before the Pinkney appointment, sending letters complaining of Madison. The Old Republicans claimed that Madison was doing serious damage to the republican cause. Randolph told Monroe that Madison's poor leadership hurt republicanism's reputation around the world, because his mistakes were "attributed to defects of the system" rather than to Madison himself. Randolph, who was prone to hyperbole, claimed that Madison was shaking "the confidence of mankind in both hemispheres" in republican government. He informed Monroe that the most "constant and influential of the old republicans . . . have beheld with immeasurable disgust" Madison's "neutralizing" their republican principles by his "cold and insidious moderation." Such attacks, especially made in Randolph's wonderfully acerbic style, eventually took their toll on Monroe.[35]

Monroe initially rebuffed the Old Republicans by telling them that it would be "impossible" for him to run for president without destroying his "antient [sic] friendships." Nevertheless, they continued to recruit him throughout 1805 and 1806. Despite his initial reluctance, Monroe was grateful for their support. He was flattered at the "confidence which you and other friends repose in me, as it is the strongest proof which can be given . . . of my past conduct in public life." The attentions of the Old Republicans offered a welcome contrast to the treatment he received from the administration. Where Jefferson and Madison ignored his advice, Randolph made it clear that he and other republican radicals preferred Monroe's ideas over the administration's. As a result, Monroe started to consider the possibility of challenging Madison. If "true" republicans such as Randolph and Taylor saw him as the obvious champion of their cause, maybe he was a better candidate than Madison to carry the party's banner in 1808.[36]

Randolph continued pressuring Monroe throughout 1806 and 1807. In a September 1806 letter, Randolph bluntly told Monroe that many of the Old Republicans supported him for the presidency over Madison. By then Monroe's disagreements with the administration made him less resistant to the idea of running. He told Randolph that "circumstances have occurr'd [sic] during my service abroad, which were calculated to hurt my feelings." His sentiments toward "the men now in power on our side of the water" had changed. Monroe concluded ominously that his problems with the administration might "produce a change in the future relation between some of them and myself." Over the next few months, the fallout from the administration's eventual reaction to the Monroe-Pinkney Treaty proved the final insult. It produced a rupture that (temporarily) sent Monroe into the arms of Randolph and the Old Republicans.[37]

Monroe recognized that Britain's policy toward America was dependent upon the makeup of the British ministry. Once Charles James Fox became the British foreign secretary after years in opposition, Monroe became more optimistic at the chances of securing a treaty with Britain. Monroe's enthusiasm was based on his expectation that he could come to an accommodation with England over commercial concerns. Unfortunately, Jefferson took Monroe's optimism to mean that he could expect Britain to give in on the question of impressment.[38] Monroe's goal for the treaty with the British was essentially to undo the harm done to American prestige over the past few years. Monroe wanted to reverse the damage caused by the administration's weakness during the negotiations with Spain. Monroe also wanted to strengthen relations with Great Britain. He saw the Monroe-Pinkney Treaty in part as a starting point for a rapprochement with the mother country, something he would look to continue as president. Monroe even told his British counterpart in the negotiations that he saw the British monarchy as "more republican than monarchical," while the French Republic under Napoleon was fast becoming "infinitely more monarchical than your monarchy."[39]

The Monroe-Pinkney Treaty marked something of a turning point for Monroe, both in terms of his republican diplomacy and his relationship with James Madison. Monroe began to see Britain increasingly as less the bastion of tyranny from his youth. He saw changes in Britain pushing the country closer to republican values, and envisioned future cooperation between the two nations, hopefully beginning with his and Pinkney's treaty. The treaty's ultimate failure and the War of 1812 would eventually put this on hold, but the seeds for future Anglo-American cooperation had been planted in Monroe's mind and would play a significant role during his presidency.

Despite Monroe's initial misgivings, he and Pinkney actually worked well together in their negotiations with Great Britain. They quickly determined that Britain would never make a major concession on the issue of the impressment of American sailors onto British ships. They therefore signed a treaty with the British that did not deal directly with this troublesome issue. When it reached the United States, the administration rejected the so-called Monroe-Pinkney Treaty out of hand, refusing even to send it to the Senate for confirmation. For Jefferson and Madison any agreement that did not end impressments was unacceptable. Jefferson bluntly told Monroe that "the British commisrs [sic] appear to have screwed every article as far as it would bear, to have taken everything, & yielded nothing." The rejection shocked Monroe, who had explained to both Jefferson and Madison that he believed a concession on impressments would come in practice if not in the actual wording of the treaty.[40] It appeared to Monroe that the administration put no faith in his abilities as a negotiator or his judgment as a diplomat. In reality, their conflict probably resulted more from a series of misunderstandings than from any malice on Madison's part. Monroe was forced to deal with certain European diplomatic realities that made a British concession on impressments nearly impossible, while Madison had to consider the American political landscape that made a treaty not dedicated to ending impressments unacceptable. News reached Monroe of the treaty's rejection in June of 1807 and, feeling betrayed, he boarded a ship for home.[41]

Upon his arrival in Washington, DC, in December of 1807, Jefferson and Madison met with Monroe but did not include him in their discussions concerning strategy toward Britain. They also failed to mention Monroe's political future, and he left the meeting convinced that he had been ostracized from the administration.[42] The situation Monroe found himself in when he arrived back home in Virginia was fraught with political dangers. He had been gone over five years, a lifetime in politics. Without Jefferson and Madison as his allies he might have been finished as a political force altogether. John Taylor of Caroline cautioned Monroe to beware the dangers a campaign against Madison would present. He warned Monroe that if he were to lose it would probably "close upon you forever the avenue to the presidency." Taylor also told Monroe that "Mr. Jefferson is unquestionably your fast friend, and earnestly desirous of advancing your prosperity." Taylor, in fact, struck upon the very strategy Monroe used to ensure he did not stay out of power for long.[43]

That same month, February 1808, Monroe told Jefferson that he felt "heavy censure" after completing the treaty, believing that it had been "wielded against me" in order to "impeach my character." Further, Monroe believed, it continued to be used to do him harm "in the publick [sic] estimation." It was therefore "impossible for me to be insensible to the effects produced" by the attacks. Monroe explained to Jefferson that "means may be found to do me justice." Monroe decided to allow his name to be brought forward as a candidate for president, which would help him prove his republican bona fides to the administration. But there were risks. If he should fail, which appeared likely considering Madison's high profile as secretary of state and his support among regular Republicans, it might destroy any hope Monroe had of remaining a power within the Republican Party. He refused to ride headlong carrying the banner of radical republicanism without an exit strategy. Coming up with a solution, he told Jefferson that though he would seek "justice" by running for office, he would also ensure that it did not cause "the slightest injury to you." He assured Jefferson that "I shall never cease to take a deep interest in your political fame." Monroe took other measures so as not to risk his standing within the party. He never sought an accommodation with the Federalists, he did not campaign for the office, and he even restricted his supporters' actions throughout the election. While trying to prove his standing as a republican by challenging Madison, Monroe worked to keep Jefferson's support.[44]

Monroe's candidacy did not offer much of a challenge to Madison, but the campaign seriously threatened their friendship, resulting in a complete break between the two. From the spring of 1808 until the middle of 1810 they had virtually no contact with one another. While the contest nearly ruined Monroe's friendship with Madison, his relationship with Jefferson improved almost immediately after he declared his candidacy. This was no accident. Monroe saw the retiring president as the best avenue back into the good graces of the Republican Party, and he took steps to preserve his friendship with Jefferson even as he cut off all communication with Madison. The idealism of his youth had been balanced by a shrewd political survival instinct. Monroe deftly managed to carry the standard for the Old Republicans by challenging Madison even as he strengthened his ties to Jefferson.[45]

Monroe's reconciliation with Jefferson began when the other man contacted him during the winter of 1808 expressing his concern over the forthcoming election. "I see with infinite grief a contest arising between yourself and another," Jefferson lamented, "who have been very dear to each other, and especially to me." Jefferson declared his neutrality in the contest, telling Monroe that he and Madison were the "two principal pillars of my happiness." He also stated his wish to carry into his retirement the "affections of all my friends." Monroe took this as an opening to lay his grievances at Jefferson's feet, and take the first steps toward rehabilitating their friendship.[46]

Monroe told Jefferson, "No occurrences of my whole life ever gave me so much concern as some which took place during my absence abroad, proceeding from the present administration." Despite his wounded feelings, he assured Jefferson that he would not dwell on the subject of their differences. Instead, Monroe declared his continued commitment to Jefferson. He recounted their early years together, explaining that he would never forget "the proofs of kindness and friendship which I received from you in early life." Throughout his career he had done all he could to "support and advance to the utmost of my power your political and personal fame." Monroe wanted Jefferson to understand two points. First, he assured his old mentor that his candidacy did not represent a break from the party. Second, he hoped to show Jefferson that he saw himself as a true Jeffersonian republican. He had built his candidacy around his devotion to the same principles that animated Jefferson. He even told Jefferson that he believed his mentor's legacy intertwined with the nation's fate. "I have seen the national interest and your advancement and fame so intimately connected, as to constitute essentially the same cause," Monroe explained. It is important to note Monroe's use of the word fame here. Because he believed that the country's future was linked to Jefferson, he believed his mentor's fame ran parallel to the nation's. In many ways Monroe saw Jefferson as the living embodiment of republicanism itself. On a more practical level, Monroe also understood that if he harbored any further political ambition, Jefferson's continued support remained paramount.[47]

Moved by Monroe's kind words, Jefferson explained away their disagreements. He blamed their misunderstanding on "falsehoods" caused by the "party spirit" affecting the nation. Monroe responded by telling his mentor that throughout the ordeal losing Jefferson's esteem had been his only concern. With Jefferson's assurances that they remained friends, Monroe considered the matter settled. The personal connection between the two helped smooth over their differences. Both men agreed, for the sake of friendship and in Monroe's case political expediency, to chalk up their grievances as misunderstandings. Even as he mended his relationship with Jefferson, and resumed a regular correspondence with his old mentor, Monroe kept his name in contention for the presidency and remained estranged from Madison.[48]

As he continued the campaign against Madison, Monroe used his renewed friendship with Jefferson as a way back into power. Jefferson's public support remained vital to the future of Monroe's political career. Monroe knew that whatever his problems with Madison, Jefferson still had the power to facilitate his reassertion into the Republican ranks. He could afford to be seen quarrelling with Madison but not with Jefferson, the patriarch of the Republican Party. The early republic represented a transitional period for American politics. The political system had not yet evolved into the mass democracy of the Jacksonian era. Most Americans distrusted political parties, and vestiges of traditional eighteenth-century deferential politics remained dominant. The emerging factions did not yet represent permanent institutions, instead coalescing around prominent national figures. As the events surrounding the election of 1808 show, Monroe saw the Democratic-Republicans as a Jeffersonian rather than a Madisonian Party. Ultimately, Monroe deferred to Jefferson in ways that he did not to Madison. For Monroe, "Little Jemmy" served as a respected colleague and occasional rival. Jefferson, on the other hand, always figured as his mentor and the central figure of the Republican Party.[49] In October 1808, Monroe prevailed upon Jefferson to allow the publication of their correspondence during the past year, in order to prove that their close connection still flourished. Though he feared having his name brought into the contest, Jefferson reluctantly agreed. By then he realized that Monroe had little chance of winning the election and that publishing the correspondence could only help speed Monroe's return to the fold. By trumpeting his relationship to Jefferson, Monroe took a major step in silencing his critics within the Republican establishment.[50]

The connection to Jefferson also gave Monroe a convenient back channel to the new president. After Madison's election, Jefferson immediately took steps to reconcile his two friends. Jefferson met with Monroe in March of 1809 and relayed the results of the meeting in a letter to Madison. Jefferson commented that Monroe appeared "sincerely cordial" to Madison's administration. Monroe's unfortunate connection to the Old

Republicans, meanwhile, had come to an end. Jefferson explained to Madison that Monroe "has quite separated himself from the junto which had got possession of him." Jefferson also hinted that the Old Republicans had duped their old friend, but now he was "sensible that they used him for purposes not respecting himself always." Monroe had removed himself from the Old Republicans and "he and J.R. [John Randolph] now avoid seeing each other." Jefferson even reported that Monroe gave up his residence in Richmond in order to distance himself from the radical faction. In all, Jefferson was hopeful that Monroe would find his way back into the Republican Party. "I have no doubt," Jefferson assured the president, "that his strong and candid mind will bring him a cordial return to his old friends." This laid the foundation for Monroe to return to Republican ranks.[51]

The first public show of reconciliation between Monroe and the regular Republicans occurred in Richmond during an October 1809 banquet in Jefferson's honor. Monroe's presence at the dinner sent a signal that he still held Jefferson's trust and friendship. A month later, Jefferson once again met with Monroe, this time concerning a position within Madison's government, where Jefferson engaged him in a "frank conversation" concerning his future in politics.[52] At this November meeting, Jefferson conveyed Madison's offer to make Monroe the governor of the Louisiana Territory. Monroe declined, telling his mentor he would rejoin the ranks of the regular Republicans only on certain terms. By now, Monroe set his sights firmly on the presidency and refused to accept a position that did not put him in a position to achieve it. Jefferson reported to Madison that Monroe refused to "act in any office where he should be subordinate to anybody but the President himself." Luckily, just such a position soon became available.[53]

Monroe continued maneuvering himself back into the good graces of the regular Republicans. During the spring of 1810 he made a public show of support for Madison's administration. Monroe delivered a speech in Charlottesville, where he took the opportunity to "lay open [his] political mind." He claimed to be astonished by the need to do so, because, as he claimed, "I have always been a Republican." Given that he had "devoted his life to the support of free government," the idea that he would abandon the party "when a Republican sits at the helm of state" he found ridiculous. He was "known in his own state and the U.S." to be a "friend to liberty." Furthermore, Monroe boasted, "the crowned heads of Europe look at [me] sternly and acknowledge [me] a republican." He supported the republican cause and claimed to be "ready to support the administration whilst I think it acts with propriety." While Monroe supported the party, he qualified his support of Madison. "I am confident," he told the crowd, "that you would not wish me to support [the administration] when it acts improperly." Monroe hoped to work with Madison's administration, but only if his conscience allowed. "Mr. Madison is a Republican and so am I," he told his supporters. Therefore, he continued, "as long as he acts in consistence [sic] with the interests of his country I will go along with him." Despite these conditions the two men moved closer to reconciliation. A face-to-face meeting with Madison eventually sealed their reunion.[54]

Jefferson arranged for Monroe to visit Washington, DC, in May of 1810 and Madison received him warmly. Afterward, Jefferson reported the good effect the meeting had on Monroe to Madison, "I have been delighted to see the effect of Monroe's late visit to Washington on his mind," he told the president. "There appears to be the most perfect reconciliation & cordiality established towards yourself," Jefferson continued. "I think him now inclined to rejoin us with zeal." And rejoin them he did.[55] Within a year, Monroe found himself thrust into the most powerful position in Madison's administration.[56]

By March of 1811 Madison had decided to remove Robert Smith from his position as secretary of state.[57] Monroe, with his experience in foreign affairs, national reputation, and personal following, offered the ideal replacement. Having shored up his status with the party during the past two years though Jefferson, Monroe could also help Madison win the support of the radicals within Republican ranks. Madison first directed Virginia senator Richard Brent to query Monroe on the idea. Shortly thereafter he sent a letter of his own offering the position and Monroe accepted, becoming secretary of state in April of 1811.[58]

Upon learning of Monroe's reconciliation with the administration John Randolph became incensed. His diary entry for the day reads simply, "James Monroe: Traitor." Later Randolph chalked up Monroe's treachery to an "insatiable thirst for office." Randolph's usual penchant for the melodramatic belies a keen observation on the Roanoke politician's part.

While he was certainly no "traitor" to the republican cause, Monroe's back channel move into the cabinet does illustrate his "thirst" for, and improved ability to attain, power. He desperately wanted to shape political affairs, and the only way to accomplish this was to achieve high office. He learned the hard way in France that republican exuberance alone would not ensure his legacy. He now knew he had to compromise to attain the kind of power needed to become a champion of the republican cause. After all, few remember failed diplomats as champions of republicanism. That title belonged to secretaries of state or, better still, presidents.[59]

## THE WAR OF 1812

The third and final example of Monroe's political evolution occurred after his reentry into the Republican hierarchy as secretary of state. As the United States careened into another war with Great Britain in June of 1812, Monroe found himself in an altogether different kind of fight, one he was becoming increasingly adept at waging, to ensure his place as Madison's successor. The same issues that had caused the rift between Monroe and his colleagues over the Monroe-Pinkney Treaty eventually led the United States and Britain down a path to war. Britain remained locked in a life and death struggle with Napoleonic France and paid little attention to how its seemingly draconian maritime policies affected the United States. Such actions hurt American pride. Republicans yearned for a final break with Britain, and while they no longer supported the French, they remained hostile to the British monarchy. In many ways, Republicans wanted to reassert their autonomy from Britain with a second war of independence. This would end the threat the former mother country posed to the new republic once and for all.[60] Jefferson was particularly eager to end American dependence on Britain. He told William Duane that "this second weaning from British principles, British attachments, British manners and manufactures will be salutary," and he hoped the war would end the "continued subordination to the interests of England."[61]

The War of 1812 was very much an ideological conflict for Monroe as well. He explained to fellow Virginian Fulwar Skipwith that the United States declared war to preserve their national honor.[62] It was critical that the country prove to the world that it was strong enough to protect its interests from encroachment by Britain and other European powers. For Monroe, it continued toward a goal he had sought since his acquisition of the Louisiana Territory. He previously advocated a more aggressive attitude in dealing with the European powers. Had the Jefferson administration heeded his advice, by either adopting the aggressive measures he proposed or by concluding the treaty with Great Britain, perhaps the conflict might have been avoided. Now, after his advice had gone unheeded, Monroe was forced to help Madison take the ultimate step in declaring war.[63]

When war finally erupted on June 18, 1812, Monroe became marginalized in his role as secretary of state. While the fighting raged around him, Monroe's personal battle to succeed Madison began when Secretary of War William Eustis proved incapable of guiding the nation through a war with a major European power. Eustis left the cabinet, and Monroe became acting head of the War Department for the next few months. The senate eventually refused to confirm him, fearing the Virginia dynasty's growing dominance over the federal government. Instead, Monroe returned to his position as secretary of state, and Madison eventually settled on John Armstrong to head the War Department.[64]

Madison chose Armstrong almost by default. He initially offered the post to William H. Crawford and Henry Dearborn, but they both turned him down. With no other obvious choices, Madison determined to find a New Yorker for the position. This would reaffirm the New York–Virginia Republican alliance and allay fears of Virginian supremacy within the administration. Armstrong came to the cabinet with a healthy dislike for the Virginia dynasty. During his term as minister to France he had run afoul of Jefferson's administration, and he had also opposed Monroe's appointment as secretary of state in 1811. Despite these strikes against him, the Senate narrowly confirmed Armstrong's appointment by an 18–15 vote.[65]

A case can be made that Monroe would have set his sights on bringing Armstrong down no matter the man's background or his dedication to republicanism, but full credit must also be given to Monroe's ideological objections to his War Department rival. Monroe distrusted Armstrong at least in part because he did not see him as a true republican. He thought the New Yorker unworthy of a public trust as important as secretary of war, and Monroe was not alone in his suspicions. Armstrong's past condemned him in the eyes of many republicans. During the Revolutionary War, Armstrong had joined a conspiracy that tried to use the military against the fledgling republic.[66]

The Newburgh Conspiracy, shrouded in controversy and mystery, remains one of the most fascinating incidents of the Revolutionary War. Though best known for Washington's famous reaction to the plot, Armstrong's role in the affair, usually reserved for a footnote in history books, did not go unnoticed by his contemporaries. During the Revolution, Armstrong served as an adjutant to General Horatio Gates. Following the 1781 victory at Yorktown, the War of American Independence had effectively ended, with only mopping-up action remaining. The Continental Army, ten thousand strong in late 1782, went to winter quarters at Newburgh while awaiting demobilization. Meanwhile, the Confederation Congress, bereft of funds and deeply in debt, found it could not fully pay the army. Specifically, Congress refused to pay the promised half-pay for life to the officer corps. Along with the considerable financial burden, members of Congress feared setting a precedent for creating a permanent class of officers on the federal payroll.[67]

A group of politicians within the Continental Congress at Philadelphia saw this controversy as an opportunity. Alexander Hamilton, Robert Morris, and Gouverneur Morris all advocated strengthening the power of the federal government, and encouraged the officers to press their claims. At Newburgh, a cabal of officers, including General Horatio Gates and Armstrong, met in secret with one of Hamilton's contacts and they decided to renew their demands. They made thinly veiled threats to Congress, alluding to the army's "alternative" should their demands not be met. Armstrong wrote a series of letters to be distributed amongst the soldiery, urging them to support the officers. Exactly what the army's "alternative" meant remains unclear. At the least, the officers were hinting that they might refuse to disband if they did not receive their pay. At the worst, the deliberately vague language led some to view the letters as a threat to use the army against Congress and possibly set up military rule.[68]

Whatever the intentions of Armstrong and his fellow conspirators, most contemporaries did not look on their actions favorably. The addresses particularly alarmed George Washington. The plotters decided not to bring the commanding general into their scheme because they realized he would oppose using the army for any political purpose. Washington received word from his friend Joseph Jones (Monroe's uncle) that the conspirators planned to "lessen your reputation in the army in the hopes ultimately that the weight of your opposition will prove no obstacle to their designs."[69] Washington took the Newburgh letters as a personal insult, a direct attack on his authority, and a serious threat to the American republic. It certainly did not help that one of the prime movers, Horatio Gates, had previously intrigued against Washington during the so-called Conway Cabal in the winter of 1777–78. Washington took immediate steps to crush the conspiracy. What resulted only added to his growing reputation.[70]

Washington confronted his troops and bade them ignore the Newburgh letters and exercise patience with Congress. During the speech, Washington revealed Jones's letter, and, as he fumbled for his glasses to read it, apologized to his men with the now-famous phrase that having "grown gray in their service" he "now found himself growing blind." This display subsequently quelled whatever revolt might have been brewing. Washington's personal prestige crushed the conspiracy then and there. Yet the Newburgh Conspiracy had branded Armstrong as an intriguer. Nearly thirty years later, Armstrong still could not shake this reputation as he entered Madison's cabinet.[71] Armstrong began his term as secretary of war fully aware of the strikes against him. He claimed to be surrounded on all sides by "personal and party malevolence." This comment, likely aimed at Monroe, contained at least a kernel of truth.[72]

Armstrong's appointment initiated a second kind of battle for Monroe, even as he helped lead the war against Britain. Though Monroe had legitimate reasons to distrust Armstrong's character, something besides republican principles led him to clash so fiercely with his new colleague. As Monroe's biographer Harry Ammon remarked, this was one of the few times when Monroe "displayed none of his usual tolerance." Monroe was openly hostile to Armstrong from the moment he entered the cabinet. Admitting that Armstrong provided energy and intelligence to the War Department, Monroe did not trust the new secretary. In fact, it may have been these very talents that threatened Monroe.[73]

Monroe knew that both he and the new secretary of war aspired to the presidency, and as John Randolph remarked, this shared ambition put them in a "deadly feud." After his years as a diplomat in Europe, his disputes with Livingston and Madison, and his return to the Republican Party, Armstrong was a final, unwanted, and unlooked-for obstacle to the presidency.[74] Monroe determined to do whatever was necessary to avoid being cheated out of the prize. As the war continued, Monroe pounced on all of Armstrong's mistakes, ultimately laying the foundation for Armstrong to become the scapegoat for military failure.

One point of contention between Monroe and Armstrong occurred over the command of the invasion of Canada. Armstrong wanted to take personal command of the northern army while maintaining his post as secretary of war. Monroe couched his argument against this scheme on constitutional grounds, stating that it was dangerous to send the sitting secretary of war to the front lines. He told the president that Armstrong would wield too much power if he commanded an army. He argued that "executive power as known to the Constitution [would be] destroyed" by such a plan, warning Madison that this scheme would effectively neuter the president by transferring all military powers "from the executive to the General at the head of the army."[75] He left unsaid the obvious fear of how Armstrong might wield this newfound authority. It would be a risky proposition to place such power in anyone's hands, but Armstrong's past made it unthinkable. He asked Madison rhetorically, and a touch sarcastically, "Does [Armstrong] possess in a prominent degree the public confidence for that trust?" The secretary of war belonged in the capital advising the president and communicating his orders to commanders in the field. If Armstrong wanted a command, Monroe reasoned, he should leave the War Department altogether. To Jefferson, Monroe accused Armstrong of wanting to conduct the entire war by himself while "know[ing] that here [in Washington] he cannot direct the army." While Monroe's ideological objections to the scheme were legitimate, personal concerns also played a role in his objections to this plan.[76]

Though he did not say so to Madison, Monroe bristled because the planned invasion of Canada had originally been his idea. He had concocted the scheme during his stint as acting secretary of war. Furthermore, like Armstrong, Monroe had also hoped to take command of the invasion of Canada himself (Monroe, at least, had the sense to offer his resignation as secretary of war in order to command the army). Madison refused to appoint him because he feared that placing Monroe above officers who possessed more extensive Revolutionary War service would cause dissension. Thus, Armstrong not only sat in Monroe's former seat as secretary of war, but he also planned to command the very invasion Monroe once hoped to lead. He appeared to be usurping Monroe's position, and it made for a bitter pill to swallow. A victory in Canada would win Armstrong the kind of laurels that might elevate him to the presidency ahead of Monroe. Madison overruled Monroe and Armstrong went to the front to command the army. Luckily for Monroe's political chances if not for the war effort, Armstrong's northern campaign ended in failure.[77]

Monroe took every opportunity to complain of Armstrong to the president. He claimed that several American generals at the front told him that Armstrong tried "seducing" officers within the army so as to win their loyalty away from Madison and the administration. By the end of 1813, Monroe pleaded with Madison that Armstrong would "ruin not you and the administration only, but the whole republican party and cause." Monroe laid the foundation so that when a true military disaster struck, Armstrong paid the political price.[78]

Throughout the summer and fall of 1814, Monroe and Madison both came to fear that the arrival of a British force near the Potomac might lead to an attack on the capital. Monroe became particularly alarmed, and requested the militia be called up. He also wanted to establish an intelligence network that could serve as an early warning system should the British march on Washington. Armstrong dismissed these reports and insisted that Baltimore was the British target. The capital, he claimed, remained secure. Monroe, with the benefit of hindsight, described Armstrong's actions to Jefferson sometime afterward. He claimed that "an infatuation seemed to have taken possession of General Armstrong relating to the danger of this place. He could never be made to believe that it was in any danger." As a result of Armstrong's inaction, when the British did march on Washington, the militia could not be mustered in time and the city's defenses proved woefully inadequate.[79]

Eventually the British army defeated the paltry American force sent against them and easily captured the city. The cabinet managed to escape, but Armstrong received much of the blame for the debacle. Afterward one soldier told Madison that "every officer would tear off his epaulettes if General Armstrong was to have anything to do with them." The fallout from the capture of Washington ultimately forced Armstrong to resign as secretary of war in September of 1814.[80] Like John Randolph before him, Armstrong blamed Monroe's boundless ambition for his political demise. When, in 1816, Monroe emerged as the front-runner to succeed Madison as president, Armstrong wrote a scathing attack on his former rival. Armstrong blamed Monroe for nearly all the problems he experienced as secretary of war. The "perpetual embarrassments" his department suffered resulted from the "unusual interference of a great civil officer of the state viz Colonel Monroe." His removal as secretary of war came after the "capture of the metropolis," which was "adroitly seized upon as a pretext for denouncing him [Armstrong]." He blamed Monroe for using this incident to land the "fatal blow to his reputation." Armstrong believed that Monroe had maneuvered Madison into making him "the scapegoat."[81]

Armstrong chalked all of Monroe's posturing to his hunger to achieve the presidency. He decried Monroe's Machiavellian scheming to remove potential rivals, explaining that "Col. Monroe has furnished unequivocal evidence that his lust for power is insatiable." Again, like Randolph, Armstrong strikes upon at least a half-truth.[82] Monroe, while a tireless and fiercely loyal lieutenant during the war, in effect ran for president during Madison's second term. He feared that a potentially strong war leader like Armstrong might swoop in and steal the presidency.

With Armstrong's dismissal Madison required a new secretary of war, and Monroe quickly stepped into the role. Madison again hesitated to make him the permanent head of the War Department for fear that critics would point to the overwhelming Virginia influence within the government. Monroe convinced the president to make the position permanent with a letter telling him quite directly that "the Department of war ought to be immediately filled. I think also, that I ought to take charge of it." He explained to Madison that "by taking charge of the Dept. twice and withdrawing from it a second time, it may be inferred that I shrink from the responsibility, from a fear of injuring my reputation." He also did not want the public to believe "that the removal of the other [Armstrong] was an affair of intrigue." He wrote Madison, "It seems due therefore to my own reputation, to go thro' with the undertaking." Monroe worried that if he did not take the job it would look like he felt guilty about taking over the War Department after having orchestrated Armstrong's downfall. In the end, Monroe got his wish. In fact, not only did Monroe direct the War Department, but he also managed to remain secretary of state when Daniel Tomkins refused the job and Monroe and others objected to Rufus King's appointment because he was a Federalist. Thus, by the end of the war, Monroe emerged with no real challengers to his succession as president. After the War of 1812 Monroe believed that he had secured both the future of American republicanism and his path to the presidency.[83]

Monroe was convinced that the war had been a success for the republican cause. Despite the peace commissioners at Ghent agreeing to return to the status quo antebellum, Monroe believed that the United States had successfully waged their war to defend their national rights. Now with the "successful" completion of the contest the union itself had been strengthened.[84] Monroe further believed that the public would recognize the role he played in the war: "I have known from the commencement of the war that it formed a crisis which would try the strength of our government and which required the greatest exertions and sacrifices of those who had to conduct it." He expected to receive his share of credit from the public and thought that, like the Louisiana Purchase, it would add his legacy. Monroe believed that his "actions and timely measures [will] do me credit when I am gone." All the things accomplished in the war from the "repulse at Baltimore" to the "victory at New Orleans" were not merely the result of the nation's "good fortune." Monroe expected Americans to see the happy results as the product of his "good service to his country."[85]

By the time the war ended in 1815 Monroe had secured everything he could have hoped for when he left France in 1797. Through his efforts in acquiring Louisiana, his various diplomatic postings, and his victory during the War of 1812, Monroe had helped secure republicanism within the United States. The war had, just barely, vindicated his aggressive approach to foreign policy. The United States had secured its national honor from encroachment by Great Britain, and the rest of the world was sure to take notice.[86] Further, the victory had landed a crippling blow to the Federalist Party after the disastrous timing of the Hartford Convention.[87] As a result the republican cause was as strong as ever in America.

Monroe's own career trajectory meanwhile put him in a prime position to do more for the republican cause. These three incidents offer insightful snapshots into Monroe's continuing evolution as a politician. Monroe's sixteen-year climb to the presidency from 1800 to 1816 offers a veritable clinic in political maneuvering. Monroe slowly climbed the Republican hierarchy during this period. His success in negotiating the Louisiana Purchase made him one of the most prominent political figures in the Republican Party, with some in the Republican camp even favoring his nomination over Madison in 1808. Similarly, after the election of 1808, Monroe managed to maintain his position within the party by attaching himself to Jefferson. That he was successful can easily be seen in his ascension to the top job at the State Department in 1811. Finally, while in Madison's cabinet, Monroe neatly eliminated a potential rival and secured his succession to the presidency. But Monroe did not abandon his principles in the pursuit of power, as Randolph, Armstrong, and Livingston all might have charged. Monroe's republicanism was joined to his increasing political acumen during his two-decades-long climb up the American political ladder. After achieving his goal of reaching the presidency, Monroe combined his idealism with his finely honed political expertise to accomplish a final act that, he hoped, would cement his legacy as a champion of republicanism.

## CONCLUSIONS

Monroe made the treacherous climb from a failed minister to France in 1797 to the presidency in 1817 through his work as a foreign policy specialist and his considerable political skills. Throughout this period, he did his best to secure republicanism in the United States even as he enhanced his own future political career. This period had important implications for the development of Monroe's republicanism, his political talents, and his concerns for his historical legacy. Because republicanism had triumphed in the United States, but looked increasingly weak in France during this period, Monroe shifted his foreign policy goals to focus more on securing the cause closer to home. Monroe's republican diplomacy took on a more traditionally realist guise during this period as he worked to safeguard the American republic from the threat posed by both monarchial Great Britain and Napoleonic France while looking for opportunities to expand its territorial boundaries across the continent.

During the Louisiana negotiations Monroe initially sought to secure the nation's access to the Mississippi through the purchase of the city of New Orleans. For Monroe, it was the culmination of his commitment to westerners' interests, dating back to the 1780s with his opposition to the Jay-Gardoqui Treaty. Napoleon's surprising offer to sell all of Louisiana gave Monroe the opportunity to extend the boundaries of the American republic across the continent. Monroe also cunningly ensured that he would receive much of the credit for this singular achievement. He wanted recognition for the Purchase, at least in part, because he hoped to be remembered as the man who had helped expand the American republic's borders into the Louisiana Territory. Monroe continually tied his career goals to the republican cause, which helped him reconcile his principles with his growing political ambitions.

During the Monroe-Pinkney negotiations, and the subsequent election of 1808, Monroe likewise had republican security on his mind. He hoped to be able to protect the American republic by negotiating a lasting treaty with Great Britain. Monroe's years in Europe convinced him that he and Pinkney had a chance to use the Napoleonic threat to bring the British closer to the side of the American republic, thus avoiding another war with the former mother country. Monroe believed that his long experience in Europe should have prompted Madison and Jefferson to defer to his judgment. The administration's failure to consider the treaty turned him against Madison, but it could not completely dampen Monroe's belief that changes in Britain provided an opportunity for the republican cause. This marked the beginning of a transition in Monroe's view of Great Britain, which even the War of 1812 did not completely alter. Monroe's extended time in London convinced him to see Britain as a potential friend, rather than the implacable enemy he remembered from the revolutionary era.

The treaty's failure put Monroe's career, and his legacy, in jeopardy. His dream of becoming a republican champion might have died with its rejection had he not taken the drastic measure of running for president in 1808. Monroe saw Madison as simply another of Jefferson's lieutenants rather than his natural heir. Support from Old Republicans like John Randolph helped convince Monroe that he could bear the standard for these true republicans. Their support would, at the least, illustrate his stature within the Republican ranks to Madison and Jefferson. Yet even as it became clear that his bid for the presidency was unlikely to succeed, the increasingly cunning Monroe used his long-standing relationship with Jefferson to maintain his position within the Republican hierarchy.

By 1811 Monroe had been appointed as Madison's secretary of state and the country was careening toward war with Great Britain due at least in part to the decision to reject the Monroe-Pinkney Treaty. Monroe believed that relations with Great Britain had deteriorated to the point that war was necessary to protect the U.S. republic's honor. During the war another threat to Monroe emerged within Madison's cabinet with the appointment of John Armstrong. Monroe feared Armstrong might be the kind of leader who would use the military to threaten American republicanism. More importantly, he stood squarely in the way of Monroe's path to the presidency. Monroe therefore undermined Armstrong and, with no small amount of help from Armstrong's own bungling of the war effort, this led to the secretary of war's dismissal. Monroe therefore viewed the end of the War of 1812 as a victory in the fight to secure republicanism, and a victory in his own fight to secure the presidency.

The Monroe who emerges from this period, on the surface, looks very different from the Monroe of revolutionary France. Here he is politically savvy in a way he did not show in Paris in 1795, when he appeared almost naïve in his zeal for the republican cause. Monroe cunningly took credit from Livingston for the Purchase, shrewdly wormed his way back into the Republican ranks after 1808, and almost ruthlessly eliminated Armstrong as a potential rival. These were the kind of political machinations that would have done a fame-seeker like Hamilton or even Julius Caesar proud. Yet Monroe saw each action as in service to the republican cause. His actions were not, in his mind, designed simply to advance his own fame, but the cause itself. Further, he justified the political intrigue precisely because he recognized that without acquiring power and position within the U.S. government he could never hope to become a champion of republican diplomacy. President Monroe applied all the lessons he learned, both as a republican diplomat and a political operative, to cement his legacy as a republican champion, by continuing to secure and expand the American republic's borders and by making one last effort to champion the cause around the world with the Monroe Doctrine.

# 5

⇢⇥  ⇤⇠

# A Bolder Attitude

*Can we . . . take a bolder attitude . . . in favor of liberty?*

JAMES MONROE TO THOMAS JEFFERSON, JUNE 2, 1823

O N AN AUTUMN DAY in Washington, DC, President James Monroe
sat in the White House surrounded by perhaps the greatest cabinet
in American history. Attorney General William Wirt and Secretary of the
Navy Benjamin Crowninshield were the least well-known of Monroe's ad-
visers. The true luminaries were John C. Calhoun, William H. Crawford,
and John Quincy Adams. They held the three most critical positions in
the administration. Calhoun, a former war hawk, current nationalist, and
future champion of southern slavery, directed the War Department. Crawford, Monroe's only Republican rival during the election of 1816 and considered the most likely successor to the presidency, occupied the top job
at the Treasury Department. Finally, and most importantly, John Quincy
Adams held the prestigious post of secretary of state, and during the next
eight years proved himself among the best ever to run the department.[1]

The meeting took place on October 25, 1817, and it marked the first
time that Monroe's entire cabinet convened. The president had recently
returned from a summer tour of the American Northeast, during which a
Boston newspaper proclaimed the beginning of an "Era of Good Feelings,"
a phrase forever linked with Monroe's administration.[2] Adams, meanwhile, had only recently arrived in the capital after a stint as the American
minister to Great Britain. Monroe began the proceedings with a series of

questions facing the government. The issue during this initial gathering involved the Spanish Empire, or rather what remained of it. Monroe wanted his cabinet to consider the mounting chaos in Spanish Florida, and the possible American response to the independence movements sweeping through Latin America. At this meeting, Monroe began outlining his republican diplomatic goals, and took the first steps toward the creation of what would become the Monroe Doctrine.[3]

The Monroe Doctrine's legacy is often linked with the rise of American dominance of the Western Hemisphere. During the late nineteenth and early twentieth centuries, as the United States emerged as a world power, Monroe's doctrine took on a nationalist tone with "Roosevelt's Corollary," in which Theodore Roosevelt declared that the United States could intervene in the affairs of Latin American nations. The doctrine's importance is often thought to lie solely in its dual role as a statement of American hegemony in the Western Hemisphere and isolation from Europe. Reading from Roosevelt's era backward, historians often interpret the doctrine as if these twentieth-century concepts alone shaped its creation in 1823. Scholars, therefore, regularly contend that these ideas formed the doctrine's primary goals at its inception. This line of thinking naturally leads historians to emphasize John Quincy Adams's role in creating it. Adams, with his strong record as a nationalist and isolationist, often receives the bulk of the credit for building this new pillar upon which so much of subsequent American foreign policy stood. Meanwhile, James Monroe's original goal for the doctrine remains largely forgotten. Monroe did not see isolationism or the projection of American power as the doctrine's most important legacies. Instead, he hoped to craft a statement of support for republican revolution. It was his final contribution to American republicanism, and his last, best attempt to cement his legacy as a champion of the cause.[4]

One of the reasons Monroe's republican aspirations for the doctrine are often overshadowed is historians' tendency to underestimate how much control Monroe exerted over his administration's foreign policy. Two of the most important, and best, works relating to the diplomacy of the Monroe administration, written almost a half century apart, come to strikingly similar conclusions concerning Adams's preeminence over foreign affairs. The first, written by one of the giants of American diplomatic history, Samuel Flagg Bemis, won the Pulitzer Prize. In this classic work, Bemis credits Adams with laying the groundwork for much of future American foreign policy. Bemis places Adams's contributions to the American republic behind only those of Abraham Lincoln.[5]

Forty-three years later, William Earl Weeks wrote a similarly important work essentially agreeing with Bemis on Adams's importance to American diplomacy. In his book, Weeks emphasizes Adams's dominance over Monroe's administration. This analysis of Monrovian foreign policy, as primarily the work of John Quincy Adams, obscures Monroe's role in crafting his administration's foreign policy. Monroe's years of diplomacy and political maneuvering helped the fifth president face the most important event of his administration: the dissolution of the Spanish American Empire.[6] The acquisition of Florida and the signing of the Transcontinental Treaty, the recognition of the Latin American revolutions, and especially the Monroe Doctrine all had their roots in Monroe's drive to be remembered as a champion of republicanism. It was the culmination of his lifelong dedication to the cause, brought about through Monroe's vast political and diplomatic experience.

## FLORIDA AND THE TRANSCONTINENTAL TREATY

When he took the presidency Monroe had one last piece of business remaining from his pre-presidential diplomatic career: the acquisition of Florida. It was in Florida where Spain's crumbling empire first caught the attention of Monroe's administration. Florida's post-1812 anarchy presented Monroe with a particularly vexing foreign policy crisis. During the war, Britain used the area to recruit runaway slaves to fight the United States, while Creek refugees from Jackson's Indian campaign flooded into the region and united with the Seminole tribes of Florida. The Spanish proved incapable of controlling the area, and the resulting instability attracted all manner of adventurers hoping to profit from the chaos.[7]

Amelia Island, a Spanish possession situated off the coast of Georgia and Florida between several major trade routes, presented an ideal target for anyone hoping to raid international shipping. Eventually a Scottish mercenary named Gregor MacGregor led his band of fifty-five adventurers and captured the island on June 28, 1817. During the almost four months between MacGregor's capture of the island and Monroe's first cabinet meeting in the fall of 1817, Amelia's new owners engaged in smuggling, piracy, and illegal slave-trading. This quickly brought the little island to the attention of the U.S. government.[8]

During his first meeting with the cabinet Monroe posed a question: "Is it expedient to break up the establishments at Amelia Island[,] . . . it being evident that they were made for smuggling, if not for piratical purposes, and already perverted to very mischievous purposes to the U. States." The cabinet unanimously agreed to send troops to the island. A month later, Monroe explained to James Madison that the pirates at Amelia Island had done the country "great injury." Monroe announced his decision in a message to Congress on December 2, and ordered General Edmund Gaines to seize the island. The mercenaries surrendered without firing a shot, but this marked only the beginning of the controversy for Monroe.[9]

In January of 1818, after news arrived of Amelia's capture, the cabinet met to decide the island's fate. Adams reported in his diary that Monroe arrived at the meeting of January 6 ready to return the island to Spain. According to Adams, he and Secretary of War John C. Calhoun alone among the cabinet members voted to retain the island, and the meeting adjourned without an agreement. Three days later, another meeting concluded without a decision. Adams took these delays as a sign of Monroe's indecision, but the president often sought consensus within his cabinet on major foreign policy questions. Monroe valued his subordinates' opinions, especially within their respective realms of expertise. Often, when his cabinet could not agree on a course of action, Monroe adjourned to find an alternative that might satisfy all parties. Monroe's experience throughout his rise to the presidency had taught him the value of patience. Rather than commit the United States to a particular course of action, he moved deliberately in the hope that more information would become available. By January 12 Monroe found his new information.

Adams reported that the president arrived at that cabinet meeting having "modified" his message to Congress, informing them that the United States would retain control of Amelia Island "for the present." Historians have argued that Adams forced Monroe's reversal, claiming that "the president's first instincts had been overturned by the powerful arguments of his secretary of state." While Monroe certainly took Adams's argument into consideration, other information changed the president's mind on the

Amelia Island question.[10] Monroe's longtime interest in Florida combined with the changing geopolitical climate, rather than Adams's "powerful arguments," precipitated Monroe's seemingly abrupt change of heart.

As seen in chapter 4, Monroe had long considered Florida critical to the continued security of American republicanism. He tried to include the territory in the Louisiana Purchase in 1803. Almost from the moment Monroe had finished negotiations with the French over Louisiana, his mind fixed on convincing Spain that West Florida, at least, was part of the purchase. Monroe tried to enlist French aid in the negotiations with Spain over Florida.[11] When the French appeared uninterested in using their influence over the Spanish government to help the United States, Monroe traveled to Spain in 1805 to personally negotiate the acquisition of the territory. Spain, meanwhile, maintained that they had retained Florida in the treaty of San Ildefonso, and thus Napoleon had not owned Florida when he sold the Louisiana Territory to the United States.[12] Though the territory remained in Spanish hands, Monroe continued to keep his eye fixed on Florida. Monroe had at least one more chance to acquire the territory as secretary of state, when, just before the outbreak of the War of 1812, Monroe and President Madison sent General George Mathews to the region. According to historians Frank Owsley and Gene A. Smith, the administration sent Mathews with secret instructions to "invade and capture east Florida," but eventually disavowed the action as the war with Britain made a conflict with Spain less desirable.[13]

When Monroe came to the presidency he had been in pursuit of the Florida Territory for over a decade. In June of 1817, just as Monroe made to leave on his tour of the Northeast, former Pennsylvania senator George Logan told him that the Spanish were willing to cede Florida as long as they were not pushed too hard.[14] While the situation in Florida offered an opportunity to secure the United States' southern border there were also inherent risks involved. Monroe feared that this crisis might eventually involve other European powers. Great Britain had emerged as the world's preeminent power at the end of the Napoleonic Wars, and British leaders viewed the United States as their primary economic rival in Latin America. Monroe believed that the British might have their own designs on Florida.[15] In 1815 Monroe, then secretary of state, wrote a letter to John Quincy Adams, then minister to Great Britain, telling him that "reports continue to circulate that the Spanish Government has ceded to Great Britain the Floridas." As he explained to Adams, East Florida was inconsequential "in itself," but as a "post in the hands of Great Britain it is of the highest importance."[16] Now, three years later, Monroe feared that the British might try to interject themselves into this new controversy over Amelia Island. Monroe also believed that excessive American aggression might prompt Spain to sell Florida to Britain, rather than risk losing the territory to the United States for nothing. He explained in a letter to Jefferson that Britain and France had offered to arbitrate the differences between Spain and the United States. To Monroe, this offer implied that Britain would move against the United States should he push Spain too hard. All these concerns shaped Monroe's response to the Amelia affair.[17]

Monroe was so heavily involved in negotiations over Florida through the years that it is difficult to imagine him deferring so completely to Adams's suggestions on the issue. Throughout the crisis he constantly directed Adams's negotiations with Don Luis de Onis, the Spanish minister to the United States. He instructed Adams to show certain papers to the Spanish ambassador that would illustrate Spain's inability to defend Florida, highlighting their need to sell the territory. He also sent a letter instructing Adams to ignore the tone of one of Onis's more heated letters, while reminding his secretary of state to make it clear to the Spanish ambassador that his position was unacceptable.[18]

As he directed the negotiations, Monroe showed considerable patience when dealing with Spain. Little would be gained and much could be lost by pushing the once-great European power into a corner. Monroe's change in attitude did not come after hearing Adams's arguments on the matter; indeed, he listened to Adams's position twice without altering his own. Monroe changed his mind only when, on January 10, Nicholas Biddle, of future Bank of the United States fame and Monroe's personal friend, visited the White House. Biddle served as Monroe's personal secretary while the two were in England in 1806, and the president later appointed him as the federal government's director of the national bank, before Biddle became the BUS's president in 1822. Biddle told Monroe that Spain was desperate to sell Florida. Monroe immediately sent his secretary of state to discuss the matter with Onis. When Adams returned, Monroe decided to "modify his message" to Congress as a result of Biddle's new information.

After receiving word from Biddle that Spain might be ready to come to terms over Florida, Monroe believed that seizing the island had broken the deadlock in negotiations going back to the Louisiana Purchase. Now, keeping Amelia seemed a calculated risk worth taking. Monroe sensed panic within the Spanish ministry over the prospect of losing Florida for nothing, and this altered his thinking on the matter. He therefore changed his message so that it made no mention of returning the island to Spain. As this controversy died, events unfolded on the Spanish border that put Monroe in another difficult situation, further complicated by the presence of Andrew Jackson.[19]

During the months before Monroe sent Edmund Gaines to capture Amelia Island, the general led American forces on the Florida border in a series of engagements against hostile native tribes. This culminated with Gaines's attack on an Indian village at Fowltown. The natives responded with a retaliatory raid on a contingent of American troops.[20] This mayhem prompted Monroe to send troops across the border into Spanish Florida. On December 16, 1817, a dispatch sent from the War Department ordered Gaines to "march across the Florida line, and to attack them [the natives] within its limits, should it be found necessary, unless they should shelter themselves under a Spanish post. In the last event you will notify this department." Monroe then directed General Andrew Jackson, hero of the Battle of New Orleans, to travel to the front and take command of the forces under Gaines's command. Thus, Gaines's orders applied to the Tennessee general as well.[21]

At this point versions of events differ. Monroe and Secretary of War John C. Calhoun later claimed that this represented the extent of Jackson's orders, while the general later insisted that he had received secret authorization to conquer the rest of Florida. This event has generated considerable controversy among historians. Not surprisingly, sympathetic Jackson biographers argue that Monroe did indeed provide such authorization. Monroe biographers, and Jackson critics, claim that the controversial Rhea letter, from which Jackson claimed this clandestine agreement, was a complete fabrication on the part of "Old Hickory."[22] For the purposes of this work the question of whether Monroe sent a secret letter to Jackson is largely irrelevant. Secret orders or no Monroe, an experienced soldier, politician, and diplomat, would not have sent a commander with Andrew

Jackson's fiery reputation into a chaotic situation like Florida without some idea as to the possible repercussions. Monroe knew from experience what to expect from the general. He had already witnessed Jackson's behavior during a similar situation during the War of 1812.[23]

During that conflict, American troops under the command of General James Wilkinson had seized Mobile and ousted the Spanish garrison at Fort Charlotte. In response, the Spanish formed an alliance with the Creek Indians, who attacked Fort Mims, an American post on the border, thus sparking the Creek War and precipitating General Jackson's involvement in the conflict. On October 21, 1814, hoping to avoid bringing a second European nation into the war, President Madison and acting secretary of war Monroe ordered Jackson not to take action against the Spanish outposts. Jackson did not receive these orders in time, and after defeating the Creeks at Horseshoe Bend, captured the Spanish city of Pensacola. Four years later, Monroe sent this same man into another chaotic situation in Florida. Monroe would not have expected anything different from the general.[24]

Jackson did not disappoint. Calling up his Tennessee veterans from the War of 1812, he departed in January 1818 with more than a thousand men under his command. In April, Jackson tracked a group of Indians to the Spanish town of St. Marks, which he captured. During the operation he seized, tried, and executed two British subjects, Robert Ambrister and Alexander Arbuthnot, for inciting the Native Americans to violence. The execution of two of the king's subjects alarmed the British, but hardly compared to the outcry over Jackson's next move. On May 28 the general, just as he had during the War of 1812, captured the city of Pensacola, giving the United States de facto control of Spanish Florida, and in essence committing an act of war against Spain.[25]

The general's actions shifted the onus to Monroe and the administration as to what should be done with the territory. Many factors weighed on Monroe. While the president understood that Jackson's activities might push the Spanish toward a settlement over Florida, he also realized that the Tennessee general's actions put the United States in a dangerous position.[26] Word of Pensacola's capture reached Washington, DC, in June 1818 and the administration received a strongly worded protest from Onis on June 25. In July the cabinet met to discuss the situation. The eventual response has often been read as evidence of Adams's "dominant influence" over the cabinet. Yet Adams's own memoir and the administration's final decision make it clear that Monroe again found a middle course.[27]

Within the cabinet, two extreme positions emerged in response to Jackson's Florida adventure. Adams wrote in his diary that the entire cabinet, save himself, believed Jackson guilty of defying orders. Calhoun appeared personally affronted that Jackson ignored him. Meanwhile, an alarmed Treasury Secretary William Crawford argued that "if the administration did not immediately declare itself and restore Pensacola it would be held responsible for Jackson's having taken it." Adams took the opposite position. He argued that Jackson's "proceedings were justified by the necessity of the case." In his diary, Adams assumed that Monroe opposed him, but a closer look at Monroe's thinking provides an alternative conclusion.[28]

In his memoirs, Adams makes an important point concerning Monroe's thoughts on the situation. "The President supposes there might be cases which would have justified Jackson's measures," Adams writes. But, Monroe argued, the general had not "made out his case."[29] Monroe never actually sided with Calhoun's position on Jackson. He simply did not make his thoughts known to Adams. Instead, he looked to his old revolutionary colleagues for guidance. Monroe's correspondence with Thomas Jefferson and James Madison during this crisis makes it clear that the president sought a middle course between the extremes of Adams's position and that of Calhoun and Crawford. Monroe tried to stay above the political infighting that occurred during his cabinet meeting, which helps explain why he did not dive too deeply into the debate. This became especially important before the election of 1824 when practically every member of his administration had his eye on the presidency. In fact, Monroe came to the meeting with a clear vision that neither of the extreme positions, keeping Florida or disavowing Jackson, was satisfactory. On July 10, five days before the first cabinet meeting, Monroe wrote to Madison describing the situation. He explained that Jackson had blamed the entire incident on "Spanish authorities" and "foreign adventurers." More significantly, Monroe confided, "I have no doubt that his opinion is correct." Already, before hearing Adams's arguments in favor of Jackson, Monroe believed the general's response to have been justified.[30]

This did not end the debate however. As Monroe maintained, "there are serious difficulties in this business, on whichever side we view it." He explained that with the United States in control of the Mississippi River and Florida, the reasons for pressing Spain were "not urgent." The United States gained nothing by putting further pressure on the Spanish, and doing so posed unnecessary risks. Monroe feared that retaining Florida might foster "a sense of injury from her and of insult." Pressuring Spain could no longer help the United States' position in Florida, and might only serve to bring about a war. Monroe recognized that with patience and tact he could gain Florida without further bloodshed.[31]

After the cabinet meetings, the president sent a letter to Jackson. In it, Monroe made clear that while he believed that the general had exceeded his orders, he understood Jackson's explanations for doing so. He also explained his reasons for giving Florida back to Spain. The president told Jackson that recent events had shown Spain that "she" could no longer "maintain her authority" in Florida. Now that Spain recognized this fact, Monroe believed that it would provide a "strong inducement to Spain to cede this territory, provided we do not wound too deeply her pride by holding it." At this point, Monroe believed that Spain could retain Florida only by involving other European powers in the struggle. Monroe explained to Jackson that "the policy of Europe respecting South America is not yet settled." Spain's best option was to push for "war with the United States, in the hope of making it general, and uniting Europe against us and her colonies." This represents the crux of Monroe's caution. The Spanish Empire itself represented no great threat, but the prospect of sparking a war with other European powers gave the president pause.[32] This was not merely a note to salve the general's pride. Monroe said the same thing in a letter to George Hay on July 20, telling his son-in-law that it had been the Spanish officers who had been responsible for the incident in Florida, rather than Jackson.[33]

A note to Onis laid out the government's official response on July 23, 1818. The product of the July cabinet meetings and largely the president's creation, this letter illustrates Monroe's ability to find an alternative path that maintained peace, and eventually led to the American acquisition of Florida only six months later. According to Adams, "the language only is mine." The secretary of state was frustrated that his point of view had been ignored. This became a regular refrain from Adams during his time as Monroe's secretary of state. Adams often commented that he served merely as Monroe's agent in these kinds of situations.[34] Yet in the text of the note, Monroe justified Jackson's actions throughout, blaming the crisis largely on the Spanish governor of Pensacola and citing Spain's inability to maintain control over Florida. This bears traces of Adams's own reasoning. Only at the end did Monroe mention returning Florida to the Spanish. Monroe designed this to appease Spain for the time being, in order to coax them back to the negotiating table. While the language bears the stamp of Adams's bellicose defense of Jackson, the substance of the note speaks to Monroe's control over national policy, and his political subtlety.[35]

Monroe discussed his reasoning in this case to various friends and fellow political leaders in the immediate aftermath of the crisis. He told Nicholas Biddle that had the United States maintained the Spanish posts they would have given Spain "just cause" for war.[36] Nevertheless, he accepted Jackson's claims that it was Spanish agents in Florida who had stirred up the native rebellions, and as he told John C. Calhoun, the entire incident could be put down to their "misconduct." Calhoun wanted an explanation as to why Monroe had effectively allowed Jackson to ignore the War Department. Monroe tried to soothe his secretary of war by explaining that if the administration had turned on Jackson and brought him to trial, "all hope of a cession [of Florida] would be at an end." Perhaps more importantly, considering Jackson's popularity, such an act would also lay "the foundation for internal feuds, the end of which we could not foresee." Monroe also explained to Calhoun that his middle path would avoid offending Spain unduly, while making them reconsider Florida's position in relation to the United States. "By surrendering the posts," he explained, "we deprive the allied powers of a motive to join against us." At the same time, it would act as a veiled hint to Spain "that we are not so much afraid of them as they may have supposed."[37]

Monroe explained the entire episode to the country in his Annual Message to Congress in November 1818. In it he claimed that returning the posts immediately to Spain had "preserved" relations between the two countries, and allowed the Spanish to review their relations with the

United States, "particularly in respect to the territory in question, with the dangers inseparable from it." This pressured Spain to come to a quick decision concerning Florida, and over the next few months Adams negotiated with Spain under the parameters Monroe created. This resulted in the Transcontinental Treaty, signed in February 1819, in which Spain, after fifteen years of work on Monroe's part, finally ceded Florida to the United States. The final acquisition of the long-sought-after territory owed as much to Monroe's dedication to securing Florida for the republican cause, and his ability to steer the United States through the various pitfalls of international geopolitics, as it did to Adams's ample negotiating powers.[38]

Adams and Monroe adopted differing approaches to the Florida crisis, and these differences highlight their opposing foreign policy philosophies. Adams wanted to use the situation to strengthen his hand in negotiating with Onis on the issue of the western border of the United States. He wanted American access to the Pacific Ocean, and thought that pressuring Spain would help achieve this. Adams saw territorial expansion as crucial for the United States to become a great power. In fact, Monroe's secretary of state can best be described as an early agent of Manifest Destiny. He laid the foundations for what historian Weeks calls the "American Global Empire." American expansion provided the key motivation for Adams, and he believed the United States would naturally come into possession of all North America.[39]

Monroe, meanwhile, had spent his youth throwing off the chains of monarchy. Nearly a half century later he still believed the European monarchs were looking for any excuse to destroy the American republic. Thus, during the Florida crisis Monroe proceeded cautiously. Monroe wanted republicanism to spread to Florida and to lay the foundation for the republic's expansion to the Pacific Ocean, but the president was not willing to risk a potential conflict with Spain or Great Britain. His caution helped ensure that the Adams-Onis negotiations were not scuttled by Jackson's invasion of Florida. As his presidency continued, however, world politics shifted to provide Monroe with another foreign policy question, and another opportunity to champion the republican cause.

## Latin American Independence

Napoleon's defeat at Waterloo in 1815 largely extinguished republicanism on the European continent. Following the Congress of Vienna, the European powers worked in concert, united by monarchial government, distrust of republicanism, and fear of revolution.[40] Czar Alexander I of Russia forged the ultraconservative "I Ioly Alliance" with Austria and Prussia. Too reactionary even for Great Britain, the Holy Alliance operated under two guiding principles: First, to preserve the settlement reached at the Congress of Vienna by maintaining peace in Europe; and second, to prevent the spread of republican revolution. France, once again under Bourbon rule, later joined this alliance, uniting with other continental powers to repress revolutions throughout Europe.[41] Meanwhile, Spain's Latin American colonies began revolting in 1808 during the Napoleonic wars. By Monroe's inauguration in March of 1817, many of these colonies had established de facto independence. Monroe was thrilled at the prospect of republicanism taking hold in Latin America, but he feared that the Holy Alliance would try to reassert Spanish power in the colonies, and envisioned Europe's war against revolution spreading to America's doorstep.[42]

As with the Florida crisis, Monroe's cabinet discussed the Latin American independence movements during their first meeting in October of 1817. Monroe asked his colleagues whether the president had the power to recognize the independence of certain Latin American colonies, and whether such a statement would lead the United States into a war with Spain.[43] As secretary of state, Monroe had discussed the possibility of recognizing the independence of the rebelling Spanish provinces as early as 1811. He told Joel Barlow, then the American minister to France, that the United States made a "very friendly answer" to the colonies' request for recognition. He believed that Americans could not possibly remain "indifferent" to the "just claims of our Southern Brethren." Monroe's concern over the progress of the Latin American revolutions continued into his presidency.[44]

Throughout his first term in office, Monroe gradually progressed toward official recognition of the Latin American republics as independent states. Some, like Speaker of the House Henry Clay, wanted Monroe to recognize the Latin American republics immediately and grant direct U.S.

military aid. But as with the crises involving Amelia and Florida, Monroe was careful not to let his zeal for republican expansion override his political good sense. In his first Annual Message to Congress, Monroe called it "natural" for Americans to sympathize with their southern neighbors, and he allowed their ships entry into U.S. ports by designating the conflict a civil war rather than a mere rebellion.[45] As he explained to fellow Virginian Fulwar Skipwith, Monroe intended to give as much support to the revolutions as possible without provoking Spain. He believed that the best course of action for both the colonies and the United States was for him to "favor" the colonies as best he could without getting directly involved. He feared that a premature American recognition of the new republics could lead to war that, he believed, would do the former colonies "more harm than good." Monroe continued with this basic policy throughout his first term in office.[46]

In 1819 Monroe declared that "the steadiness, consistency, and success with which" the Latin American republics had pursued independence gave "them a strong claim" to recognition from other nations. The next year, Monroe alluded to a sense of inevitability concerning the colonies' independence, announcing that soon "an adjustment will finally take place on the basis proposed by the Colonies." In other words, he believed that Spain would soon be forced to listen to the colonies' demands for independence. "To promote that result," Monroe assured the American public, "has always been the uniform policy of the government." While Monroe slowly brought the United States closer in line with the independence movements, he waited until after his reelection in 1820 to take a stronger approach.[47]

Despite Monroe's fervent support of republicanism, his hardened political instincts kept him from bringing the United States more firmly on the side of the Latin American republics. Threats from Europe forced Monroe to tread carefully for fear of bringing one or more of the European Allies into the conflict. In an 1820 letter to Andrew Jackson, Monroe explained his reasoning. He told the Tennessee general that his goal had always been for the United States to throw its "moral weight in the scale of the Colonies," while not directly involving itself in the war. American "moral weight" became a key concept for Monroe when considering the Latin American revolutions, one he used time and again to describe U.S.

policy in the region.[48] He likewise told Albert Gallatin that he hoped to throw the full force of the United States, in a "moral sense," behind the revolutionary cause. The United States did not possess great armies to aid their republican brethren, but as the birthplace of modern liberal republicanism their support lent ideological backing to the Latin American cause. Monroe wanted to back the movements without making the United States an active "party to the contest."[49]

Monroe believed that his decision to move cautiously had kept the Holy Allies on the sideline during the Latin American revolutions. "Europe has remained tranquil spectators of the conflict," he told Jackson, whereas if the United States had recognized the colonies' independence too early, "it is presumable that several powers would have united with Spain." In Monroe's mind, active American involvement would prove counterproductive to the cause. It might, he feared, precipitate a more powerful European nation entering the war on Spain's side. He had learned over the years to balance his "éclat" for the republican cause with diplomatic caution.[50]

Monroe had good reason to move carefully so as to not provoke either Spain or the other European monarchies. Rumors continued to swirl that the British were still irritated by the executions of their subjects by Jackson during his invasion of Florida, and that they might even conspire with the Spanish to prevent the implementation of the Transcontinental Treaty of 1819 that Adams had signed with Onis.[51] Minister to Great Britain Richard Rush reported that Spanish foreign policy was specifically designed to ignite British hostility to the United States, in the hopes that the two European powers would join hands against the upstart Americans.[52] Monroe also realized that recognition from the European powers would give the fledgling republics legitimacy. A hasty announcement from the United States, on the other hand, might "alarm" Europe and "defeat our own objects."[53]

The United States officially recognized the Latin America republics in a special message to Congress in 1822. By then, Monroe claimed that the revolutions were "manifestly settled," and explained that the new governments had conclusively made their case for recognition.[54] Once he made up his mind to support the republics, Monroe wanted to ensure that American recognition made a serious impact. When Virginia congressman Robert Garnett remained the lone vote against recognition, Monroe sent a letter urging the young politician to change his mind. He stressed the need for unanimity to put the full weight of a unified U.S. government behind the declaration of support.[55]

As with Florida, Monroe took a hand in directing U.S. diplomacy in South America. After recognition, the United States planned to dispatch envoys to the new South American republics. Before sending the instructions to his two subordinates, Adams sent a copy to Monroe in order to ensure that everything in them reflected the president's position on Latin America.[56] This illustrates a key to understanding the differing approaches to policy between Adams and Monroe in this period. Adams was not as sanguine concerning the future of the Latin American republics as his president. In fact, there was no real consensus among American policymakers when it came to Latin America, but rather three distinct approaches.

Speaker of the House Henry Clay was perhaps the loudest American voice in favor of recognition. Adams thought Clay was essentially using this topic to score political points against the president and Adams, who had the seat at the State Department that Clay had coveted when Monroe took office. Clay wanted, in part, to use the Latin American revolutions as a weapon against the administration. He suggested allowing the outfitting of privateers in the United States to be used against the Spanish. Monroe and Adams opposed such measures as likely to bring the United States more directly in the contest, which in turn might spark full-scale war between European monarchists and American republicans. Though Monroe was as dedicated to Latin American republicanism as any, he knew an actual military conflict between the two sides would mean disaster for the republican cause. Clay was heedless of the international repercussions that forced Monroe to take a more realist approach, and continued berating the administration for its policy in Latin America until Monroe finally recognized the republics in 1822. Interestingly, Clay was not the only prominent figure irritated by Monroe's Latin American policy.[57]

After John Quincy Adams completed the Transcontinental Treaty with Spain, providing the United States with both Florida and a claim to the Pacific Ocean, the Spanish government was slow in ratifying the agreement. Adams lamented in his diary that the major reason Spain had failed to sign the treaty was Monroe's constant support of the Latin American independence movements.[58] Adams was particularly annoyed that Monroe continued to declare his support for the revolutions in his annual messages to Congress, which Adams saw as more favorable to the colonies than the "facts" warranted.[59] Adams even went on to tell Henry Clay that he did not think the Latin American republics would ever become free and "liberal" governments like the United States.[60] Monroe, meanwhile, adopted a middle course between Clay's more idealistic approach and Adams's harsh diplomatic realism. He pursued a policy that supported the colonies, but moved slowly toward recognition to avoid provoking Spain and her European allies, thus paving the way for the Monroe Doctrine a year later.

## The Monroe Doctrine

The Latin American revolutions rekindled Monroe's long-cherished dream of becoming a champion of worldwide republicanism. His optimism was at least partially tempered by the increasingly chaotic situation in Europe. During Monroe's first term the European allies, with Great Britain leading the way, remained content to simply maintain the balance of power. But after 1820, the Holy Allies moved beyond the British vision, voting to give the Austrians a mandate to crush republican revolutions underway in nearby Naples and Piedmont. They pursued the same course in Verona the following year, in spite of British dissent. Finally, with a restored Bourbon king on the French throne, the Holy Alliance authorized French intervention against the newly created republican regime in Spain. This time, the Alliance even announced their intention to move against Britain if she stood in the way. In 1822 King Louis XVIII launched a sixty-thousand-man army into Spain, to crush the liberal regime in place there and restore Ferdinand VII to the throne. Monroe was concerned with the news he received from Europe, but he also held out hope that perhaps the monarchists had overextended themselves. He was especially encouraged by the news of a revolution in Greece, where the inventors of republicanism worked to shake off the rule of the Ottoman Empire in 1821.[61]

Monroe's view of events in Europe was colored by reports from various correspondents in that part of the world. After being ignored by his superiors in Washington when he served as a diplomat, Monroe had learned to heed the warnings from those closest to events. The Marquis de Lafayette kept Monroe informed of the situation in restoration France. The former French and American revolutionary told the president that the European reactionaries were determined to suppress liberal movements throughout the continent. Lafayette, meanwhile, favored a kind of American independence movement for the South American republics.[62] In London, Minister to Great Britain Richard Rush told Monroe that he was unsure whether Britain would remain neutral in the war between Spain and France.[63] Monroe even received news from his friend John Jacob Astor, the wealthy New York businessman, of growing rumors of a more general revolution brewing throughout the European continent.[64]

Monroe hoped that this might be the beginning of a new birth of republicanism in Europe. As he told Jefferson in June of 1823, Monroe believed that a Bourbon military disaster in Spain might "put at issue its own future[,] . . . perhaps its existence." He hoped that a French defeat would undermine the restored Bourbon regime and hopefully even spark a renewed revolution by the French people. Monroe refused to "believe that the revolutionary spirit has become extinct" in France. The president held to his original revolutionary-era ideals. He still believed in the righteousness of the French Revolution's original tone and spirit. In fact, the remainder of Monroe's letter to his former mentor exhibits an almost remorseful tone. He regretted that the United States had squandered past opportunities to advance the republican cause. Now, fate granted him a chance to rectify those mistakes, as the United States faced another critical period analogous to his own experience in France thirty years earlier. "The state of Europe . . . and our relation to it," Monroe told his mentor, "is pretty much the same, as it was, in the commencement of the French Revolution." Monroe, now in a position to direct foreign affairs, questioned the long-standing U.S. policy of isolation. He began to contemplate a more powerful statement in favor of republicanism. He asked Jefferson, "Can we, in any form, take a bolder attitude in regard to it [revolution], in favor of liberty, than we then did? Can we afford greater aid to that cause, by assuming any such attitude, than we now do?" In the coming months events provided Monroe with an opportunity to assert this new "bolder attitude."[65]

During the summer and fall of 1823 Monroe learned that the French army had succeeded in suppressing the Spanish revolutionary government.

Rumors swirled that the Holy Alliance, emboldened by their victories over republicanism in Europe, next planned to reassert Spanish control over the Latin American colonies.[66] For Monroe, the one saving grace to this near-calamitous turn of events was British opposition to the alliance. As the preeminent maritime power Britain wanted free access to Latin American markets, not the reestablishment of Spanish rule over the region. By 1823 Foreign Minister George Canning realized that Britain had lost control of the concert of Europe. The Holy Alliance, increasingly led by Russia, who had its own designs on the American Pacific Northwest, adopted increasingly aggressive tactics against revolutionary regimes, and Canning began to see the United States as a potential ally in preventing European interference in Latin America. In October of 1823 Canning formally suggested Anglo-American cooperation to achieve this end. He asked Monroe to agree to the following:

1. We conceive the recovery of the colonies by Spain to be hopeless.
2. We conceive the recognition of them, as independent states, to be one of time and circumstance.
3. We are, however, by no means disposed to throw any impediment in the way of an arrangement between them and the mother country by amicable negotiations
4. We aim not at the possession of any portion of them ourselves
5. We could not see any portion of them transferred to any power with indifference.[67]

This amounted to an Anglo-American alliance for the preservation of Latin American independence against the Holy Allies, something unthinkable less than a decade before. Canning's offer intrigued Monroe, who sent a letter to Jefferson seeking advice on how to respond. Monroe posed a startling proposition, "Shall we entangle ourselves, at all, in European politics?" A joint proclamation meant abandoning the most sacred principle of American foreign relations. Monroe recognized the country's long-standing policy of neutrality toward the European powers, most famously enunciated in Washington's farewell address that Monroe had so vehemently castigated in 1797. Jefferson himself continued the principle during his presidency. Nevertheless, Monroe asked the former president, "if a case can exist" where the American policy of avoiding entangling alliances could be "departed from, is not the present instance precisely that case?"[68]

It should not be surprising that Monroe considered departing from the American aversion to entangling alliances. As far back as 1801 he had criticized Jefferson's inaugural address, especially with regard to foreign policy. He bristled that Jefferson had pledged not to involve the United States in "entangling alliances." Monroe considered this a slap in the face of France after the Federalists had effectively torn up the Treaty of Alliance of 1778. Further, as France slid back into monarchy under Napoleon, Monroe thought that if the United States had maintained a strong connection to France it would have made it far more difficult for that country to "leave the republican standard." He believed that if France had been tied to another republican government "the sentiment of the people would be doubly shocked, in the approach of her government towards monarchy."[69] In other words, Monroe believed that a strong Franco-American alliance would have made it harder for France to accept Napoleon's rule. But it was not just Monroe's attitude toward foreign alliances that made him interested in this offer. Canning's proposal also offered an opportunity to detach the mightiest nation in the world from the other monarchial powers.

It is important to understand Monroe's mindset when he considered a response to Canning's offer of cooperation. The proposal had not come out of nowhere for the president. He had seen signs of just this sort of reconciliation during his negotiations over the Monroe-Pinkney Treaty a decade previously. Since then the British had increasingly softened their fiercely anti-republican posture of the French revolutionary and Napoleonic eras. Combined with the obvious signs of rapprochement between the two former enemies, Monroe became convinced that this was an opportunity to separate Britain from the rest of monarchial Europe. As early as 1818 Richard Rush had reported rumors of British aid to the revolutionary governments in South America.[70] Rush had also told Monroe that the British were beginning to see the United States in a more favorable light after the War of 1812. Rush, perhaps hoping to score points with the president, told Monroe that in the minds of the British "we have sprung . . . into the rank of the great nations of the world."[71] Combined with the Rush-Bagot Treaty of 1818, which had demilitarized the Great

Lakes and Lake Champlain, the signs of rapprochement between the two sides were unmistakable.[72]

More specifically, the accession to the head of the British foreign office in 1822 of George Canning, who was, according to Rush, decidedly "moderate and conciliatory" in his attitude toward the United States, offered an opportunity to bring the two former enemies closer together.[73] To add to the positive vibes from the former mother country, Canning's cousin Stratford had been posted as the British minister to the United States, and had boasted to Adams that it was now Britain who contended in favor of liberty in Europe. Stratford Canning told the American secretary of state that Britain would be happy to see constitutional governments placed in nations that were seeing revolt, like Spain and Naples, in stark contrast to the Holy Allies' policy of repression.[74] George Canning even reversed course on Britain's previous anti-independence stance on the revolution in Greece when he granted belligerent rights to the Greek rebels.[75] Rush had also offered some proof of this new attitude toward the United States when he reported that the British ministry was eager to make certain trade deals if the Americans were willing to make the first move.[76]

Monroe tried to act on these positive developments from England. In April of 1823 he wrote to Henry Vassal-Fox (Lord Holland), the British diplomat he had negotiated the failed Monroe-Pinkney Treaty with in 1806. Monroe suggested that the British take action to resist the Holy Allies' advances against Spain. Monroe told Holland that Europe was once again involved in a war over the "principles of the French Revolution." It was, he explained, a contest to decide whether the people "derive their rights from their rulers" or the reverse. The French king, in Monroe's mind, was going to war to prove that the people had no rights other than those granted by the monarch, and only Great Britain could stop him. If Britain moved to prevent this French attack on the people's rights it would place her on "high ground in favor of human rights." Monroe also warned Lord Holland that the Holy Allies would not stop with Spain. Eventually they would look to the United States and England as targets.[77] Canning's proposal for an alliance to protect Latin America, coming a few months after Monroe's request to Lord Holland, may have seemed to the president as a response to his making the first move toward an alliance in favor of republicanism. And while it may have been too late for the British and Americans to link arms to act in Spain, Latin American republicanism still hung in the balance. All in all, this new proposal from Canning appeared to Monroe to be genuine. More to the point, it was also the diplomatic opportunity of a lifetime, a chance to win a key victory for the republican cause.

For two decades Monroe had watched the promise of the French Revolution fade. Now a potential rift between Britain and the Holy Allies appeared possible. Britain had been French republicanism's most implacable foe, but now Monroe told Jefferson, "I think a change has since been wrought" in them. As the Holy Allies moved in a more reactionary direction, British liberals looked askance at their activities. The British constitutional monarchy increasingly had more in common with the American republic than it did with autocrats like the Russian czar.[78] Monroe wanted to force Great Britain to stand either with the "monarchs of Europe" and despotism, or with the "U. States and liberty." He thought the opportunity great enough to take the risk, even if it meant reversing nearly half a century of American foreign policy. "My own impression," he told Jefferson, "is that we ought to meet the proposal of the British government and to make it known that we would view interference on the part of the European powers [or] an attack on the Colonies . . . as an attack on ourselves." Jefferson's response only added to Monroe's fervor.[79]

Jefferson weighed Monroe's concerns carefully. He called Canning's offer "the most momentous [question] . . . offered to my contemplation since that of Independence." Jefferson believed that Monroe's decision would shape the future of republicanism for years to come. While he reiterated his desire never to "entangle ourselves in the broils of Europe," Canning's offer provided an opportunity too enticing to ignore. Jefferson saw Europe increasingly descending back into the "domain of despotism." He hoped that accepting Canning's offer might "draw to our side" the "most powerful member" of the European community, and ultimately "bring her into the scale of free government." It would mark a pivotal victory in the struggle for the republican cause. And after all, by bringing Britain into the fight to secure republicanism in the Western Hemisphere the United States would not be entangling itself in "their" war, "but ours."[80]

Monroe also wrote to James Madison for advice. Though the former president refused to trust the British, he too responded eagerly. After reading Monroe's letter on the subject, Madison told Jefferson that "in the great struggle of the Epoch between liberty and despotism we owe it to ourselves to sustain the former, in this hemisphere at least." Madison suggested that Monroe ask Britain to extend their efforts not only to Latin American, but also to "the French invasion of Spain." He even wanted "to make Greece an object of some favorable attention."[81]

Madison hoped to press the British to support the cause of liberty in Europe as well as the Western Hemisphere, and he was not alone. In fact, Monroe had been bombarded with advice from another eminent revolutionary over this same point. The Marquis de Lafayette had written to Monroe from France several times over the past year imploring the president to take a stronger stance on the Greek revolutionary movement. In January of 1822 Lafayette explained that with the rest of Europe, led by the Holy Allies, engaged in counterrevolution across the continent it was the United States alone who could provide the proper support to the Greek cause. In Lafayette's typically ebullient style he told Monroe that, "It seems to me that the flag of American independence can nowhere be displayed so honourably and advantageously than in forming the establishment of Grecian republics."[82] Lafayette wrote again in September of 1822 saying much the same thing, explaining that with the "cloudy situation" in France, the "counterrevolutionary intrigues" in Spain, and the Holy Alliance poised to unveil "new conspiracies against the rights of mankind," the Greek cause was sure to fail without American intervention.[83] Lafayette's and Madison's advice resonated with Monroe's own thinking. He had mentioned the Greek rebellions during his annual message of 1822, in the process drawing the ire of John Quincy Adams, who believed that Monroe was dangerously close to involving the United States in Europe's constant wars.[84] Nevertheless, after conferring with the revolutionary generation's leading lights, Monroe's concern over Greek independence helped convince him to consider discarding one of the bedrock principles of American foreign policy.

For the obvious reason that it was not one of the Latin American republics, Greece is usually not included in historians' discussions of the

Monroe Doctrine. And while Monroe did not, in the end, include the birthplace of republicanism in the doctrine, he made reference to the movement in the annual messages of both 1822 and 1823, lending as much moral weight to the cause as he thought prudent. The Greek rebellion was meaningful to Monroe, who had been steeped in the classics both as a student at William and Mary and during his apprenticeship to Thomas Jefferson. Further, he had delved deeply into the histories of the Greek republics during the ratification debates of the 1780s, and he would later go into greater detail in *The People the Sovereigns* after his retirement. Thus, Greece's plight concerned Monroe deeply and played a major part in convincing him to consider Canning's proposal.[85]

Canning's offer provided Monroe with an opportunity to guide the United States toward the kind of robust support of republicanism he thought it should have extended to France in the 1790s. He wanted to grasp this chance to force the United States to take a stronger stance in favor of republican government around the world and to take its place as the defender of the cause. This would, he was sure, secure his own legacy as republicanism's greatest diplomat. With Lafayette, Jefferson, and Madison all in favor of his new direction for American policy, Monroe convened his cabinet on November 7, 1823, to discuss Canning's proposal. Only then did he receive an entirely different perspective from Adams.

The secretary of state agreed with the general idea of warning the European powers against reestablishing colonies in the New World, but thought that by accepting Canning's proposal the United States would "come in as a cock-boat in the wake of the British man-of-war."[86] Adams did not perceive a world locked in a life-and-death struggle between the proponents of monarchy and republicanism. To him the United States stood alone as the last bastion of freedom in the world. In his famous July 4, 1821, speech to Congress, in response to the calls for American aid to the revolutionary regimes in Latin America, Adams declared that the United States "goes not abroad, in search of monsters to destroy. . . . She is the well-wisher to freedom and independence of all but she is the champion and vindicator only of her own."[87] He saw Great Britain as another rival for power in the New World, not a potential ally in a grand concert for liberty. He wanted the United States to assert itself as the dominant power in the Western Hemisphere. Accepting Canning's proposal would only invite future British incursions into Latin America, potentially weakening American influence in the region.[88] Adams also feared that the notoriously fickle British policymakers would soon reverse course, leaving the Americans standing alone in a war against the Holy Allies. Further, he disliked the idea of swearing off any future American territorial expansion into the former Spanish empire, specifically Cuba and Texas.[89]

Monroe's cabinet met on November 13 and 15 to discuss the proposal. Adams confided to his journal that the president appeared terrified "far beyond anything that I could have conceived possible with the fear that the Holy Alliance are about to restore immediately S. America to Spain." Adams disagreed, "I no more believe that the Holy Allies will restore the Spanish dominion upon the American continent than that the Chimborazo will sink beneath the Ocean." The fact that Adams turned out to be correct in his assessment of the Holy Allies' intention should not diminish what Monroe and his cabinet saw as a very real threat in the autumn of 1823. Adams himself admitted that the Holy Allies might intervene in the revolutions. According to the secretary of state, this would merely delay Latin American independence by "three, four, or five years." But even a temporary delay was unacceptable to Monroe, and a long-term suppression of republicanism in the New World akin to that taking place in Naples, Spain, and Greece was a horrifying prospect, and made an alliance with Great Britain all the more enticing.[90]

The situation changed abruptly on November 16 when Rush sent word that Canning had received assurances from France that the Holy Alliance would not interfere in the Western Hemisphere. Rush reported that Canning was now uninterested in pursuing a joint venture with the Americans. According to Adams, Monroe was in such "an extraordinary degree of dejection" after learning this that Adams was sure that "there must be something that affects him beside the European news." Adams could not understand why these events caused Monroe such anguish. He failed to realize the importance of this moment to the former republican revolutionary. For Monroe and his former brothers in arms the chance to pull the old enemy Great Britain away from the Holy Allies, while securing republicanism in the new world, represented an opportunity nearly as important as the

American Revolution itself. The lingering trauma of Monroe's past experience in France only made the question more personal. A few weeks later, Monroe explained in a letter to Jefferson just how disappointing Canning's reversal had been. He called the new British position an "unpleasant circumstance" and lamented that "Mr. Canning's zeal" had "abated." By now Latin American independence was so dear to the president that, just as he had with the French a generation before, Monroe considered their cause "as essentially our own."[91]

On November 21, Adams learned exactly what "affected" the president. Without British backing, Monroe still intended to commit the United States to unilateral support of republicanism, not just in Latin America as the British had suggested but around the globe. When Monroe read his initial outline of what became the Monroe Doctrine to the cabinet, it struck Adams like a bolt of lightning. The president began by warning of the "formidable dangers" facing the country, urging Americans to prepare themselves to defend the cause of liberty against its enemies. He harshly criticized the French invasion of Spain, and tacitly recognized Greek independence with joyous praise of their "heroic revolutionary struggle." Taking Jefferson and Madison's suggestions to heart, Monroe declared the United States the champion of republicanism, not only in the west but in Europe as well. An alarmed Adams called Monroe's draft "a summons to arms . . . against all Europe." He warned the president that his message might enrage the Holy Allies and drive the country to war. Europe, he claimed, had always gone through "convulsions," while the United States meanwhile looked upon these "safe in our distance" and wisely maintained a "forbearance to interfere." With this message Monroe, in his zeal for the revolutionary movement, would "buckle the harness and throw down the gauntlet." It would entangle the United States in Europe's incessant wars. Worse, it did so for reasons that Adams called "exclusively European." He urged the president to soften his message. Adams could not understand why Monroe, whose presidential temperament was usually so sensible, would look to entangle the United States into European affairs so rashly. He did not fully understand that this was Monroe's chance to defend republicanism the way he believed the United States should have during the 1790s.[92]

During the cabinet meeting Monroe appeared unwilling to change the message. Then on November 22 Adams again met with the president, this time in private. This appears to have been the meeting that swayed Monroe toward a compromise position between his initial draft and Adams's position. Adams argued for a message that stated the government's "earnest remonstrance against the interference of the European powers by force with South America, but to disclaim all interference on our part with Europe." It was the meddling in European affairs that alarmed Adams. At heart, Adams wanted the message to be defensive, warning Russia against meddling in the Pacific Northwest as well as warning the rest of Europe, Britain included, against continued Latin American colonialism. Monroe meanwhile thought that throwing American moral weight into the republican cause in Europe was almost as important as doing the same in Latin America. Ultimately, Adams convinced Monroe by appealing to his legacy. The secretary of state knew that Monroe feared war with the Holy Allies. The president said as much during previous cabinet meetings. Adams convinced the president that issuing a statement pledging the United States to a defense of republicanism in Europe would be the surest way of bringing such a conflict to America's doorstep. A war with the Holy Allies would have a devastating effect on the republican cause, both in the United States and around the world. More to the point, Monroe would be forever remembered as the president who embroiled the United States in this disastrous confrontation, irreparably damaging Monroe's legacy. Up to this point Monroe's presidency, Adams told him, would be "looked back to as the golden age of this republic." This would remain true only if Monroe could manage to hand the reins to his successor with the United States "at peace and amity with all the world."[93]

Adams's argument was well aimed. Many years' devoted struggle inclined Monroe to see monarchial conspiracies wherever he looked. The entire revolutionary movement focused on kingly plots to subvert American liberty. In Monroe's mind, British monarchists had conspired to destroy the American colonies in the years preceding independence. During the 1790s the same monarchists had contrived to extinguish the French Revolution, while their Federalist allies in the United States labored to corrupt the American republic. Now the European rulers linked arms to crush revolutionary movements on the continent. It did not take a great leap of imagination for Monroe to think them capable of targeting the United States if he tried to champion the republican cause in their own backyard.

Monroe and Adams had, in fact, discussed the possibility of Holy Alliance attacks on the United States. As early as 1821 Adams reported in his diary that Monroe "believed that we could not have a quarrel with any one member of the Holy Alliance without bringing the whole body of them upon us." The European Allies all "hated us for our principles" and "dreaded the effect of our example, the standing refutation of their doctrines in our prosperous condition, and the danger to themselves in our constantly growing power."[94] Further, Monroe knew just how costly war could be to the republican cause. His last experience fighting a war with a European power had seen the two great symbols of American republicanism, the White House and the Capitol, burned. Though the United States had emerged more or less whole from that conflict, there was no guarantee that the same would hold true in the next war against the monarchists.[95]

These last few days before Monroe issued his annual message on December 2 were obviously trying for the president. His entire diplomatic career had been building to this moment. He had his fellow revolutionaries' thoughts fresh in his mind, including Lafayette's pleas for the United States to take up the cause of the Greek revolutionaries, as well as Madison's urging Monroe to work with the British to do something about the French invasion of Spain. But he also shared Adams's fears concerning the threat the Holy Allies posed to the United States if provoked. Were Latin American, Greek, and Spanish republicanism worth the risk of another war that might fatally wound the American republic? How far could the United States threaten the Holy Allies before they responded directly? And what of the British? Was this an opportunity to bring the British closer to the side of "free government"? These were issues, in the abstract, that he had wrestled with since the 1790s, and he had learned that there were no easy answers.

Monroe again needed to find a middle course, this time between his initial aggressive message of support for the republican cause and John Quincy Adams's safer approach. He ultimately mixed ideology-driven republicanism with calculating diplomatic realism. He chose to focus on the cause in the Western Hemisphere, but he also kept strong support for budding European republicanism. Once again, Monroe chose to wield the "moral weight" of the United States in favor of liberty while hinting to the world, without expressly committing to a course of action, that the United States would defend republicanism in the Western Hemisphere. On November 24, two days after his private meeting with the president, Adams learned that Monroe had changed the message, removing the most controversial passages from the text.[96] Nevertheless, Monroe's unwavering support for the movement comes through in the words of the actual doctrine. For him, the heart of the Annual Message of 1823 was his support of the republican cause. Monroe hoped that his statement would still be seen as a great blow for republicanism, carving out a space for it in the Western Hemisphere.

The republican thread in Monroe's thinking is easy to spot in the Annual Message of 1823. Monroe began the message by harking back to the halcyon days of the revolution. He opened with a warning for his fellow citizens: there "never was a period since the establishment of our Revolution when" more was required of Americans. While he softened the language preparing Americans for a war against Europe, Monroe stressed the need for Americans to practice "virtue and patriotism," to live up to the example set by his generation.[97] Adams had bristled at the warlike footing that Monroe had adopted in his first draft, but as Monroe explained in a private letter to his son-in-law, George Hay, he still wanted the United States to be "on its guard."[98]

While the final enunciation of the Monroe Doctrine focused primarily on Latin America, Monroe nevertheless declared a kind of tacit American support for the revolutionary struggle in Europe.[99] Monroe continued on a theme from his message of the previous year when he declared that the Greek republican movement filled Americans "with the most exalted sentiments," and lamented that "such a country should have been overwhelmed . . . under a gloomy despotism." Taking Lafayette's advice to heart, Monroe claimed that the fate of the Greeks filled Americans with "unceasing and deep anger." Now that the birthplace of democracy "contend[ed] in favor of their liberties" to "recover their independence," just as the United States had done in 1776, it could not help but elicit "sympathy and excitement" from Americans.[100]

Next, Monroe moved on to the ideas he had discussed with James

Madison by setting his sights on the European monarchies themselves. Though he removed the passages that Adams called a "summons to arms," he did criticize the Holy Allies. After mentioning in his message of 1822 that Spain and Portugal were taking steps to "improve the condition of the people," a year later he lamented the interference from the Holy Allies.[101] Americans kept an eye on the cause of liberty in Europe, "cherish[ing] sentiments the most friendly in favor of the liberty and happiness of their fellow men on that side of the Atlantic." This signaled to the world that the United States supported the revolutionary cause in Europe.[102] The president claimed that "Europe is still unsettled," and he held out hope for republicanism on that continent. The monarchists' reactionary measures amounted to nothing more than a feeble attempt to hold back the tide. Proof of this lay in the allied powers decision to meddle in the "internal concerns of Spain."[103] Monroe wanted the Holy Allies to know that Americans disapproved of their attempts to foist a restored monarchy upon the Spanish people.

Finally, Monroe moved on to the ideas he and Jefferson had discussed: the spread of republicanism in Latin America. Monroe explained that his government was "more immediately connected" with things in the Western Hemisphere. The "causes" of which, he continued, "must be obvious to all enlightened and impartial observers." These "causes" were the Latin American revolutions. He declared victory for republicanism in the Western Hemisphere, trumpeting not only that the Latin American governments had won their independence, but also that under his leadership the United States had recognized these new states on "just principles." Those "just principles" primarily concerned the inherent differences between the governments of Europe and the United States. "The political system of the allied powers is essentially different in this respect from that of America," Monroe explained. Latin America's choice of government, as much as proximity, imbued the region with particular importance. With republicanism taking root in Latin America, the United States refused to stand idle while the allied powers forced their style of government on the Western Hemisphere. To allow that would threaten America's "peace and happiness." Monroe also criticized the quality of monarchial government, claiming that no nation would ever knowingly choose monarchy over republicanism. He argued that no one believed "that our southern brethren, if left to themselves, would adopt it [monarchy] of their own accord." The Latin American republics shared a connection to the United States and "we could not view any interposition for the purpose of oppressing them, or controlling in any other manner their destiny, by any European power in any other light than as the manifestation of an unfriendly disposition toward the United States." It was this republican connection as much as their proximity that induced Monroe to make a vigorous show of support for Latin America.[104]

Finally, Monroe outlined the words that helped define much of subsequent American foreign policy: "We owe it, therefore, to candor and to the amicable relations existing between the U.S. and those powers to declare that we should consider any attempt on their [Europe's] part to extend their system to any portion of this hemisphere as dangerous to our peace and safety." This, the core of the doctrine, had its origins in Monroe's republicanism. The attempt to keep European powers out of the affairs of the Western Hemisphere stemmed directly from Monroe's dedication to the cause. Despite softening his stance, Monroe still saw his message as a great victory for republicanism.

Almost from the moment he delivered the Annual Message to Congress, Monroe received words of praise from many different corners of the world. A week after it was delivered Chief Justice John Marshall sent Monroe a brief line complimenting his message, telling the president that he agreed with the president that the United States could not "look on the present state of the world with indifference."[105] In France, Lafayette was equally pleased with Monroe's message. Though it did not go so far as to engage the American military on behalf of the Greeks, the hero of Yorktown was satisfied with the "moral weight" the United States had placed on the scale of free government. Lafayette commented on the positive effect Monroe's doctrine made in Europe, where his message was "hailed by every friend of liberty." Its importance in Lafayette's mind lay in its dual nature. He thought it wonderful that "the independence of the American continent is now under the protection of the noble stars and stripes," but to Lafayette it was just as important that Monroe had shown that "the heroic effort of Greece find[s] due sympathy in the heart of the people of the U.S." Lafayette saw Monroe as wielding both the moral strength and the potential military might of the United States in favor of republicanism.[106]

Monroe was particularly proud of this letter. He gushed with pride in repeating to James Madison that the European "friends of liberty" lauded his message.[107]

Monroe received welcome news from other revolutionaries across the globe. An American in Paris named John Brown told the president that the French revolutionary and diplomat Francois Barbe-Marbois, Monroe's opposite number during the Louisiana negotiations, approved of the doctrine.[108] Caesar A. Rodney, a diplomat in Buenos Aires and son of one of Monroe's fellow revolutionaries, congratulated the president on his message, telling Monroe that "the state of the world required this frank and manly avowal of your patriotic sentiments." Rodney even harked back to his father's era when he told the president, "You breathe a spirit worthy of the purest and proudest days of the Revolution." Finally, he expected the doctrine to have a powerful effect because the "weight of the moral character" of the United States was worth "armies in the field."[109] A prominent Virginia politician living in London, Alexander McRae, who had backed Monroe for president in 1808, told the president not only that his message had met with "universal approbation from the American public," but also that the people of Europe in general "pronounce it to be the greatest state paper, or as Mr. Canning puts it 'Document,' that has been given to the world." Further, "it has secured immortality to its author and has elevated the American name high above that of every other nation."[110] Such praise convinced Monroe that his message made an important contribution to republicanism and just as importantly that he had secured his own republican legacy.

Six months after the creation of the doctrine Monroe gave some indication of what he thought he had accomplished in a letter to Jefferson. He wrote to his old mentor in alarm when word reached him that the French government had sent an envoy to Colombia, offering the new nation recognition in exchange for a promise that the Colombians establish a monarchial form of government. Monroe wrote that the "attitude" the United States took in this crisis was "in the highest degree important to the whole civilized world," primarily because the United States had stood alone against the monarchs of Europe. Monroe thought such an act might even lead the United States to war. Though the French were willing to leave a monarchial Latin America alone, this did not satisfy

Monroe. Latin American independence meant little without Latin American republicanism.[111]

Exactly one year after creating the doctrine, Monroe sat down to compose his final message to Congress. In this last statement to the country Monroe spoke with pride of his accomplishment, and again linked the republican cause around the world. He referred to the revolutions in Latin America as well as to the one in Greece, claiming that the cause of "liberty and humanity continues to prevail" throughout the world. Latin America, in part because of his doctrine, was "settling down under governments elective and representative, in every branch, similar to our own." The "deep interest" the United States took in that region, "especially in the very important one of instituting their own government[,] . . . has been declared and is known to the world." Monroe left the presidency believing that his doctrine had helped ensure the future of republicanism in the Western Hemisphere.[112]

From his first days in office until his final annual message to the American people, Monroe dealt constantly with the dissolution of the Spanish Empire. The crisis combined perhaps the two most important aspects of Monroe's career, foreign policy and the republican cause. After serving in almost every conceivable important public office, playing a key role in nearly every major event of the founding era, Monroe hoped that the doctrine would cap his legacy as republicanism's greatest diplomat.

## Conclusions

Monroe's presidency was the culmination of his career-long struggle to champion republicanism. It should not be surprising then that his actions during his eight years in office bear all the hallmarks of Monroe's republican diplomacy, including both his dedication to the republican cause and the skills he had learned over a lifetime of fighting to climb the American political ladder.

During the contest over Florida, Monroe dealt with Jackson's invasion in conjunction with John Quincy Adams's Transcontinental Treaty negotiations with Don Luis de Onís. Monroe declined to chastise the Tennessee general, but he also refused to risk war with the Spanish Empire, or more importantly one of its stronger monarchial allies. What he sought, and ultimately achieved, was to illustrate to the Spanish that their continued control of Florida was untenable, and that selling to the United States would allow them to profit from the territory before they lost the region for nothing. Monroe applied the lessons learned from decades dealing with the deteriorating Spanish government going as far back as the Jay-Gardoqui negotiations in the 1780s, and continuing through his own negotiations over Florida in 1803. In the end, Monroe secured the United States' southern border with the acquisition of Florida, and helped lay the groundwork for the Adams-Onis Treaty of 1819, which expanded the American republic's reach across the continent to the Pacific Ocean.

As with the Florida Crisis, the debate over recognition of the fledgling Latin American republics was also a continuation of Monroe's other foreign policy goal: to spread republicanism to other nations. Monroe saw the upheaval in Latin America, and in European countries like Greece, as a republican renaissance, a repeat of the 1790s. He saw people on both sides of the Atlantic once again throwing off the shackles of monarchy and embracing republican government. Monroe wanted to ensure that under his leadership the United States deployed its full moral weight on the side of this cause. He recognized that the United States was in no position to undertake the spread of republicanism to Latin American, much less Europe, through its military might. Yet he also did not want to repeat the mistake of the Washington administration, by keeping other revolutionary regimes at arm's length.

What emerged was Monroe's policy of moving slowly toward recognition, while indicating his support through public statements, which satisfied neither Henry Clay, who wanted more direct action, nor John Quincy Adams, who wanted the United States to stay out of the controversy entirely. Despite this opposition, Monroe steadily provided moral support to the republics, but refrained from action that might have antagonized the Holy Allies into joining the conflict, a concern Monroe took seriously. While he continued to see the world engaged in a contest between republicanism and monarchy, it was not part of his plan to engage the United States in an actual worldwide military conflict between the two sides, as such a struggle would distinctly favor the monarchies and threaten republicanism both at home and abroad. As the Latin American revolutions enjoyed more successes in their quest for independence in the early 1820s,

Monroe's language in support grew bolder, until he eventually pushed the United States toward a full diplomatic recognition of the new republics in 1822, setting the stage for the Monroe Doctrine a year later.

As Monroe's final act in support of republicanism, the Monroe Doctrine combined issues Monroe had struggled with throughout his presidency, indeed his entire career. Greek independence, and various liberal and republican movements in Europe, filled Monroe with the kind of hope reminiscent of the headiest days of the French Revolution. More ominously though, the specter of Holy Allies' interference in Latin America also filled him with the same fear of monarchial reprisals against republicanism that he had witnessed during both the American Revolution and its French counterpart. The Holy Allies' increasingly aggressive military response to European republicanism, combined with hints that they might consider using the same measures in the Western Hemisphere, represented a serious threat to the cause. Britain's offer to cooperate in favor of Latin American independence therefore offered a golden opportunity for Monroe.

The convergence of these separate yet interconnected developments provided Monroe with a rare opportunity to build republican bridges among various nations in opposition to the Holy Allies. This alliance would have included the United States, the Latin American republics, Great Britain, and even revolutionaries in places like Greece who were, in Monroe's mind, rekindling the flame European republicanism. Seen like this, an Anglo-American version of the Monroe Doctrine can be viewed as Monroe's attempt to correct the United States' diplomatic mistakes of the past. By entering into an agreement to support republicanism, Monroe would have corrected what he saw as the Washington administration's mistakes during the negotiations with France in the 1790s. But it would also have corrected the mistakes Jefferson and Madison made in 1806, when they rejected the Monroe-Pinkney Treaty. At one stroke Monroe might have been able to secure an alliance to challenge the monarchial Holy Allies. When George Canning rescinded the British offer Monroe altered his strategy, but he did not give up the dream of championing the cause entirely. Antagonizing the European monarchs without a British alliance made a Monroe Doctrine in Europe too risky, but he felt more secure in Latin America.

Monroe, true to form, did not commit the United States to any specific military action with his doctrine. Instead he utilized what he saw as the most powerful weapon in the United States' arsenal: unequivocal moral support for republican revolution. As he left the presidency he hoped that this would be enough to cement his legacy as a champion of the republican cause on par with George Washington or Thomas Jefferson.

# Conclusion

## Making the World Safe for Republicanism

*An effort in favor of liberty by the people of any country
has always commanded my highest respect.*

JAMES MONROE, ON THE FRENCH REVOLUTION OF 1830

JAMES MONROE left politics in 1825. His six-year retirement from public life offers a sad conclusion to one of the great, if underappreciated,
political careers in American history. Nearly bankrupt, Monroe spent his
final years petitioning Congress to compensate him for the massive debts
he accrued while serving in various diplomatic posts. It made for a humiliating task for the former president. Worse, after his wife Elizabeth's death,
health concerns forced Monroe to leave Virginia to live with his daughter
in New York. Despite this sad state of affairs, news from France once again
managed to raise Monroe's spirits. In 1830 a new generation of French citizens rebelled against the restoration Bourbon crown.[1] Showing the same
enthusiasm he had fifty years earlier, Monroe hoped that *this* revolution
would finally sweep monarchism away forever. In January of 1831 Monroe wrote to his former secretary of state, John Quincy Adams, with the
same passion for the republican cause that he had shown throughout his
life. He believed that the news from France would open "a new epoch to
that country and to the world." Ever the optimist, Monroe expected this
round of revolution would succeed where the others failed, because it "occurred under much more favorable circumstances." Monroe believed that
his doctrine had helped change the climate, allowing republicanism a more

favorable hearing. Monroe was comforted with the thought that the movement he had spent his life promoting would "extend its influence . . . to other people, to Spain and Italy and even to the North." Despite his ill health, he even agreed to attend a Tammany Hall meeting to "celebrate the late glorious revolution in France." Monroe died a few months later on July 4, 1831—the fifty-fifth birthday of the republic he had fought so hard to defend.[2]

Monroe never doubted the justice of the cause. He supported republicanism with a consistency rarely seen in politicians. For half a century nearly every key moment in Monroe's life surrounded the movement. On the cold Christmas Day in 1776 when the teenaged Monroe suffered a bullet wound at Trenton, it was in defense of republicanism. When he returned to the United States in 1797 after his humiliating recall from France, the presence of his fellow republicans reminded Monroe that his struggles in Paris served the cause. During his ascent from a disgraced envoy in 1797 to the presidency in 1817, Monroe convinced himself that each political maneuver put him in a better position to champion the American republic. As president, Monroe tried to turn American foreign policy toward a defense of worldwide republicanism. Finally, at the end of his life, Monroe watched a new revolution in France with great hope, believing that his legacy had been fulfilled and that Americans would remember him as a champion of republicanism.

Unfortunately, he was wrong. Monroe's legacy is nothing like what he hoped it would be when he died in 1831. Monroe has never been placed beside his more illustrious colleagues. In fact, compared to the other founders, Monroe has been mostly forgotten. To the general public Benjamin Franklin, Thomas Jefferson, and George Washington have always loomed as the greatest of the American founders, but even less obviously heroic figures have earned acclaim recently. John Adams received popular attention with the commercial success of the HBO miniseries based on David McCullough's bestselling biography of the second president. Alexander Hamilton has a popular Broadway musical based on his life. Conversely, in the popular imagination, Monroe has almost no historical legacy. There is no history channel documentary focused on Monroe, to say nothing of a big-budget Hollywood movie or Netflix series dedicated to his life. In fact, Monroe does not even appear in either the *John Adams* miniseries or

*Hamilton: The Musical.* The general public has never embraced the fifth president, and among historians he hardly fares better.

Over the years there have been only a handful of scholarly works focused on Monroe. John Quincy Adams wrote a dual biography of James Madison and Monroe in the mid-nineteenth century.[3] Then, in the wake of Theodore Roosevelt's revitalization of the Monroe Doctrine in the early part of the twentieth century, two biographies of the fifth president appeared from Daniel Gilman and George Morgan in 1911 and 1921, respectively. Yet despite this brief revival, scholarly interest quickly waned, and only two major Monroe biographies appeared during the rest of the twentieth century, with William Cresson's work in 1946 and Harry Ammon's biography in 1972. Ammon's work is still the best scholarly treatment of the fifth president.[4]

This paltry list pales next to the work done on Monroe's longtime mentor Thomas Jefferson. In the twenty-first century alone, eminent scholars such as Peter Onuf, Andrew Burstein, Joyce Appleby, and Annette Gordon-Reed have all published works on the "sage of Monticello." Similarly, popular authors such as Jon Meachem and Joseph Ellis have written award-winning biographies of the third president. Meanwhile, Monroe continues to be overlooked. And while James Madison suffers something of the same fate as Monroe among the general public, scholars at least tend to reserve a special place for the author of the Virginia Plan, Bill of Rights, and *Federalist* no. 10, even if the average American often forgets "Little Jemmy's" contributions to the founding.[5]

There may be a glimmer of hope on the horizon for Monroe's legacy. With the two hundredth anniversary of Monroe's election, scholars have begun reappraising his contributions to the American founding. The "founders chic" that became so popular in the 1990s has continued unabated in the twenty-first century, and appears to have belatedly included the fifth president. Robert Pierce Forbes recently argued that Monroe was instrumental in procuring the Missouri Compromise of 1820. Jay Sexton published a work on the Monroe Doctrine's impact on subsequent American foreign policy. In addition, Stuart Leibiger's edited work on Madison and Monroe provides a number of important essays on Monroe. Harlow Giles Unger attempted to bring the study of Monroe to a wider audience in 2009 with a popular biography of the fifth president.[6]

Perhaps most important is that with the ongoing publication of Daniel Preston's *Papers of James Monroe* series Monroe has finally been given his own papers project.[7] This only underscores how little attention has been paid to Monroe over the years. Several of the American founders were the subjects of multigenerational efforts to print their papers during the twentieth century, but, as usual, James Monroe was overlooked. Stanislaus Murray Hamilton did publish seven volumes of Monroe's selected writings beginning in 1898, but until recently, no effort had been made to collect and publish Monroe's correspondence. This renewed scholarly interest in Monroe will hopefully bring more attention to the fifth president. In the meantime, it is important to note some of the reasons why Monroe has been ignored.[8]

There are several explanations as to why Monroe has been overlooked through the years. First, the written record works against his memory. Though he was desperate to secure his republican legacy, Monroe was not terribly effective at influencing the evidence historians would later use to evaluate him. In particular, he failed to adequately shape the historical record (at least compared to his contemporaries). Historians are limited to the sources their subjects leave behind, and Monroe's actions in this realm may have done his legacy a disservice. He burned most of his personal correspondence, including nearly every letter he and his wife wrote to each other. Thus, we know very little of Monroe's personal life and almost nothing of Elizabeth Monroe. Though we have much of Monroe's public life to sift through, our picture of him is incomplete. Consider that one of the reasons for the renewed interest in John Adams has been his relationship with Abigail Adams. In fact, perhaps the most absorbing aspect of the Adams miniseries is the relationship between husband (played by Paul Giamatti) and wife (Laura Linney) amidst the political drama of the era. Similarly, one of the most compelling features of James Madison's presidency is his relationship with his wife, the dynamic Dolly Madison. Elizabeth Kortright Monroe, meanwhile, like her husband, is seen as diffident, almost cold compared to other first ladies. But the truth is we simply do not know enough to form much of an opinion of her or her relationship with her husband. Would we see Monroe in a different light if scholars were privy to his personal life as well as they are to his political life? This is impossible to answer, but it clarifies just one of a number of reasons why Monroe is often lost in the shuffle when historians discuss the founders.

The lack of insight into his family life notwithstanding, less is known about James Monroe's personality than about those of his fellow founders. Unlike Jefferson, Monroe showed little interest in anything outside of politics, at least not in the letters that survived Monroe's purge of his personal correspondence. Unlike some of Jefferson's other correspondents, Monroe was not someone with whom his mentor often engaged in nonpolitical discussion. Further, the writings Monroe did leave behind are, at times, difficult to decipher. For one thing, he was overly fond of dense sentence structure. He had neither Jefferson's nor Madison's skill for eloquent prose, nor Franklin's simple, more accessible, style.[9] He also had terrible handwriting, which he acknowledged on at least one occasion.[10]

Monroe also failed to take certain measures that might have helped shape his legacy. Unlike Jefferson, Monroe did not organize his papers in any practical way before his death. Jefferson actively tried to shape the record after the fact. From meticulously organizing his papers to his personal selection of his tombstone's epitaph, Jefferson cultivated his legacy in a number of ways. He probably even took steps to hide what most historians now believe was a long-term sexual relationship with his slave Sally Hemmings.[11] Monroe, meanwhile, as far as we know, took none of these kinds of steps. Unlike either John or John Quincy Adams, Monroe also left no diary to reveal his innermost thoughts on the personalities and issues of the day.[12] And, while Monroe did begin work on his autobiography and *The People the Sovereigns*, he failed to finish either before his death. Thus, perhaps one of the major reasons historians spend so little time on Monroe is that, compared with his contemporaries, he gave them so little with which to work. But no matter how scant the record, few historians would argue that that alone keeps Monroe from a place beside Jefferson and Washington on Mt. Rushmore. Most would agree that Monroe simply did not match his predecessors.

In many ways, Monroe suffers from comparison to some of the giants, of not just the American founding, but all of U.S. history. The four men who preceded Monroe, while not always considered great presidents, are still regarded as some of the most influential figures in American history.

Further, like Monroe, each of the first four presidents built their legacies by defending republicanism. George Washington was called "the father of his country" by his contemporaries, and eulogized by Henry Lee as "the first in war, first in peace, first in the hearts of his countrymen."[13] John Adams, though perhaps not the most effective president, did more than almost anyone else to push the cause of independence and help establish the American republic. But, most importantly, Monroe suffers from the natural comparison to his two closest colleagues and immediate predecessors, Thomas Jefferson and James Madison.

Historians have always viewed Monroe as the third of the Virginia Republican Dynasty, both in sequence and ability. After all, Jefferson was the author of the Declaration of Independence and James Madison was the "father" of both the Constitution and the Bill of Rights. His two best friends had literally created the American republic's three most important founding documents. Monroe was conscious that he followed in the footsteps of the greatest of his generation, and often mentioned his more illustrious predecessors.[14] He summed up his thoughts on them in a letter to his son-in-law, George Hay: "It is my opinion that Mr. Jefferson and Mr. Madison have done more since the establishment of the revolution (in which Genl. W. was preeminent) than any two persons on the continent."[15]

He also made public references to his predecessors. Monroe undertook a presidential tour of the Northeast after his election in 1817, where only a few years before New England Federalists had hinted at secession at the end of the War of 1812. The trip itself was in some ways an homage to the tours Washington undertook during his presidency. During this trip, and those to the Chesapeake and the southern states that followed in 1818 and 1819 respectively, Monroe praised Jefferson, Madison, and Washington.[16] Monroe explained that during his presidency he would "take example from the conduct of the distinguished men who have preceded [him] in this high trust."[17]

Most historians agree that Monroe ultimately fell short of living up to the "example" set by his predecessors. But this was not entirely his fault. The first four presidents all made their mark on the United States during the late eighteenth century, when republican ideas were at their zenith. Monroe was too young to have made the kind of impact on the revolution as had older men like Washington, Jefferson, and Adams. He was also just slightly too junior within the ranks of politicians in Virginia to earn a place beside Madison at the Constitutional Convention in 1787. By the time Monroe had achieved high office and tried to make his mark on history, a new generation was moving away from the obsession with American republicanism. When Monroe entered the presidency he tended to look backward to the revolution, while the next generation looked forward to new challenges.

Monroe came of age in a monarchial world, where republicanism had to fight for its very survival. As the revolution unfolded, that same world became divided between republicans and monarchists. Monroe believed the United States needed to use its status as the birthplace of republican government to sound the trumpet for the cause, even at the risk of conflict with the monarchies of Europe. Once republicanism prevailed in that contest it would change the world forever. Unlike John Quincy Adams, Monroe saw monarchism as a monster that needed slaying. Near the end of his presidency, Monroe and his fellow Democratic-Republicans had emerged victorious over the "monarchist" Federalists in the United States, but things looked bleak for the future of republicanism in Europe after the Congress of Vienna. Monroe had spent his life contesting every inch, both in the United States and abroad, to expand the boundaries of republicanism. As the last of the founders, Monroe wanted to continue the fight. The new generation of Americans, born after the revolution, had other ideas.

The dynamic, experimental nature of the founding generation's republicanism was commonplace to 1820s Americans. While Monroe continued to look to spreading republicanism abroad, his constituents were increasingly occupied with the economy, westward expansion, and the growing sectional divide. Younger Americans simply did not see the cause in the same way. They were no longer obsessed with the republican experiment. Monroe's desire to spread republicanism landed awkwardly with his fellow Americans of the 1820s, and within the wider currents of American foreign policy. It was in part why he decided to write *The People the Sovereigns*, and ultimately why it failed to excite much interest.

Monroe's republicanism connects generally within a long line of thinkers who have articulated, in the broadest sense, an idea of American mission. The concept of a "City on a Hill," first uttered by John Winthrop, has resonated with Americans both before and after Monroe's time. The idea has retained its relevancy even in the twenty-first century. During the 2016 presidential campaign former Republican nominee Mitt Romney claimed that a Donald Trump presidency would mean that the United States would "cease to be a shining city on a hill."[18] When Winthrop spoke of this "City upon a Hill" in his famous sermon in 1630, he wanted the Massachusetts Bay Colony to become a model of Christian charity for the world to follow.[19] Other politicians since have also adopted the broader idea that the United States has a special purpose. Monroe was no different. Though he did not see the American mission in the kind of explicitly Christian terms Winthrop did, Monroe had a religion-like fervor for the cause nonetheless. For Monroe, the United States was a model of republicanism rather than of Christian charity. Monroe wanted other nations to follow in the American example, adopting republicanism of their own accord. His entire diplomatic career was dedicated to the idea that republicanism could be spread throughout the globe, and his devotion to this singular cause makes Monroe something of an outlier within the major currents of American foreign policy, even among his contemporaries.

Perhaps the most important pillar of American diplomatic principle during Monroe's lifetime was the policy of avoiding "entangling alliances" with foreign powers. In his farewell address in 1796 George Washington, perhaps with Monroe's behavior in France in mind, famously warned his fellow Americans to "steer clear of permanent alliances with any portion of the foreign world."[20] Four years later, President Jefferson agreed with Washington. The new Democratic-Republican president explained that under his leadership the United States would maintain "peace, commerce, and honest friendship with all nations, entangling alliances with none." Washington and Jefferson were the two most important men upon whose examples Monroe tried to model his own career, yet he largely rejected perhaps their most important diplomatic principle.[21]

Monroe did not fear "foreign entanglements," as long as they helped spread republicanism abroad. He advocated an alliance with France in the 1790s, tried to make a lasting peace with Britain in 1806, and was ready to sign an agreement allying the United States with the former mother country in defense of Latin American republicanism had George Canning not reversed course in 1823.[22] Because of this difference between Monroe and his contemporaries it has been difficult to define his place in the foreign policy of the early republic.

Monroe differed, to one degree or another, from all of his contemporaries on the issue of republican diplomacy. As two of the most prominent scholars of Jefferson's diplomacy have stated, Monroe's mentor hoped to "reform" the world but feared "contamination" from Europe in particular.[23] Another scholar has stated that nearly all of the major policymakers of the early republic on both sides of the Federalist-Republican divide saw "political separation from Europe and neutrality in Europe's endemic wars" as essential to the United States' survival.[24] Monroe agreed that war was to be avoided, but he did not fear contamination from Europe, nor did he believe in separation from the world. In fact, it is interesting to consider, though ultimately impossible to say with any certainty, what the fifth president envisioned a joint Monroe-Canning Doctrine might have entailed, with warnings aimed at the Holy Allies' movements in Europe as well as in Latin America. Monroe surely considered that any such agreement would have made the United States a party to various European diplomatic disputes, and would have essentially done away with Washington and Jefferson's proscription against entangling alliances. Yet he was ready to go forward despite these risks. Thus among the founders Monroe remains something of an oddity.

But Monroe is no less an outlier compared with leaders of the second generation of American policymakers, most notably his own secretary of state, John Quincy Adams. Adams was a realist whose diplomacy was, in the words of one scholar, a "realism grounded in a tragic sense of politics." Adams saw the United States' mission as "not to bring enlightenment or happiness to the rest of the world, but to ensure the life, liberty, and happiness of the American people."[25] Thus even in his own administration Monroe's foreign policy was something of an oddity, and it is no less challenging to appreciate Monroe's impact on subsequent American policy. While many eras of American diplomacy bear traces of the fifth president's vision, no one period can be called truly "Monrovian."

Monroe's sense of American mission also differed from the Jacksonian ideal of westward expansion. Monroe died only a few years before Americans became infatuated with a new version of American mission known as Manifest Destiny. Certain traces of Monroe's foreign policy can be linked to Manifest Destiny. Monroe played a vital role in American expansion throughout his career. He helped ensure access to the Mississippi River when he helped scuttle the Jay-Gardoqui treaty in the 1780s. He negotiated the Louisiana Purchase in 1803, and acquired Florida in 1819. Throughout his career he wanted the American republic to spread across the continent, just as Jacksonian-era expansionists did a generation later. But the practitioners of Manifest Destiny strayed from Monroe's republican vision in at least one key respect.

The Jacksonian version of American mission was built on the idea of American exceptionalism. In *Democracy in America*, published during the Jacksonian era, the French theorist Alexis de Tocqueville stressed the unique characteristics of American republicanism and democracy. One of the most perceptive observers of antebellum American ideology, Tocqueville argued that "the position of the Americans is therefore quite exceptional, and it may be believed that no democratic people will ever be placed in a similar one." He concluded that the American experiment could not be replicated, saying, "Let us cease, then, to view all democratic nations under the example of the American people."[26] Manifest Destiny itself was driven by this idea of American exceptionalism.

Jacksonian expansionists were largely unconcerned with the spread of republican ideas, at least in part because they did not hold other republics in the same esteem Monroe did. They did not see other republics as the equal of the United States. Andrew Jackson was indifferent to the rights of the Cherokee, who had created republican institutions based on the American version.[27] President James K. Polk had no qualms about insulting and eventually going to war with Mexico in 1846, at least nominally a republic, and one of the nations Monroe's doctrine had been meant to support. Polk was wholly unconcerned with spreading republicanism. He wanted American expansion across the continent. Manifest Destiny therefore had a more restricted version of the American mission at its core, one that was explicitly built on American exceptionalism rather than on worldwide republicanism.[28]

When the United States emerged as a world power at the end of the nineteenth century the Monroe Doctrine was used to justify foreign policy decisions that appeared connected to Monroe's diplomacy but were in reality far removed from his republican vision. It is tempting to view the American war against Spain in 1898 as a more extreme version of the kind of support for republican government that Monroe had offered Latin America in 1823. The Spanish government, under a Bourbon monarch, fought to prevent Cuban independence, and many Americans saw it as similar to their own revolutionary movement a century earlier. Monroe, on the other hand, was leery of direct military intervention, so it is difficult to say whether he would have approved of President William McKinley's decision to ask Congress to declare war. But where the policymakers of 1898 surely departed from Monroe's vision for worldwide republicanism was in the conflict's aftermath. American Gilded Age and Progressive Era leaders were mostly uninterested in the people of the Philippines, Cuba, or Puerto Rico creating republican institutions. Interest in these overseas possessions centered on the creation of an American empire. Monroe, conversely, wanted other nations to build republican governments, and explicitly rejected American imperialism. In 1804 Monroe discussed the possibility of the U.S. conquest of South America. The subjugation of the Spanish colonies would "offer an extensive field for jobs and plunder to individuals." But it would ultimately "corrupt and debauch" any American who engaged in the takeover. Conquering these territories offered "nothing to the United States as a nation." Again, republicanism rather than American imperialism was the key to Monroe's foreign policy.[29]

After the Spanish American War ended in the creation of an American overseas empire, Monroe's doctrine was used as a tool to overhaul much of American foreign policy. During the twentieth century a series of alterations made by American policymakers such as Teddy and Franklin Roosevelt, Woodrow Wilson, and others discarded Washington and Jefferson's proscription on interventionism and entangling alliances. Teddy Roosevelt's "Corollary" to the Monroe Doctrine was built on so-called big stick diplomacy and American military power. The United States began to use the doctrine to protect Latin America from foreign influence, even if that meant interfering in their domestic affairs. This marked the beginning of a more interventionist American foreign policy in the years to come.

American experiences in the twentieth century convinced policymakers to completely abandon their distrust of "entangling alliances." Modern American foreign policy began to shift away from nonintervention and toward what appears, on the surface, to be a more Monrovian direction. In

1917, a century after Monroe's presidency, Woodrow Wilson led the nation into World War I. Wilson told Americans the war was fought to "make the world safe for democracy," a phrase that smacks of Monrovian ideology. If we simply replace "republicanism" for "democracy" it is easy to imagine Monroe writing something similar about either the French or Latin American revolutions. After World War I American policymakers sought to defend the United States from new dangers. The threats to American democracy and republicanism were now fascism and communism, rather than monarchy. The United States embraced alliances to defeat fascism in the Second World War and the lesson was applied during the Cold War against communism.

As historian Jay Sexton has explained, Monroe saw his era in similar terms to the way Americans viewed the Cold War. The way Monroe perceived the conflict between monarchy and republicanism was similar to the way capitalists and communists viewed their struggle in the late twentieth century. Neither were simple conflicts over national interests, but rather wars to preserve a particular way of life. Monroe saw the world locked in a titanic ideological struggle between republicanism and monarchy, the same way the late twentieth century was a fight between two competing ideologies. It was not a simple contest over national borders, but an ideological boundary where the front lines could be found almost anywhere on the globe.[30]

NATO and other American alliances around the globe are, in some respects, the kind of grand coalitions Monroe had in mind for the defense of republicanism. The American policy of communist containment could be viewed as just the kind of "bolder attitude" Monroe might have considered to protect republicanism during the founding era. Further, the U.S. occupation of Japan and Germany after World War II was designed to infuse those governments with republican principles. Later the United States tried, with only limited success, to use military force to protect republics in South Korea and South Vietnam from the communist threat. Even during the twenty-first century, after the communist threat was all but eliminated, the United States has shown no sign of reverting back to Washington and Jefferson's idea of nonintervention. With many Cold War treaties intact "entangling alliances" have outlived the Cold War. Meanwhile the United States has dedicated itself to "nation-building" in places like Iraq and Afghanistan, essentially attempting to force republican government on other nations. On the surface then American foreign policy of the past seventy-five years contains at least a kernel of Monrovian ideas. But Monroe would be uneasy with this kind of legacy. Even if he did not fear foreign entanglements the way Washington and Jefferson did, Monroe was not the kind of statesman who valued aggressive military intervention. Monroe's legacy should instead be tied to a less militaristic and more ideological brand of diplomacy than the one practiced by modern American policymakers.[31]

It is tempting to view Monroe's wish to spread republican values as a precursor to American interventionism in the twentieth century. Today something like 150 countries and territories are home to upward of eight hundred American military bases around the world. All of this, to one extent or another, is part of the United States' perceived mission to protect certain republican (or democratic) values around the world. But it is critical to remember that Monroe never advocated American military intervention in France in the 1790s or in Latin America during the 1820s. That was not Monroe's aim in championing republicanism. He wanted the same ends as American policymakers in the twentieth and twenty-first centuries: to preserve and extend republican government. Where he differed was in the means. For Monroe the United States' role was ideological. He saw the United States as a beacon of liberty, lighting the world's path to republicanism. Throughout his life he continually argued that the United States should make an unequivocal, definitive statement of moral support for the cause. Monroe's doctrine was the culmination of his vision—an announcement to the world that the United States supported republican ideals wherever they flourished. He did not envision military intervention in favor of republicanism because, for Monroe, a statement of support for the cause had far more power.

For Monroe ideas were as important as actions. Fighting the War of Independence was of course critical, but it was the ideas found in the writings of John Locke, Thomas Paine's *Common Sense*, and Jefferson's Declaration of Independence that made the movement truly revolutionary. Monroe was willing to declare his support for republicanism in stark terms, and if that offended European monarchs it was a price worth paying. He would not seek war with the monarchists, but neither would he temper his language to avoid offending them. Monroe understood that no amount of military intervention could sweep monarchism away. Only republican ideas could accomplish that task. The U.S. military would not win the war against monarchy. Victory for the republican cause would come only after it won the hearts and minds of people around the world. And it is here where Monroe deserves more credit from posterity.

In 1806 while living in England Monroe told a friend that "every year of tolerably successful government" within the United States "produces an effect in favor of that cause throughout the world."[32] For Monroe, the United States truly was a city on a hill. The example of American republicanism had real concrete value to Monroe. He believed that a closer relationship with France could have made the difference during their revolution. His belief was not founded in the idea that American troops could turn the tide of battle, as they later did in World War I. Instead, Monroe believed that American "moral weight," as he often called it, would act as an ideological anchor making it nearly impossible for a fellow republic like France "to leave the republican standard." Monroe was convinced that American support for the cause would ultimately push back the borders of monarchy in favor of republican government.[33] For Monroe, republican ideology was the most powerful weapon in the American arsenal, and to a remarkable degree he has been proven correct in this assessment. Republican ideals have transformed the world in ways American military intervention could never dream.

If we look at Monroe's legacy as part of the larger republican movement, it may be time to give him his due. Republican ideas have spread far and wide, and the boundaries of republicanism have expanded exponentially since he assumed office in 1817. When Monroe was elected president, apart from the United States, there were only a handful of republican governments around the world in small countries like San Marino and Switzerland. With the help of the Monroe Doctrine, republicanism had taken hold in Argentina, Venezuela, Colombia, Panama, Costa Rica, Honduras, and Bolivia by the time of the fifth president's death in 1831. Later it spread to Liberia, whose capital, Monrovia, was named after the fifth president. By 1870, a generation after his death, republicanism once again took hold in France just as Monroe had dreamed.

Monroe once accused monarchists of portraying republican revolution as a disease they feared would spread around the world. And in many ways this was an apt description of the movement. Monroe did all he could during his life to spread the republican "virus" as far abroad as he dared. By the middle of the twentieth century there were too many republics in the world to list. By the twenty-first century, two hundred years since Monroe's presidency, only a handful of monarchs on earth retain any actual power. Republicanism has, in a relatively short period of time, become the dominant form of government after millennia of monarchial rule. Monroe's career was dedicated to achieving that goal, and maybe that is as fine a legacy as he could hope for, as perhaps not *the* champion of republicanism, but at least one of its most dedicated warriors.

# NOTES

## INTRODUCTION

1. James Monroe, "Address to the French National Convention," Aug. 15, 1794, *The Papers of James Monroe*, ed. Preston, 3:30–31; Ammon, *James Monroe*, 119.

2. Cunningham, *In Pursuit of Reason*, 349; Ammon, *James Monroe*, 571–72.

3. "Columbia Centinel," Boston, MA, July 12, 1817, in *Papers of James Monroe*, ed. Preston, 1:226.

4. Donovan, *Mr. Lincoln's Proclamation*, 118–19.

5. Bush, *Decision Points*, 580–83.

6. David Remick, "On and Off the Road with Barack Obama," *New Yorker*, Jan. 27, 2014; see also David Herszenhorn, "Obama Signs Healthcare Overhaul Bill, with a Flourish," *New York Times*, Mar. 23, 2010. After President Obama passed his controversial healthcare reform bill in 2010, the microphone picked up Vice President Joseph Biden telling his boss, "This is a big *fucking* deal." Biden's off-color comment underscores that the reformation of the American health care system would go a long way in shaping Barack Obama's legacy.

7. Scarry, *Millard Fillmore*, 270–71; Boller, *Presidential Anecdotes*, 112; see also Clinton, *My Life*, 911–16, 923–27. Similarly, at the end of his presidency Clinton seemed to be searching for something upon which he might build a legacy that would eclipse the Monica Lewinsky scandal. He tried to achieve a lasting peace in the Middle East.

## CHAPTER 1. THE CELESTIAL CAUSE

1. Thomas Jefferson to John Holmes, Apr. 22, 1820, *Thomas Jefferson*, ed. Peterson, 1434.

2. Preston, *Papers of James Monroe*, xxi. Monroe often referred to parties as "the curse of the country."

3. James Monroe to John C. Calhoun, Aug. 4, 1828, *Writings of James Monroe* (hereafter JM Writings), 7:173.

4. Thomas Jefferson to John Holmes, Apr. 22, 1820, *Thomas Jefferson*, ed. Peterson, 1434.

5. Monroe, *The People the Sovereigns* (hereafter *TPtS*).

6. Ammon, *James Monroe*, 561. Ammon, the fifth president's foremost biographer, dedicated only a paragraph of his seven-hundred-page book on Monroe to *The People the Sovereigns*. For a brief analysis of Monroe's unfinished manuscript, see Scherr, "James Monroe's Political Thought."

7. *TPtS*, 17. Monroe also wrote *The People the Sovereigns* in part to convince Congress to reimburse him for his expenses from his days as a diplomat.

8. *TPtS*, 17–18.

9. *TPtS*, 19.

10. One of the early historians to tackle the impact the ancients had on the founders was Gummere in *American Colonial Mind and the Classical Tradition*. See also Richard, *Founders*. Richard explains that the founders saw the ancients as both models and "anti-models" for their own behavior. Richard's most recent book, *Greeks and Romans Bearing Gifts*, is designed to bring the discussion to a more general audience. See also Shalev, *Rome*, and Winterer, *Culture*.

11. Aristotle, "Politics," in *Aristotle*, ed. Loomis, 250. Aristotle explained that ancient republicanism's fundamental presumption was that "man is by nature a political animal." For an explanation of the difference between the two forms of republicanism see Rahe, *Republics*, 15–17. See also Pangle, *Spirit*.

12. Cicero, "De re publica," In *Cicero*, 29. Cicero claimed that "there is no other occupation in which human virtue approaches more closely the august function of the gods than that of founding new states or preserving those already in existence."

13. Aristotle, "Politics," in *Aristotle*, 250; See also Pangle, *Spirit*, 43–46; Rahe, *Republics*, 1:16, 44, 97,103–25.

14. See generally Rahe, *Republics*, and Pangle, *Spirit*, 62–73. In his three-volume work Paul Rahe outlines the progression of republican government from the ancient world until the creation of the liberal, modern republic. Pangle, meanwhile, identifies the fundamentals of American republicanism. Both authors show that the fundamental difference between the republics of the ancient world and the modern American republic was the relationship between politics and society.

15. An entire "classical republican revisionist" school of historical thought has been devoted to claiming that the founders adopted classical republicanism as the basis of their republic. The "founder" of the republican revisionist school is generally thought to be Caroline Robbins. See generally Robbins, *Eighteenth-Century Commonwealthman*. Some of the most important works of classical republican revisionism are Bailyn, *Ideological Origins*; Wood, *Radicalism*; Wood, *Creation*; and Pocock, *Machiavellian Moment*, 545. Not surprisingly, classical republicanism has come under scrutiny. See generally Appleby, "Republicanism in Old and New Contexts"; and Banning, "Jeffersonian Ideology Revisited," 4–19. These two articles do an excellent job summarizing the state of the argument in the late 1980s. See also

Appleby, *Capitalism and the New Social Order*. Appleby contends that while classical republicanism played a key role in the nation's ideology it was by no means more important than liberalism. She focuses her attention on the Jeffersonian republicans, who represented a radical strand of thought in American history. In Appleby's estimation, the Federalists represented the kind of "country party" that Wood and Bailyn discuss, while Jefferson and his Republican Party believed in an individualistic, essentially liberal, philosophy. Appleby argues that the capitalist revolution was already under way during the revolutionary era. She explains that capitalism, specifically commercial agriculture, played the major role in forming Jeffersonian thought; see also Diggins, *Lost Soul*. The revisionists have given some ground on the importance of classical republicanism in recent years; see Wood, *Creation of the American Republic*, v–xiii. In his preface to the 1998 version of *Creation of the American Republic* Gordon Wood concedes a number of points to the proponents of "liberalism." He agrees that American republicanism "was never as severely or as thoroughly classical as perhaps I and others suggest." Indeed, he admits that "to picture the republican revolution as something undertaken in a pervasive mood of anxiety over corruption and the loss of virtue misses all the optimism and exuberance of the period."

16. *TPtS*, 201.

17. *TPtS*, 171, 196.

18. *Federalist*, no. 9 (Alexander Hamilton), in *Federalist Papers*, by Hamilton, Jay, and Madison, 71–72.

19. Thomas Jefferson to John Adams, July 5, 1814, *Adams-Jefferson Letters*, ed. Cappon, 430–33. On Plato, see Durant, *Story*, 32.

20. Benjamin Rush to John Adams, Oct. 2, 1810, *Spur of Fame*, by Adams and Rush, 169.

21. The Roman Senator Cato the Elder famously ended every speech with this phrase, translated as "Carthage must be destroyed," during the period between the Second and Third Punic Wars.

22. Adair, "Fame and the Founding Fathers," in *Fame and the Founding Fathers*.

23. Rahe, *Republics*, 1:15–17, 1:44, 1:70–75; Pangle, *Spirit*, 43–46.

24. Heraclitus, *Vorsokr*, 22 B29, in Rahe, *Republics*, 1:30.

25. Xenophon, "Hiero," 7.3, quoted in Strauss, *On Tyranny*, 14–15; Plato, "Symposium," in *Plato*, 199–201; see generally Rahe, *Republics*, 1:28–32.

26. Homer, *Iliad*, trans. Hammond, 143.

27. Polybius, in Lewis, *Mammoth Book*, 43, italics added. In a society where the afterlife reserved itself only for those heroes chosen to ascend to Mount Olympus to join the gods, as Hercules had, achieving honor and glory represented the only way to secure immortality. On the Roman afterlife see MacMullen, *Christianizing*, 11; on service to the greater glory of Rome see Braudy, *Frenzy of Renown*, 115.

28. Cicero, "In Defence of Aulus Licinius Archias," *Orations*, 119. Cicero also wrote two books on glory, which are lost.

29. Cicero, "De re publica," 253.

30. Adair, "Fame and the Founding Fathers," 7. In the spring of 1965, at a meeting of the Organization for American Historians in Kansas City, Douglass Adair delivered a lecture entitled "Fame and the Founding Fathers." In this paper, Adair attempted to explain why America's founding generation produced such a disproportionately large number of what he calls "great men." Adair argued that the founders were "fantastically concerned with posterity's judgment of their behavior," and the desire to be remembered spurred them to achieve greatness. Adair proclaimed that "the greatest of the great generation develop[ed] an almost obsessive desire for fame."

31. James Monroe, "Speech to the Virginia Ratification Convention," June 10, 1788, *Papers of James Monroe*, ed. Preston, 429–30.

32. Pangle, *Spirit*, 23; see also Rahe, "Eighteenth Century," in *Noblest Minds*, 21–29; John Locke, "Of Study," in *Educational Writings*, 409–10. In their distrust of fame, as in so many things, the founders took after John Locke. Locke thought of history's most famous men as little more than butchers, conquerors, and tyrants. He went so far as to denounce the study of history because he feared that impressionable children would be unduly influenced and infatuated by the deeds of great conquerors. See Locke, "Of Study," 409–10.

33. Franklin, *Complete Poor Richard's Almanacks*, 2:1748.

34. Paine, "The Age of Reason," in *Complete Writings*, 543.

35. Adams "Diary," Apr. 23, 1756, *Diary*, 1:22.

36. Adams, "Diary," Oct. 18, 1761, *Diary*, 1:222.

37. *TPtS*, 164.

38. Sharp, *American Politics*, 1–14.

39. Thomas Jefferson to Benjamin Rush, Jan. 16, 1811, *Papers of Thomas Jefferson*, ed. Looney, 3:304–8.

40. Douglass Adair uses this anecdote specifically to prove the dominant role fame played for both Jefferson and Hamilton. See Adair, "Fame and the Founding Fathers," in *Fame and the Founding Fathers*, 13.

41. Thomas Jefferson to George Washington, Sep. 9, 1792, *Something*, ed. Dunn, 289.

42. John Adams to Abigail Adams, Dec. 31, 1796, *Founders*, ed. Kaminski, 200.

43. Alexander Hamilton, "The Farmer Refuted," *Papers of Alexander Hamilton*, ed. Syrett, 1:126; *Federalist*, no. 1 (Alexander Hamilton)," in *Federalist Papers*, by Hamilton, Jay, and Madison, 4; See also McNamara, "Alexander Hamilton," in *Noblest Minds*, 141–62.

44. James Monroe to Thomas Jefferson, June 17, 1791, *Papers of James Monroe*, ed. Preston, 2:503–6.

45. James Monroe to James Sullivan, Aug. 29, 1806, *Papers of James Monroe*, ed. Preston, 5:520–21.

46. James Monroe to the Virginia House of Delegates, Dec. 1810, *Papers of James Monroe*, ed. Preston, 5:781.

47. Monroe, "Speech to the Virginia Ratification Convention," June 10, 1788, *Papers of James Monroe*, ed. Preston, 2:429–30.

48. Paine, *Common Sense*, 120.

49. *Federalist*, no. 14 (James Madison), in *Federalist Papers*, by Hamilton, Jay, and Madison, 66–67.

50. Monroe, "Some Hints Directing the Measures to be Taken to Form a Monarchy out of Several Confederate Democracies," June 1788, *Papers of James Monroe*, ed. Preston, 2:445–46.

51. James Madison, "Charters," *National Gazette*, Jan. 19, 1792, *James Madison*, ed. Rakove, 502.

52. *TPtS*, 39.

53. Boller, *Presidential Anecdotes*, 53.

54. *TPtS*, 18.

55. Paine, *Common Sense*, 63; George Washington to James Warren, Mar. 31, 1779, *George Washington*, ed. Rhodehamel, 342; Benjamin Franklin to Samuel Cooper, May 1, 1777, *Papers of Benjamin Franklin*, 24:7. Paine declared that "the Cause of America is in great measure the cause of all mankind." Washington echoed his statements: "Our cause is noble; it is the cause of mankind!" Benjamin Franklin agreed: "It is a common observation here that our cause is the cause of all mankind, and that we are fighting for their liberty in defending our own."

56. John Adams to William Cushing, June 9, 1776, *John Adams*, 80.

57. *TPtS*, 18.

58. Ammon, *James Monroe*, 562–63; Monroe, *Autobiography*.

59. James Monroe, "Speech to the Virginia Ratification Convention," June 10, 1788, *Papers of James Monroe*, ed. Preston, 2:429–30.

60. James Monroe, "Liberty and Tyranny," 1798, *Papers of James Monroe*, ed. Preston, 4:313–20.

61. James Monroe to James Sullivan, Aug. 29, 1806, *Papers of James Monroe*, ed. Preston, 5:520–21.

62. James Monroe, "First Inaugural Address," Mar. 4, 1817, in *Compilation*, ed. Richardson, 2:4–10.

63. James Monroe, "Second Inaugural Address," Mar. 5, 1821, in *Compilation*, ed. Richardson, 2:86–94.

64. James Monroe, "Seventh Annual Message to Congress," Dec. 2, 1823, JM *Writings*, 6:340.

65. James Monroe, "Eighth Annual Message to Congress," Dec. 7, 1824, in *Compilation*, ed. Richardson, 2:248–64.

66. James Monroe to Chapman Johnson, Jan. 14, 1811, *Papers of James Monroe*, ed. Preston, 5:785.

67. James Monroe to Henry Dearborn, Apr. 22, 1820, James Monroe Papers, New York Public Library (hereafter NN).

68. Monroe, *Autobiography*, 26, 31, 35. Like *The People the Sovereigns*, Monroe's *Autobiography* was also designed to convince Congress that the government should reimburse him for his expenses from his days as a diplomat.

### CHAPTER 2. REPUBLICAN APPRENTICE

1. Fischer, *Washington's Crossing*, 1–6.
2. Eaton, *Historical Atlas*, 15–18.
3. Monroe, *Autobiography*, 21–22.
4. See generally Selby, *Revolution*, 1–5.
5. Quoted in Peterson, *Thomas Jefferson*, 69–70.
6. Ammon, *James Monroe*, 4–7.
7. Bland, *Bland Papers*, 1:xxiii; Ammon, *James Monroe*, 5–7.
8. Monroe, *Autobiography*, 22; Ammon, *James Monroe*, 7.
9. Monroe, *Autobiography*, 25.
10. Monroe, *Autobiography*, 25, 230.
11. Paine, "American Crisis," no. 1, Dec. 19, 1776, in *American Revolution*, 238.
12. Monroe, *Autobiography*, 24.
13. Stryker, *Battles of Trenton and Princeton*, 360–64.
14. Wilkinson, *Memoirs*, 130. Interestingly, while Wilkinson praised Monroe's actions, some thirty years later Monroe told Thomas Jefferson that he'd rather be shot than serve under Wilkinson.
15. Monroe, *Autobiography*, 25–26, 223–24. Note that Monroe wrote his autobiography in the third person.
16. Fischer, *Washington's Crossing*, 222, 231, 247; Monroe, *Autobiography*, 25–26.
17. James Monroe to John Thornton, July 3, 1777, *Papers of James Monroe*, ed. Preston, 2:4–5; Ammon, *James Monroe*, 15–17.
18. Ammon, *James Monroe*, 18–27.
19. Monroe, *Autobiography*, 26–31.
20. Monroe, *Autobiography*, 24.
21. George Washington to Lewis Nicola, May 22, 1782, *Writings of George Washington*, 24:272–73.
22. Quoted in Furstenberg, *Name*, 66.

23. George Washington to the Legislature of Pennsylvania, Sep. 12, 1789, *Papers of George Washington*, 24.

24. George Washington, "Circular to the States," June 8, 1783, *George Washington*, 517–18, 525, italics added.

25. Marquis de Lafayette to George Washington, July, 22, 1783, *Founders*, ed. Kaminski, 486.

26. Elkanah Watson, "Memoir," Jan. 23–25, 1785, in *Founders*, ed. Kaminski, 492.

27. Marquis de Lafayette to George Washington, Jan. 10, 1784, in *Founders*, ed. Kaminski, 489.

28. George Washington to Lewis Nicola, May 22, 1782, *Writings of George Washington*, 24:272–73; Boller, "George Washington," 14–16; Boller, *Presidential Anecdotes*, 13–16.

29. Monroe, *Autobiography*, 24.

30. The similarities between Washington's and Monroe's presidential cabinets are fascinating. During their presidencies each enjoyed a period of nonpartisan harmony (for Washington this lasted only a few years before it became clear that Jefferson's vision for the country contrasted sharply with Hamilton's). Both tried desperately to unite the country and thereby head off the insidious power of faction and party. Yet each saw the very thing they tried so hard to stamp out rise again under the very men they appointed to the cabinet.

31. James Monroe to William Woodford, Sep. 1779, *Papers of James Monroe*, ed. Preston, 2:14–15, exact date unknown.

32. James Monroe to John Thornton, Nov. 21, 1777, *Papers of James Monroe*, ed. Preston, 2:6–7; James Monroe to John Thornton, July 3, 1777, *Papers of James Monroe*, ed. Preston, 2:4–5. In these letters, Monroe told Thornton of his failed efforts to raise a regiment.

33. James Monroe to John Thornton, Nov. 21, 1777, *Papers of James Monroe*, ed. Preston, 2:6–7.

34. Monroe, *Autobiography*, 31.

35. Joseph Jones to George Washington, Aug. 11, 1777, *Letters of Joseph Jones*, 77–87; Ammon, *James Monroe*, 15.

36. Joseph Jones to James Monroe, Mar. 1, 1780, *Papers of James Monroe*, ed. Preston, 2:16–17.

37. Ammon, *James Monroe*, 29–31; Monroe, *Autobiography*, 31; Cunningham, *Jefferson and Monroe*, 15.

38. James Monroe to Thomas Jefferson. Sep. 9, 1780, *Papers of James Monroe*, ed. Preston, 2:26–27. Monroe also may have had a brief feud with his uncle that might have contributed to his "disappointments," but the record is unclear.

39. Stuart Gerry Brown, preface to *Autobiography*, by Monroe, v–vii.

40. Monroe, *Autobiography*, 33.

41. James Monroe to Thomas Jefferson, Sep. 9, 1780, *Papers of James Monroe*, ed. Preston, 2:26–27; see also Cresson, *James Monroe*, 63.

42. Ammon, *James Monroe*, 29–32; Joseph Jones to James Monroe, Mar. 1, 1780, *Papers of James Monroe*, ed. Preston, 2:16–17.

43. George Washington, "Circular to the States," June 8, 1783, *George Washington*, 517.

44. Gay, *Enlightenment*, 1:3.

45. See Gay, *Enlightenment*, 2:555–68.

46. Peterson, *Jefferson Image*, 401–5.

47. Ammon, *James Monroe*, 17–19.

48. James Monroe to Thomas Jefferson, Oct. 1, 1781, *Papers of James Monroe*, ed. Preston, 2:31–32; Ammon, *James Monroe*, 30; Monroe, *Autobiography*, 32; Cresson, *James Monroe*, 53.

49. Thomas Jefferson to Robert Skipwith, Aug. 3, 1771, *Thomas Jefferson*, 740.

50. Thomas Jefferson, "List of Books Sold to James Monroe," May 10, 1784, in *Papers of James Monroe*, ed. Preston, 2:96–97.

51. Monroe, *Autobiography*, 32.

52. James Monroe to George Washington, Aug. 15, 1782, *Papers of James Monroe*, ed. Preston, 2:44.

53. James Monroe to William Alexander Lord Stirling, Sep. 10, 1782, *Papers of James Monroe*, ed. Preston, 2:45.

54. James Monroe to Thomas Jefferson, June 17, 1791, *Papers of James Monroe*, ed. Preston, 2:505.

55. Thomas Jefferson to William Short, Oct. 31, 1819, *Writings of Thomas Jefferson*, 10:143–46. Jefferson called himself an epicurean on at least one occasion.

56. Thomas Jefferson to Archibald Stuart, Dec. 23, 1791, *Thomas Jefferson*, ed. Peterson, 983–84.

57. See Mayer, *Constitutional Thought*. See also David Mayer, "'The Holy Cause of Freedom': The Libertarian Legacy of Thomas Jefferson," in *Noblest Minds*, by McNamara, 98; quotes are from Thomas Jefferson, "Response to Address of Welcome by the Citizens of Albemarle," Feb. 12, 1790, *Papers of Thomas Jefferson*, ed. Boyd, 16:179.

58. James Monroe to Thomas Jefferson, May 11, 1782, *Papers of James Monroe*, ed. Preston, 2:34. See also Peterson, *Thomas Jefferson*, 242–44.

59. Jefferson is referencing Virginia's Declaration of Rights, written by George Mason in 1776.

60. Thomas Jefferson to James Monroe, May 20, 1782, *Papers of James Monroe*, ed. Preston, 2:34–35. Jefferson's practical reason for not joining was his wife's sickness. She had recently given birth to her last child and would die only a few months later.

61. Cogliano, *Thomas Jefferson*, 138–47; Becker, *Declaration of Independence*; Wills, *Inventing America*. Locke's influence on Jefferson's philosophy has been the source of considerable debate. Much of it has centered on the Declaration of Independence, which stands as the most prominent example of Jefferson's political philosophy. In fact, some of Jefferson's contemporaries accused him of lifting the Declaration's main ideas wholesale from Locke. Since Carl Becker's famous 1923 work on the Declaration, the most common interpretation is that Locke, especially his "Second Treatise on Government" and his "Essay Concerning Human Understanding," provided the framework upon which Jefferson built his philosophy as it appears in the Declaration. Monroe, for his part, firmly believed that the American republic was built on Lockean principles.

62. *TPtS*, 144–48.

63. *TPtS*, 144–48.

64. Thomas Jefferson to Monsieur A. Coray, Oct. 31, 1823, *Writings of Thomas Jefferson*, 15:480; *TPtS*, 154.

65. Thomas Jefferson to William Hunter, the Mayor of Alexandria, Mar. 11, 1790, *Papers of Thomas Jefferson*, ed. Boyd, 16:225.

66. Jefferson, "Inscription for His Tombstone," *Works of Thomas Jefferson*, ed. Ford, 12:483.

67. Cogliano, *Thomas Jefferson*, 138–41, 160–61.

68. Thomas Jefferson to Roger O. Weightman, June 24, 1826, *Writings of Thomas Jefferson*, 476–77; see also Peterson, *Jefferson Image*, 5.

69. James Monroe to Thomas Jefferson, Sep. 9, 1780, *Papers of James Monroe*, ed. Preston, 2:26–27.

70. James Monroe to Thomas Jefferson, June 17, 1791, *Papers of James Monroe*, ed. Preston, 2:503–6.

71. Monroe, *Autobiography*, 52.

72. Monroe, *The People the Sovereigns*, 36.

73. Monroe, "First Inaugural Address," Mar. 4, 1817, in *Compilation*, ed. Richardson, 2:4–10.

74. *TPtS*, 64–68.

75. Jefferson, "First Inaugural Address," Mar. 4, 1801, *Something*, ed. Dunn, 303.

76. Monroe, *Autobiography*, 26.

77. *TPtS*, 23.

78. It is important to note that Monroe was wrong in his belief that the Federalists were not committed republicans, at least in the broad sense.

79. Monroe, *Autobiography*, 51–52.

80. Monroe, *Autobiography*, 36.

81. See Monroe, *Autobiography*. Monroe's account of his life reaches only 1805 and his ministry in Spain. The seven chapters are as follows: 1. "Soldier in the

Revolution"; 2. "Lawyer and Legislator"; 3. "Minister from America to the French Revolution"; 4. "Vindication" (justifying his actions in France); 5. "Minister to Napoleon"; 6. "At the Court of St. James"; 7. "Minister to Spain."

82. James Monroe to Thomas Jefferson, July 16, 1786, JM Writings, 1:140; James Monroe to James Madison, Aug. 10, 1786, JM Writings, 1:143–51; James Monroe to James Madison, May 31, 1786, JM Writings, 1:132; Monroe, *Autobiography*, 44–45; James Monroe to Arthur St. Clair, Aug. 20, 1786, JM Writings, 1:343.

83. James Monroe to Thomas Jefferson, June 16, 1786, *Papers of James Monroe*, ed. Preston, 2:310; James Monroe to Patrick Henry, Aug. 12, 1786, *Papers of James Monroe*, ed. Preston, 2:331–34; James Monroe, William Grayson, Edward Carrington, and Henry Lee, "Motion to the Continental Congress," Aug. 29, 1786, *Papers of James Monroe*, ed. Preston, 2:345–54; James Monroe, "Speech to the Virginia Ratification Convention," June 13, 1788, *Papers of James Monroe*, ed. Preston, 2:437–40; James Monroe to John Henry, Apr. 23, 1794, *Papers of James Monroe*, ed. Preston, 2:714–15.

### CHAPTER 3. UNNECESSARY ÉCLAT

1. Ammon, *James Monroe*, 157–58; Albert Gallatin to Hannah Gallatin, June 28, 1797, in *Albert Gallatin*, by Raymond Walters, 104–5.

2. For a general treatment of the French Revolution and the early American republic see Wood, *Empire*, 174–208; see also Elkins and McKitrick, *Age*, 303–65.

3. "Gazette of the United States," Oct. 10, 1789, in *Age*, by Elkins and McKitrick, 310.

4. See Sharp, *American Politics*, 69–92; DeConde, *Entangling Alliance*. During the early days of the Revolution most Americans maintained their positive attitude toward the French. They mostly cheered the calling of the Estates General in May of '89 as well as the fall of the Bastille on July 14, 1789. They appreciated when the French-American hero Lafayette sent his surrogate father, George Washington, the key to the hated prison that symbolized of the old regime's tyranny.

5. For an account of Jefferson's time in France during the final years of the Old Regime see O'Brien, *Long Affair*, 38–68. Quotes are from Thomas Jefferson to James Monroe, Aug. 9, 1788, *Papers of James Monroe*, ed. Preston, 2:450.

6. Thomas Jefferson to James Monroe, Aug. 9, 1788, *Papers of James Monroe*, ed. Preston, 2:450.

7. Thomas Jefferson to John Adams, Aug. 30, 1787, *Thomas Jefferson*, ed. Peterson, 908.

8. Thomas Jefferson to Richard Price, Jan. 8, 1789, *Papers of Thomas Jefferson*, ed. Boyd, 14:420–24.

9. Thomas Jefferson to John Jay, Mar. 9, 1789, *Papers of Thomas Jefferson*, ed.

Boyd, 15:110. Immediately following this statement Jefferson told Jay of various riots in the streets of Paris.

10. Thomas Jefferson to Count Diodati, Aug. 3, 1789, *Papers of Thomas Jefferson*, ed. Boyd, 15:326–27.

11. Cunningham, *Jefferson and Monroe*, 15; McColley, *Federalists*, 19. Many historians casually refer to Jefferson and Monroe as unabashed Francophiles. While both men exhibited a certain fondness for French culture, it was only with the beginning of the Revolution that they became so overwhelmingly pro-France.

12. Monroe took the pen name Aratus from the Greek statesman Aratus of Sicyon who deposed the Sicyonian Tyrant Nicocoles in 251 BC and helped lead the Achaean League. See Ammon, *James Monroe*, 86–87; see also Fenessy, *Burke*. Monroe's defense of the Revolution was only a small part in the massive transatlantic debate occurring between those who supported the Revolution and those who feared its outcome. Edmund Burke, an ardent supporter of America's revolution, published *Reflections on the Revolution in France* in 1790. He argued that the Revolution was ultimately doomed to failure because it was based on vague, abstract principles. Burke defended hereditary rule and the nobility. Thomas Paine responded to this by writing *The Rights of Man*, throughout which he defended citizens' right to overthrow their government. Paine was tried for treason in absentia in England after leaving for France to aid the Revolution.

13. Quotes are from James Monroe, "Aratus Number I," Nov. 9, 1791, *Papers of James Monroe*, ed. Preston, 2:511–53; Ammon, *James Monroe*, 87–88.

14. Quotes are from James Monroe "Aratus Number II," Nov. 22, 1791, *Papers of James Monroe*, ed. Preston, 2:514; James Monroe "Aratus Number III," Dec. 17, 1791, *Papers of James Monroe*, ed. Preston, 2:521; Cresson, *James Monroe*, 127.

15. Cunningham, *Jefferson vs. Hamilton*, 106–10.

16. Thomas Jefferson to James Monroe, June 4, 1793, *Papers of James Monroe*, ed. Preston, 2:625; See also Thomas Jefferson to James Monroe, June 28, July 14, 1793, *Papers of James Monroe*, ed. Preston, 2:629–30, 2:632–33. On July 14, Jefferson claimed that America's declaration of neutrality made the "disgust of France inevitable"; on the neutrality debate see Elkins and McKitrick, *Age*, 336–41.

17. James Monroe to Thomas Jefferson, Jan. 11, 1792, *Papers of James Monroe*, ed. Preston, 2:525; James Monroe to St. George Tucker, Jan. 24, 1792, *Papers of James Monroe*, ed. Preston, 2:528–29. See also Monroe's attack on American neutrality in his Agricola Essays: James Monroe, "Agricola," Oct. 8, 1793, *Papers of James Monroe*, ed. Preston, 2:646.

18. James Monroe to George Washington, Apr. 8, 1794, *Papers of James Monroe*, ed. Preston, 2:710. Monroe wrote to Washington personally explaining exactly what the Republican reaction might be if Hamilton were nominated. Washington's

chilly response can be found in George Washington to James Monroe, Apr. 9, 1794, *Papers of James Monroe*, ed. Preston, 2:710–11. On Morris's mission see DeConde, *Entangling Alliance*, 311–41; on Washington's presidency and neutrality see McDonald, *Presidency*, 113–38.

19. James Monroe to Thomas Jefferson, May 27, 1794, *Papers of James Monroe*, ed. Preston, 3:1. Randolph had replaced Thomas Jefferson, who resigned as secretary of state in December of 1793.

20. James Monroe to Thomas Jefferson, July 23, 1793, *Papers of James Monroe*, ed. Preston, 2:634–35.

21. Ammon, *James Monroe*, 112–15.

22. James Monroe to Thomas Jefferson, Aug. 21, 1793, *Papers of James Monroe*, ed. Preston, 2:635–36.

23. The French revolutionaries wanted to wipe out any and all evidence of the old regime's existence, and one of their targets became Christianity itself. They attacked even the Christian calendar by dating events from the beginning of the Revolution rather than the birth of Christ.

24. Ammon, *James Monroe*, 108; for an evaluation of Robespierre see McPhee, *Robespierre*.

25. James Monroe to Edmund Randolph, Aug. 15, 1794, *Papers of James Monroe*, ed. Preston, 3:25.

26. James Monroe to Edmund Randolph, Aug. 15, 1794, *Papers of James Monroe*, ed. Preston, 3:25–26.

27. James Monroe to Edmund Randolph, Aug. 15, 1794, *Papers of James Monroe*, ed. Preston, 3:25–26.

28. James Monroe to Robert R. Livingston, Feb. 23, 1795, *Papers of James Monroe*, ed. Preston, 3:242–43.

29. James Monroe to Edmund Randolph, Mar. 6, 1795, *Papers of James Monroe*, ed. Preston, 3:253–56.

30. James Monroe to Edmund Randolph, Aug. 15, 1794, *Papers of James Monroe*, ed. Preston, 3:27–28.

31. James Monroe to Edmund Randolph, Aug. 15, 1794, *Papers of James Monroe*, ed. Preston, 3:27; James Monroe to Thomas Jefferson, July 30, 1796, *Papers of James Monroe*, ed. Preston, 4:61–64.

32. James Monroe to Edmund Randolph, Jan. 13, 1795, *Papers of James Monroe*, ed. Preston, 3:202–6.

33. Monroe was wildly optimistic concerning the new French Constitution. For an evaluation of the new constitution see Furet, *French Revolution*, 162–68; James Monroe to Timothy Pickering, Nov. 5, 1795, *Papers of James Monroe*, ed. Preston, 3:506. See also James Monroe to Timothy Pickering, Dec. 6, 1795, *Papers of James Monroe*, ed. Preston, 3:534–35; Monroe to Thomas Jefferson, Nov. 18, 1795, *Papers*

*of James Monroe*, ed. Preston, 3:516–20; and Monroe to James Madison, Jan. 12, 1796, *Papers of James Monroe*, ed. Preston, 3:563–565. Monroe marveled in his letter to Madison of the "wise, steady and energetic" progress of the French government.

34. Scherr, "Limits," 6–11, 33, 41–44; James Monroe to Thomas Jefferson, July 30, 1796, *Papers of James Monroe*, ed. Preston, 4:61–64.

35. Bond, *Monroe Mission*, 15–16.

36. James Monroe to Philippe Merlin de Douai, Aug. 13, 1794, *Papers of James Monroe*, ed. Preston, 3:24; Monroe, *Autobiography*, 59  61.

37. James Monroe, "Address to the French National Convention," Aug. 15, 1794, *Papers of James Monroe*, ed. Preston, 3:30–31.

38. James Monroe, "Address to the French National Convention," Aug. 15, 1794.

39. James Monroe to James Madison, Sep. 2, 1794, *Papers of James Monroe*, ed. Preston, 3:47–49.

40. James Monroe to Edmund Randolph, Aug. 25, 1794, *Papers of James Monroe*, ed. Preston, 3:40. The French government had even offered the new minister a house to live in at the expense of the French government that Monroe was forced to turn down because of its unconstitutionality.

41. Edmund Randolph to James Monroe, Dec. 2, 1794, *Papers of James Monroe*, ed. Preston, 3:172. ("Éclat" roughly translates to "brilliant display.")

42. James Madison to James Monroe, Dec. 4, 1794, *Papers of James Monroe*, ed. Preston, 3:174.

43. See also John Brown to James Monroe, Dec. 5, 1794. *Papers of James Monroe*, ed. Preston, 3:182–84.

44. James Monroe to Edmund Randolph, Feb. 12, 1795, *Papers of James Monroe*, ed. Preston, 2:224–27. For the concessions Monroe achieved during his mission see James Monroe to Edmund Randolph, Jan. 13, 1795, *Papers of James Monroe*, ed. Preston, 2:202–206; and James Monroe to Committee of Public Safety, Jan. 4, 1795, *Papers of James Monroe*, ed. Preston, 2:195–96.

45. Bond, *Monroe Mission*, 13. Quotes are from Edmund Randolph to James Monroe, Sep. 25, 1794, *Papers of James Monroe*, ed. Preston, 3:7–11.

46. Though he may have suspected. See James Monroe to Thomas Jefferson, May 4, 1794, *Papers of James Monroe*, ed. Preston, 2:720–21: "'Tis said the envoy will be armed with extraordinary powers . . . and 'authorized to form a commercial treaty.'" Monroe did not relish the prospect of giving the man who had "bartered away" the Mississippi such power; for Jay's instructions see John Jay's Instructions as Envoy Extraordinary to Great Britain, May 6, 1794, *Correspondence*, 4:10–21.

47. See Edmund Randolph to James Monroe, Sep. 25, 1794, *Papers of James Monroe*, ed. Preston, 89; see also Bond, *Monroe Mission*, 14.

48. James Monroe to the Committee of Public Safety, Dec. 27, 1794, *Papers of James Monroe*, ed. Preston, 3:193.

49. John Jay to James Monroe, Nov. 24, 1794. *Papers of James Monroe*, ed. Preston, 3:158.

50. The Committee of Public Safety to James Monroe, Dec. 26, 1794, *Papers of James Monroe*, ed. Preston, 3:191; Bond, *Monroe Mission*, 30–31.

51. James Monroe to Edmund Randolph, Dec. 18, 1794, *Papers of James Monroe*, 3:188, 3:190; James Monroe to the Committee of Public Safety, Dec. 27, 1794, *Papers of James Monroe*, ed. Preston, 3:192. Monroe was beginning to believe that the treaty was a "project" conceived by "Messrs. [British prime minister William] Pitt and Jay . . . to weaken our connection with France and put us again under the influence of England."

52. James Monroe to John Jay, Jan. 17, 1795, *Papers of James Monroe*, ed. Preston, 3:207.

53. John Jay to James Monroe, Feb. 5, 1795, *Papers of James Monroe*, ed. Preston, 3:222.

54. James Monroe to Edmund Randolph, Mar. 17, 1795, *Papers of James Monroe*, ed. Preston, 3:271–73; James Monroe to Edmund Randolph, Apr. 14, 1795, *Papers of James Monroe*, ed. Preston, 3:290; Ammon, *James Monroe*, 143.

55. Benjamin Hichborn to James Monroe, Mar. 31, 1795, *Papers of James Monroe*, ed. Preston, 3:282; Ammon, *James Monroe*, 144.

56. James Monroe to James Madison, Sep. 8, 1795, *Papers of James Monroe*, ed. Preston, 3:438.

57. James Monroe to John Beckley, June 23, 1795, *Papers of James Monroe*, ed. Preston, 3:368–72.

58. Ammon, *James Monroe*, 146–47.

59. James Monroe to Timothy Pickering, Feb. 16, 1796, *Papers of James Monroe*, ed. Preston, 3:590.

60. James Monroe to Charles Delacroix (Foreign Minister for the French Directory), Feb. 17, 1796, *Papers of James Monroe*, ed. Preston, 3:591–92; James Monroe to James Madison, July 5, 1796, *Papers of James Monroe*, ed. Preston, 4:39–40.

61. Timothy Pickering to James Monroe, June 13, 1796, *Papers of James Monroe*, ed. Preston, 4:35–36. Pickering also furnished the June 1795 letter Monroe wrote to George Logan, founder of the Democratic-Republican Societies, in which he condemned Jay's Treaty. See James Monroe to John Beckley, June 23, 1795, *Papers of James Monroe*, ed. Preston, 368–72.

62. James Monroe, "Address to the Executive Directory," Jan. 1, 1797, *Papers of James Monroe*, ed. Preston, 4:138–39.

63. For Monroe's letters demanding an explanation for his recall see the following correspondence between him and Timothy Pickering: James Monroe to Timothy Pickering, July 6, 1797, *Papers of James Monroe*, ed. Preston, 4:157–58; Timothy Pickering to James Monroe, July 17, 1797, *Papers of James Monroe*, ed.

Preston, 164–65; James Monroe to Timothy Pickering, July 19, 1797, *Papers of James Monroe*, ed. Preston, 4:165–66; Timothy Pickering to James Monroe, July 24, 1797, *Papers of James Monroe*, ed. Preston, 4:170–71; James Monroe to Timothy Pickering, July, 31, 1797, *Papers of James Monroe*, ed. Preston, 4:173–76.

64. James Monroe to James Madison, Jan. 1, 1797, *Papers of James Monroe*, ed. Preston, 4:140.

65. James Monroe, "Response to Scipio," Mar. 1798, *Papers of James Monroe*, ed. Preston, 4:261–62.

66. James Monroe, "War with France," 1798, *Papers of James Monroe*, ed. Preston, 4:308–13.

67. James Monroe, "A View of the Political Situation of the United States in the Commencement of the French Revolution," 1798–99, *Papers of James Monroe*, ed. Preston, 4:304–8.

68. James Monroe, "A View of the Conduct of the Executive," Dec. 23, 1797, *Papers of James Monroe*, ed. Preston, 4:227.

69. James Monroe, "A View of the Conduct of the Executive," 4:227.

### CHAPTER 4. JAMES MONROE: TRAITOR

1. David Gelston, "Account of an Interview between Alexander Hamilton and James Monroe," July 11, 1797, in *Papers of James Monroe*, ed. Preston, 4:158–60; James Monroe to James Madison, June 8, 1798, *Papers of James Monroe*, ed. Preston, 4:272.

2. Peterson, *Thomas Jefferson*, 628. Peterson claims that 18 Brumaire "crushed the last hopes" Jefferson had for the Revolution.

3. Thomas Jefferson to Robert R. Livingston, Apr. 18, 1802, *Papers of Thomas Jefferson*, ed. Oberg, 37:266; Brecher, *Negotiating*, 1–3. Monroe wrote a series of essays on the subject that was "exciting much interest" throughout the nation during the spring of 1802. In these essays, Monroe, true to form, blamed the previous, Federalist administration for the crisis. See also James Monroe, "Richmond Examiner," May 5, 12, 1802, *Papers of James Monroe*, ed. Preston, 4:593–95.

4. Thomas Jefferson to Robert R. Livingston, Apr. 18, 1802, *Papers of Thomas Jefferson*, ed. Oberg, 37:264–65; See generally Lewis, *Louisiana Purchase*, 18–24.

5. Thomas Jefferson to Robert R. Livingston, Apr. 18, 1802, *Papers of Thomas Jefferson*, ed. Oberg, 37:266; Lewis, *Louisiana Purchase*, 31–53.

6. Lewis, *American Union*, 16; Ammon, *James Monroe*, 203–5.

7. Thomas Jefferson to James Monroe, Jan. 13, 1803, *Works of Thomas Jefferson*, ed. Ford, 8:190–92.

8. Thomas Jefferson to James Monroe, Jan. 10, 1803, *Works of Thomas Jefferson*, 9:416–17; James Monroe to Thomas Jefferson, Mar. 7, 1803, JM Writings, 4:4; Monroe, *Autobiography*, 153.

9. Robert R. Livingston to James Madison, Jan. 24, 1803, *Papers of James Madison*, ed. Hackett, 4:277–78; Brecher, *Negotiating*, 46.

10. Ammon, *James Monroe*, 212; James Monroe to James Madison, Apr. 15, 1803, *Papers of James Madison*, ed. Hackett, 4:520–22. He used the fact that Monroe had not been officially introduced to the emperor as a pretext.

11. See Brecher, *Negotiating*, 80–105; Dangerfield, *Chancellor*, 376–78; Ammon, *James Monroe*, 215.

12. James Monroe to James Madison, Apr. 15, 1803, JM Writings, 4:9.

13. James Monroe to Virginia Senators, May 25, 1803, JM Writings, 4:31–33.

14. James Monroe to Virginia Senators, May 25, 1803, JM Writings, 4:31–32.

15. James Monroe to James Madison, Sep. 17, 1803, *Papers of James Madison*, ed. Hackett, 5:440.

16. James Monroe to James Madison, Nov. 25, 1803, JM Writings, 4:102–3.

17. James Monroe to James Madison, May 18, 1803, JM Writings, 4:24–27; James Madison to James Monroe and Robert R. Livingston, July 29, 1803, *Papers of James Madison*, ed. Hackett, 5:238–40.

18. James Monroe to Madison, Aug. 31, 1803, *Papers of James Monroe*, ed. Preston, 5:114–16.

19. James Monroe and Robert R. Livingston to James Madison, May 13, 1803, *Papers of James Monroe*, ed. Preston, 5:96. Monroe also wrote that the Purchase would place the United States outside "the market of political intrigue in Europe[,] . . . without asking or accepting favors of any one." Monroe also believed it would continue the "republican revolution" in New England. See James Monroe to James Madison, Dec. 15, 1803, *Papers of James Monroe*, ed. Preston, 5:157–59.

20. John Randolph to James Monroe, Nov. 7, 1803, *Papers of James Monroe*, ed. Preston, 5:144.

21. For an overview of the election of 1800 see Ammon, "James Monroe."

22. Peterson, *Thomas Jefferson*, 269; Monroe, *Autobiography*, 32–33; Ammon, *James Monroe*, 43; Thomas Jefferson to James Madison, May 8, 1784, *Republic*, ed. Smith.

23. James Monroe to Thomas Jefferson, July 27, 1787, *Papers of James Monroe*, ed. Preston, 2:391; Ammon, *James Monroe*, 60. Monroe was already bitter that he had not been chosen to serve on the Virginia delegation to Philadelphia in 1787 and told Jefferson that Madison had entered into efforts to try to "thwart him."

24. Ammon, *James Monroe*, 69–75; James Monroe to Thomas Jefferson, Feb. 15, 1789, *Papers of James Monroe*, ed. Preston, 2:461.

25. Some historians refer to the "Old Republicans" as the conservative wing of the Democratic-Republican Party. This is certainly true when considering them in a twenty-first-century light, but in the early nineteenth century, conservatism was associated with monarchy and a powerful central government. As the defenders of

"old school" republicanism, the Old Republicans positioned themselves in direct opposition to any form of traditional conservatism. Thus I refer to them as the radical wing of the party.

26. On the "Old Republicans" see generally Sheldon and Hull, *Liberal Republicanism*; and Risjord, *Old Republicans*, 72–73. For specific reasons why John Randolph disliked Madison see Kirk, *John Randolph*, 87–88.

27. John Randolph to James Monroe, Sep. 16, 1806, JM Writings, 4:486–87; Ammon, *James Monroe*, 244–45; Risjord, *Old Republicans*, 18 39; James Monroe to John Randolph, June 16, 1806, JM Writings, 4:467.

28. James Monroe to James Madison, Aug. 15, 1803, *Papers of James Monroe*, ed. Preston, 5:109–10.

29. James Monroe to James Madison, June 30, 1805, NN.

30. James Monroe and Charles Pinckney to James Madison, May 25, 1805, *Papers of James Monroe*, ed. Preston, 5:400–401.

31. Monroe's disagreements with the administration over Spanish policy can be found in the following letters: James Madison to James Monroe, May 18, 1803, *Papers of James Madison*, ed. Hackett, 5:12–13; James Madison to James Monroe, May 23, 1803, *Papers of James Madison*, ed. Hackett, 5:24–25; James Monroe to Thomas Jefferson, June 15, 1806, JM Writings, 4:457. This final letter outlines Monroe's thoughts on Spain, but he never sent it and thus Jefferson was not aware of the extent of Monroe's disgruntlement until after 1808; see also Ammon, *James Monroe*, 243–46.

32. James Monroe, "Journal of the Negotiation at Aranjuez," Apr. 20, 1805, *Papers of James Monroe*, ed. Preston, 5:386. Monroe thought Jefferson should build a small naval fleet to ensure American interests on the high seas.

33. James Monroe to Thomas Jefferson, Nov. 1, 1805, *Papers of James Monroe*, ed. Preston, 5:429–32.

34. James Monroe to James Madison, Feb. 2, 1806, JM Writings, 4:403; Ammon, *James Monroe*, 251; James Monroe to John Randolph, June 16, 1806, JM Writings, 4:460. Monroe unloaded his grievances toward the administration in this letter to Randolph; see also Ammon, *James Monroe*, 251–55.

35. John Randolph to James Monroe, Sep. 16, 1806, JM Writings, 4:486–88.

36. James Monroe to John Randolph, June 16, 1806, JM Writings, 4:460; see also Risjord, *Old Republicans*, 38, 75.

37. John Randolph to James Monroe, Sep. 16, 1808, JM Writings, 4:486–88; James Monroe to John Randolph, Nov. 12, 1806, JM Writings, 4:484–94; Risjord, *Old Republicans*, 87.

38. Ammon, James Monroe, 264.

39. Holland, *Memoirs*, 2:101; Gilman, *James Monroe*, 99; see also James Monroe to Peace Commissioners, June 27, 1814, *American State Papers* (hereafter *ASP*),

3:704. During the height of the War of 1812, Monroe told the peace commissioners at Ghent that the United States would be willing to drop their demands that the British cease the practice of impressment.

40. See James Monroe and William Pinkney to James Madison, Jan. 3, 1807, *Papers of James Monroe,* ed. Preston, 5:562–72, for the negotiators' explanation of the treaty to Madison; see also James Monroe to Thomas Jefferson, Jan. 11, 1807, JM Writings, 5:2, for Monroe's explanation to Jefferson that this was the best deal he could get from the British.

41. Thomas Jefferson to the United States Minister to Great Britain (James Monroe), Mar. 21, 1807, *Works of Thomas Jefferson,* 10:374–77; Ammon, *James Monroe,* 261–62; Risjord, *Old Republicans,* 87–88. On the treaty itself see generally Hickey, "Monroe-Pinkney Treaty," 65–88.

42. Ammon, *James Monroe,* 270; James Monroe to James Madison, Dec. 13, 1807, JM Writings, 5:20–22; Ammon, "James Monroe," 42–43.

43. John Taylor to James Monroe, Feb. 22, 1808, *Papers of James Monroe,* ed. Preston, 5:673.

44. James Monroe to Thomas Jefferson, Feb. 27, 1808, JM Writings, 5:24–26; Ammon, "James Monroe," 46–48, 53; Ammon, *James Monroe,* 277.

45. Ammon, *James Monroe,* 274; Ammon, "James Monroe," 40; Preston, *Comprehensive Catalogue,* 1:199–204.

46. Ammon, *James Monroe,* 273; Thomas Jefferson to James Monroe, Feb. 18, 1808, *Works of Thomas Jefferson,* 11:10–11.

47. James Monroe to Thomas Jefferson, Feb. 27, 1808, JM Writings, 24–27; Ammon, *James Monroe,* 273–74.

48. Thomas Jefferson to James Monroe, Mar. 10, 1808, JM Writings, 11:11–14; James Monroe to Thomas Jefferson, Mar. 22, 1808, JM Writings, 5:27–35; Ammon, *James Monroe,* 274.

49. For a discussion of deferential politics in the early republic see Formisano, "Deferential Participant Politics"; see also Freeman, *Affairs of Honor.* For a discussion of "proto-parties" see Sharp, *American Politics,* 1–14. For the view that Madison was equal to Jefferson as the central figure in the Republican Party see Cunningham, *Jeffersonian Republicans.*

50. James Monroe to Thomas Jefferson, Sep. 13, 1808, James Monroe Papers, Library of Congress, Washington, DC (hereafter DLC); Thomas Jefferson to James Monroe, Oct. 13, 1808, DLC.

51. Thomas Jefferson to James Madison, Mar. 30, 1809, *Republic,* by Smith, 3:1580.

52. Ammon, *James Monroe,* 280. Jefferson wrote to Madison concerning this meeting; see Thomas Jefferson to James Madison, Nov. 30, 1809, *Republic of Letters,* by Smith, 3:1610.

53. James Monroe, "Account of a Conversation with Thomas Jefferson," Nov. 30, 1809, *Papers of Thomas Jefferson*, ed. Looney, 2:44–46; Thomas Jefferson to James Madison, Nov. 30, 1809, *Papers of Thomas Jefferson*, ed. Looney, 2:42–44; James Monroe to Richard Brent, Feb. 25, 1810, JM Writings, 5:110–11; Ammon, *James Monroe*, 280. Jefferson also suggested a military command. Monroe responded that he would "sooner be shot than take a command under Wilkinson," the erstwhile commanding general of the U.S. Army. Monroe's instincts on Wilkinson proved to be spot on. It was later revealed that while serving as a general in the U.S. Army, he was also an agent in the pay of the Spanish Empire.

54. James Monroe, "Election Day Speech," Apr. 10, 1810, *Papers of James Monroe*, ed. Preston, 5:762–64. See also Ammon, *James Monroe*, 282.

55. Ammon, *James Monroe*, 283; Thomas Jefferson to James Madison, May 25, 1810, *Papers of Thomas Jefferson*, ed. Looney, 2:416–17.

56. Brant, *Fourth President*, 300–309; Ammon, *James Monroe*, 274–75, 285; James Monroe to James Madison, Mar. 29, 1811, JM Writings, 5:181–84; James Monroe to Thomas Jefferson, Apr. 3, 1811, JM Writings, 5:184–85; James Monroe to Thomas Jefferson, Jan. 21, 1811, JM Writings, 5:160–61. Throughout the remainder of 1810 and into early 1811 Madison continued to search for a way to get Monroe back into a major political office. An opportunity arose when Cyrus Griffin died, opening up a federal judgeship. Madison quickly moved to appoint John Tyler, then governor of Virginia. This left the governorship open for Monroe's election. By rallying his own personal following, and with the backing of Madison's administration, in January 1811 Monroe once again became governor of Virginia.

57. On Robert Smith's removal see Pancake, "Invisibles"; and Ammon, *James Monroe*, 285. Madison's administration came under fire during the early months of 1811. Many of the president's problems stemmed from the so-called Invisibles, a nebulous group of influential Washington politicians with Maryland senator Samuel Smith at their head. They opposed many of Madison's measures throughout his early term in office and even blocked the nomination of Albert Gallatin as secretary of state in favor of Samuel Smith's younger brother Robert, who proved ineffective as the nation's chief diplomat.

58. Ammon, *James Monroe*, 286–88; James Monroe to Richard Brent, Mar. 18, 1811, JM Writings, 5:178–80; James Madison to James Monroe, Mar. 20, 1811, JM Writings, 181; James Monroe to James Madison, Mar. 23, 1811, JM Writings, 5:181–83; James Monroe to James Madison, Mar. 29, 1811, JM Writings, 5:183–84.

59. Quoted in Ammon, *James Monroe*, 285; see also James Monroe to John Taylor, Jan. 23, 1811, JM Writings, 5:161–69, for Monroe's explanations for taking the post. No one was better respected as a thinker than John Taylor was, and contemporaries certainly admired his Atticus-like existence away from the pressures

of politics, but of course almost no one outside the history profession remembers Colonel Taylor of Caroline.

60. See Thomas Jefferson to William Duane, Apr. 20, 1812, *Papers of Thomas Jefferson*, ed. Looney, 4:632–33. As secretary of state, Madison attempted to carry out Jefferson's policy of non-importation and an embargo of British goods as means of dealing with British insults. With his move to the executive mansion and the addition of Monroe, who knew full well from his familiarity with European politics that such soft measures were destined to fail, Madison decided to adopt a harder line against the British. New elements within the government aided the administration. Younger, more aggressive members of Congress began pushing for war. These so-called war hawks, led by Henry Clay, Felix Grundy, and John C. Calhoun, supported a tougher stance against British obstinacy. Eventually Madison called on Congress to declare war; see Stagg, *Mr. Madison's War*.

61. See Thomas Jefferson to William Duane, Apr. 20, 1812, *Papers of Thomas Jefferson*, ed. Looney 4:632–33.

62. James Monroe to Fulwar Skipwith, Aug. 12, 1813, NN.

63. See generally Smith, *Republic*, 3:1681; Ketcham, *James Madison*, 508–9; Ammon, *James Monroe*, 289–301.

64. James Monroe to William H. Crawford, Dec. 3, 1812, JM Writings, 5:227; Ketcham, *James Madison*, 542–46.

65. Skeen, *John Armstrong Jr.*, 58–112, 120, 123, 124; Ammon, *James Monroe*, 317.

66. Skeen, *John Armstrong Jr.*, 202; Ammon, *James Monroe*, 317–18. Skeen states that Armstrong had virtually no defenders in Washington.

67. Skeen, *John Armstrong Jr.*, 9–10, 13; Ammon, *James Monroe*, 317–18; see also Kohn, "Inside History."

68. Skeen, *John Armstrong Jr.*, 13; Middlekauff, *Glorious Cause*, 603–5; In *Critical Period* (110), John Fiske writes of the Newburgh letters that "better English has seldom been wasted in a worse cause."

69. Alexander Hamilton to George Washington, Feb. 13, 1783, *Papers of Alexander Hamilton*, Ed. Syrett, 3:253–55; Joseph Jones to George Washington, Feb. 27, 1783, *Letters of Joseph Jones*, 97–102.

70. Skeen, *John Armstrong Jr.*, 5. For the Conway Cabal see Ward, *American Revolution*, 115–18.

71. John Quincy Adams, Sep. 23, 1822, *Memoirs of John Quincy Adams* (hereafter JQA Memoirs), 6:66. John Quincy Adams explained in his memoirs that Armstrong had always "been supposed" to be the author of the Newburgh letters.

72. Quoted in Skeen, *John Armstrong Jr.*, 14, 124.

73. Ammon, *James Monroe*, 317–18; Skeen, *John Armstrong Jr.*, 1, 115–23. Personal issues also divided Armstrong and Monroe. Armstrong married Robert R. Livingston's sister and shared the family's dislike of Monroe.

74. Quoted in Ammon, *James Monroe*, 323.

75. James Monroe to James Madison, Feb. 25, 1813, JM Writings, 5:245.

76. James Monroe to James Madison, Feb. 25, 1813, JM Writings, 5:244–50; James Monroe to Thomas Jefferson, June 7, 1813, JM Writings, 5:266.

77. James Monroe "Notes on a Plan of Campaign for the Year 1813," JM Writings, 5:235–41.

78. James Monroe to James Madison, Dec. 1813 [specific date unknown], JM Writings, 5:275  77. Monroe even considered resigning because he felt so useless. See James Monroe to George Hay, Mar. 11, 1814, NN; Monroe's son-in-law George Hay told him not to resign. He said that Monroe's resignation would "materially . . . injure" the republican cause. He also hinted that it would come back to haunt him prior to the election of 1816 and hurt his chances at the presidency. Hay claimed that it would not be worth becoming the next president anyway if the United States did not make peace with Great Britain. As Hay put it, "Unless we have peace, I would not exchange my gardener's house for the presidential palace." See George Hay to James Monroe, Mar. 14, 1814, NN.

79. James Monroe to the president (James Madison), Aug. 21, 1814, JM Writings, 5:289–90; Ketcham, *James Madison*, 573–74; Ammon, *James Monroe*, 323, 330. Quote is from James Monroe to Thomas Jefferson, Dec. 21, 1814, JM Writings, 303–4.

80. James Madison, "Memorandum on the Battle of Bladensburg," Aug. 24, 1814, *James Madison*, 700–706.

81. Armstrong, *Exposition*.

82. Armstrong, *Exposition*, 6–7.

83. James Monroe to James Madison, Sep. 25, 1814, JM Writings, 5:293–95. With the possible exception of William H. Crawford.

84. James Monroe to John Holmes, Apr. 3, 1815, NN.

85. James Monroe to George Hay, Mar. 5, 1815, NN.

86. James Monroe, "First Inaugural Address," Mar. 4, 1817, *Compilation*, ed. Richardson, 2:4–10. Monroe specifically said, "National honor is national property of the highest value."

87. Stagg, *Mr. Madison's War*, 469–86.

### CHAPTER 5. A BOLDER ATTITUDE

1. John Quincy Adams, Oct. 25, 1817, JQA Memoirs, 4:13. Monroe proved an excellent judge of talent. Before settling on John C. Calhoun, he offered the job at the War Department to Henry Clay, who declined. Clay had set his sights on becoming secretary of state, and when Monroe did not select him to head that department Clay proceeded to act as the de facto head of the opposition to the government as speaker of the House of Representatives.

2. "Columbia Centinel," Boston, MA, July 12, 1817, *Papers of James Monroe*, ed. Preston, 1:226.

3. James Monroe's Questions for the Cabinet, Oct. 25, 1817, JM Writings, 6:31; Ammon, *James Monroe*, 413; John Quincy Adams, Oct. 25, 1817, JQA Memoirs, 4:13. The term "Monroe Doctrine" did not come into use until the Civil War, when Napoleon III authorized a French invasion of Mexico, but I will use the term so as to avoid confusion.

4. See a variety of works in Rappaport, *Monroe Doctrine*: For evaluations of the doctrine's legacy, see Luis Quintanilla, "A Latin American View: Machiavellian Due to Corollaries," and Gaston Nerval, "Egoistic from Its Pronouncement"; for a discussion of the purpose of the doctrine see Dexter Perkins, "To Deter the Continental Allies in the Western Hemisphere," and Arthur P. Whitaker, "To Frustrate France's Plans in South America"; for discussions on who formulated the doctrine see Worthington C. Ford, "The Work of John Quincy Adams." Historians have also stressed other concerns leading to the doctrine's creation, including the threat Russia posed to Oregon and the politicking prior to the election of 1824, when three members of Monroe's cabinet, John C. Calhoun, William H. Crawford, and John Quincy Adams, vied for the presidency. For a discussion of the role domestic politics played in the creation of the Monroe Doctrine see May, *Making*. See also Perkins, *Monroe Doctrine*. While Perkins's book, perhaps still the most important work on the Monroe Doctrine, highlights Adams's contribution to what he believes are the more important parts of the doctrine, he does give credit to Monroe on the question of Latin American independence. The most recent account of the Monroe Doctrine is Sexton, *Monroe Doctrine*. Sexton also emphasizes the role various members of the cabinet played in the doctrine's creation, calling it essentially a compromise.

5. See generally Bemis, *John Quincy Adams*.

6. See generally Weeks, *John Quincy Adams*.

7. Owsley and Smith, *Filibusters*, 118–19; Weeks, *John Quincy Adams*, 57.

8. Don Luis de Onis to James Monroe, July 9, 1817, ASP, 4:442; Owsley and Smith, *Filibusters*, 140.

9. First quote from James Monroe to the cabinet, Oct. 25, 30, 1817, JM Writings, 6:31–32. See also John Quincy Adams, Oct. 30, 1817, JQA Memoirs, 4:14–16; James Monroe to James Madison, Nov. 24, 1817, JM Writings, 6:32–33. Second quote is from James Monroe, "First Annual Message to Congress," Dec. 2, 1817, JM Writings, 6:36; John C. Calhoun to James Monroe, Jan. 12, 1817, *Papers of John C. Calhoun*, 2:69; James Monroe to the Senate and House of Representatives, Jan. 13, 1817, JM Writings, 6:71.

10. John Quincy Adams, Jan. 12, 1818, JQA Memoirs, 4:39; Weeks, *John Quincy Adams*, 65–66.

11. James Monroe and Robert R. Livingston to Francois Barbe-Marbois, May 2, 1803, DLC; James Monroe to Charles Talleyrand, Nov. 8, 1804, *ASP*, 2634; James Monroe to Robert R. Livingston May, 1803 DLC (not sent); James Monroe to James Madison, May 23, 1803, DLC. Monroe initially planned to travel to Spain immediately after finalizing the Purchase. He first traveled to Great Britain in 1804 before heading to Spain to negotiate in 1805.

12. James Monroe and William Pinkney to Mr. Cevallos, Apr. 9, 1805, *ASP*, 2:658; James Monroe and William Pinkney to James Madison, May 23, 1805, *ASP*, 2:667; Monroe warned the Spanish that the United States was poised to take their possessions in the New World if Spain did not give in on Florida; see James Monroe to Manuel de Godoy, May 14, 1805, *Papers of James Monroe*, ed. Preston, 5:391–93.

13. Owsley and Smith, *Filibusters*, 61–81.

14. George Logan to James Monroe, June 5, 1817, DLC.

15. James Madison to James Monroe, July 29, 1803, *Papers of James Monroe*, ed. Preston, 5:101–4.

16. Lewis, *American Union*, 75; Ammon, *James Monroe*, 409–12. Quotes are from James Monroe to John Quincy Adams, Dec. 10, 1815, JM Writings, 5:381–82.

17. James Monroe to Thomas Jefferson, Dec. 23, 1817, JM Writings, 6:46–47.

18. James Monroe to John Quincy Adams, Jan. 13, 1818, Adams Family Papers: Letters Received, Massachusetts Historical Society; James Monroe to John Quincy Adams, Feb. 12, 1818, Monroe, *Comprehensive Catalogue*, 2:719; see also James Monroe to John Quincy Adams, Mar. 11, 1818, Monroe, *Comprehensive Catalogue* 2:722.

19. See John Quincy Adams, Jan. 10, 1818, JQA Memoirs, 4:37–38; Don Luis de Onis to Secretary of State James Monroe, Jan. 2, 1816, *ASP*, 4:424; James Monroe, "Special Message to the House of Representatives," Jan. 13, 1818, JM Writings, 6:36–39.

20. Owsley and Smith, *Filibusters*, 150–51.

21. John C. Calhoun to General Edmund P. Gaines, Dec. 16, 1817, *Papers of John C. Calhoun*, 2:20; John Quincy Adams, Dec. 26, 1817, JQA Memoirs, 30–31; John C. Calhoun to Andrew Jackson, Dec. 26, 1817, *Papers of John C. Calhoun*, 2:38–40.

22. Remini, *Andrew Jackson*, 130–62; Ammon, *James Monroe*, 412–17. See also Heidler and Heidler, *Old Hickory's War*, 121.

23. It may interest readers to note that Monroe signed a sworn affidavit insisting that he had never sent any such authorization through Rhea or anyone else only a week before his death in 1831.

24. James Madison to Andrew Jackson, Oct. 21, 1814, *Papers of Andrew Jackson*, 3:170; Andrew Jackson to James Madison, Oct. 26, 1814, *Papers of Andrew Jackson*, 3:173; Andrew Jackson to John Coffee, August 10, 1814, *Papers of Andrew Jackson*, 3:112; Owsley, *Creek War*, 88–89.

25. Remini, *Andrew Jackson*, 143–62; Owsley and Smith, *Filibusters*, 153–60.

26. James Monroe to James Madison, Feb. 13, 1818, JM Writings, 6:47–49; Cunningham, *Presidency*, 59–60. If we take it for granted that Monroe sent Jackson to Florida knowing that the general might take aggressive action against the Spanish, he almost certainly did not anticipate Jackson's execution of two British subjects.

27. Don Luis de Onis to the secretary of state, June 25, July 8, 1818, *ASP*, 4:478–97; Weeks, *John Quincy Adams*, 117.

28. John Quincy Adams, July 15, 1818, JQA Memoirs, 4:108; John Quincy Adams, July 16, 1818, JQA Memoirs, 4:109.

29. John Quincy Adams, July 15, 1818, JQA Memoirs, 4:108.

30. James Monroe to James Madison, July 10, 1818, JM Writings, 6:53–56.

31. James Monroe to James Madison, July 10, 1818, JM Writings, 6:53–56.

32. James Monroe to Andrew Jackson, July 19, 1818, JM Writings, 6:54–61. Monroe was right to be concerned over British involvement. In August, Richard Rush wrote to the president informing him of increased British hostility over the executions of Ambrister and Arbuthnot. See Richard Rush to James Monroe, Aug. 3, 1818, DLC.

33. James Monroe to George Hay, July 20, 1818, NN.

34. John Quincy Adams, Aug. 2–9, 1823, JQA Memoirs, 6:168–71. Specifically Adams said that in all cases "for which Mr. Monroe, as the head of the administration[,] is responsible, I submit my judgment to his."

35. John Quincy Adams, July 18, 1818, JQA Memoirs, 6:112; John Quincy Adams to Don Luis de Onis, July 23, 1818, *ASP*, 4:497–99.

36. James Monroe to Nicholas Biddle, July, 24, 1818, NN.

37. James Monroe to John C. Calhoun, Aug. 31, 1818, NN.

38. James Monroe "Second Annual Message," Nov. 16, 1818, JM Writings, 6:80.

39. John Quincy Adams, "Speech to the U.S. House of Representatives," July 4, 1821, University of Virginia, Miller Center database, http://millercenter.org/president/speeches/detail/3484; see also Weeks, *John Quincy Adams*, 19–21; Bemis, *John Quincy Adams*, 341–42.

40. Rappaport, *Monroe Doctrine*, 2–8; Lewis, *American Union*, 75.

41. Rappaport, *Monroe Doctrine*, 2–8; Davies, *Europe*, 762–63.

42. For information on the United States and the revolutions in Latin America see Whitaker, *United States*.

43. James Monroe, "Questions for the Cabinet," Oct. 25, 1817, JM Writings, 6:31; see also Ammon, *James Monroe*, 413.

44. James Monroe to Joel Barlow, Nov. 27, 1811, JM Writings, 5:364.

45. James Monroe "First Annual Message to Congress," Dec. 2, 1817, JM Writings, 6:33–35. In the following year he expressed similar thoughts concerning

American sympathy for the revolutions; see also James Monroe's Second Annual Message to Congress, Nov. 16, 1818, JM Writings, 6:81–82.

46. James Monroe to Fulwar Skipwith, Apr. 21, 1818, NN.

47. James Monroe, "Third Annual Message to Congress," Dec. 7, 1819, JM Writings, 6:112; James Monroe, "Fourth Annual Message to Congress," Nov. 14, 1820, JM Writings, 6:158–59.

48. James Monroe to Andrew Jackson, May 23, 1820, JM Writings, 6:128.

49. James Monroe to Albert Gallatin, May 26, 1820, JM Writings, 6:132–33. In another interesting letter to an unknown correspondent on the same day Monroe made nearly the exact same point; see James Monroe to unknown, May 26, 1820, NN.

50. James Monroe to Andrew Jackson, May 23, 1820, JM Writings, 6:128. Monroe may even have had some hope of coming to an accommodation with the Holy Allies when he received word from Rush that a Russian diplomat planned to make inquiries concerning a "association" between the United States and the Holy Alliance; see Richard Rush to James Monroe, Aug. 25, 1818, DLC.

51. Richard Rush to James Monroe, Jan. 17, 1819, DLC; John Forsyth to James Monroe, Aug. 7, 22, 1819, NN.

52. Richard Rush to James Monroe, May 30, 1818, DLC.

53. James Monroe to Jonathon Russell, Mar. 12, 1822, JM Writings, 6:211–12; see also James Monroe to James Madison, May 10, 1822, JM Writings, 6:284–85. Monroe lays out his thinking to Madison on the subject in the first two pages of this letter.

54. James Monroe, "Special Message to Congress Concerning South American Affairs," Mar. 8, 1822, JM Writings, 6:204.

55. James Monroe to Robert Garnett, Mar. 29, 1822, JM Writings, 6:214–15.

56. John Quincy Adams to James Monroe, May 10, 1823, DLC. Some proof that Monroe took a firm hand in the South American affairs can be found in a letter from Adams to the president with the secretary of state asking Monroe for specific instructions to give to two important American diplomats to Buenos Aires and Colombia: "I am exceedingly anxious not only that they should meet your approbation, but that they should fill up entirely to your satisfaction the outline of your own ideas and intentions."

57. Heidler and Heidler, *Henry Clay*, 136; Fritz, *Our Sister Republics*, 156–93.

58. John Quincy Adams, May 10, 1820, JQA Memoirs, 5:108–11.

59. John Quincy Adams, Nov. 12, 1820, JQA Memoirs, 5:200.

60. John Quincy Adams, Mar. 9, 1821, JQA Memoirs, 5:324–25.

61. Bemis, *John Quincy Adams*, 369–71.

62. Lafayette to James Monroe, July 13, 1822, NN; The Marquis de Lafayette to James Monroe, Mar. 16, 1823, DLC.

63. Richard Rush to James Monroe, Jan. 30, 1823, DLC. Rush was a close friend of Monroe's and the president valued his judgment. He defended Rush from his political opponents, who claimed the young man had risen too quickly, see John Quincy Adams, May 25, 1820, JQA Memoirs, 5:132.

64. John Jacob Astor to James Monroe, Apr. 15, 1820, NN.

65. James Monroe to Thomas Jefferson, June 2, 1823, JM Writings, 6:310; Cunningham, *Presidency*, 61.

66. In fact, Monroe had heard rumors that the French would intervene in South America at least as far back as 1820 when Rush told him of discussions he had had with British officials concerning a French plot to establish a Bourbon king in Buenos Aires; see Richard Rush to James Monroe, July 21, 1820, DLC.

67. Mr. Canning to Mr. Rush, Aug. 23, 1823, JM Writings, 6:365. Rush had reported rumors of British aid to the revolutionary governments in South America as early as 1818; see Richard Rush to James Monroe, Nov. 1, 1818, DLC.

68. James Monroe to Thomas Jefferson, Oct. 17, 1823, JM Writings, 6:323–25.

69. James Monroe, "Memo," 1801–2, *Papers of James Monroe*, ed. Preston, 4:557–59.

70. Richard Rush to James Monroe, Nov. 1, 1818, DLC.

71. Richard Rush to James Monroe Oct. 1. DLC; Richard Rush to James Monroe, Jan. 17, 1819, DLC. Rush told Monroe that the British cabinet was essentially unconcerned by the executions of Ambrister and Arbuthnot; Monroe had even contemplated just such an alliance during his years as minister to Spain in 1805. He had warned the Spanish that an Anglo-American alliance could easily "sever forever from France and Spain their American possessions"; see James Monroe, "Journal of the Negotiation at Aranjuez," Apr. 5, 1805, *Papers of James Monroe*, ed. Preston, 5:365–66.

72. Ammon, *James Monroe*, 349–50, 386.

73. Richard Rush to James Monroe, Aug. 6, 1820, DLC.

74. John Quincy Adams, Oct. 30, 1820, JQA Memoirs, 5:193–94.

75. Dixon, *George Canning*, 238–39.

76. Richard Rush to James Monroe, Mar. 4, 1822, DLC. Specifically Rush told Monroe that the British were inclined to come to terms in the West Indies.

77. James Monroe to Lord Holland, Apr. 24, 1823, NN.

78. James Monroe to Thomas Jefferson, June 2, 1823, JM Writings, 6:309.

79. Ammon, *James Monroe*, 476–77; Davies, *Europe*, 762–63; James Monroe to Thomas Jefferson, Oct. 17, 1823, JM Writings, 6:323–25.

80. Thomas Jefferson to James Monroe, Oct. 24, 1823, *Works of Thomas Jefferson*, ed. Ford, 12:318–19.

81. James Madison to Thomas Jefferson, Nov. 1, 1823, *Republics of Letters*, ed.

Smith, 3:1879; James Madison to James Monroe, Oct. 30, 1823, JM Writings, 6:394–96.

82. The Marquis de Lafayette to James Monroe, Jan. 22, 1822, NN.

83. The Marquis de Lafayette to James Monroe, Sep. 22, 1822, NN.

84. John Quincy Adams, Nov. 16, 1822, JQA Memoirs, 6:102.

85. See chapters 1 and 2 above.

86. John Quincy Adams, Nov. 7, 1823, JQA Memoirs, 6:179.

87. John Quincy Adams, "Speech to the U.S. House of Representatives," July 4, 1821, University of Virginia, Miller Center database, http://millercenter.org/president/speeches/detail/3484; see also Weeks, *John Quincy Adams*, 19–21; Bemis, *John Quincy Adams*, 341–42.

88. John Quincy Adams, Nov. 7, 1823, JQA Memoirs, 6:176–77.

89. John Quincy Adams, Nov. 7–Dec. 2, 1822, JQA Memoirs, 6:177–236. Monroe had opposed annexation of Cuba in a letter to Madison: James Monroe to James Madison, Sep. 26, 1822, DLC. Summary found in *Comprehensive Catalogue*, ed. Preston; see Sexton, *Monroe Doctrine*, 47–62.

90. John Quincy Adams, Nov. 13, 15, 1823, JQA Memoirs, 185–86; James Monroe to Thomas Jefferson, June 2, 1823, JM Writings, 6:309.

91. John Quincy Adams, Nov. 17, 18, 1823, JQA Memoirs, 187, 190; James Monroe to Thomas Jefferson, Dec. 4, 1823, JM Writings, 6:342.

92. John Quincy Adams, Nov. 21, 22, 1823, JQA Memoirs, 6:195–97; Ammon, *James Monroe*, 481–82; James Monroe, "Seventh Annual Message to Congress," Dec. 2, 1823, JM Writings, 325–41; John Quincy Adams, Nov. 24, 1824, JQA Memoirs, 6:199.

93. Adams, Nov. 22, 1823, JQA Memoirs, 6:198. Czar Alexander had issued an *ukase*, or proclamation, in 1821 asserting Russian claims over the American Pacific Northwest. See Sexton, *Monroe Doctrine*, 48.

94. John Quincy Adams, Nov. 28, 1821, JQA Memoirs, 5:424–26.

95. Monroe had received letters from Richard Rush as early as 1818 detailing rumors of Spanish plans to raid American shipping, as well as French and British support designed to prevent further U.S. territorial expansion; see Richard Rush to James Monroe, May 20, June 5, 1818, DLC.

96. Adams, Nov. 24, 1823, JQA Memoirs, 6:199.

97. James Monroe, "Seventh Annual Message to Congress," 6:338.

98. James Monroe to Samuel L. Gouverneur, Dec. 4, 1823, NN.

99. James Monroe, "Seventh Annual Message to Congress," 6:338.

100. James Monroe, "Sixth Annual Message to Congress," Dec. 3, 1822, JM Writings, 6:298–99; James Monroe, "Seventh Annual Message to Congress," 6:338.

101. James Monroe, "Sixth Annual Message to Congress," 6:298–99; James Monroe, "Seventh Annual Message to Congress," 6:338.

102. Monroe, "Seventh Annual Message to Congress," 6:338.

103. Monroe, "Seventh Annual Message to Congress," 6:338.

104. Monroe, "Seventh Annual Message to Congress," 6:339–41.

105. John Marshall to James Monroe, Dec. 9, 1823, DLC.

106. The Marquis de Lafayette to James Monroe, Jan. 11, 1824, NN.

107. James Monroe to James Madison, Mar. 22, 1824, JM Writings, 7:12.

108. John Brown to James Monroe, Apr. 15, 1824, DLC.

109. Caesar A. Rodney to James Monroe, Feb. 10, 1824, JM Writings, 7:3.

110. Alexander McRae to James Monroe, Feb. 7, 1824, DLC.

111. See James Monroe to Thomas Jefferson, July 12, 1824, JM Writings, 7:29–30; see also James Monroe to James Madison, Aug. 2, 1824, JM Writings, 7:31.

112. James Monroe, "Eighth Annual Message to Congress," Dec. 7, 1824, JM Writings, 7:46–47.

### CONCLUSION: MAKING THE WORLD SAFE FOR REPUBLICANISM

1. Blanning, Short Oxford History, 162–63.

2. James Monroe to John Quincy Adams, Jan. 25, 1831, JM Writings, 7:216–18; James Monroe to A Committee of Tammany Hall, 1831, JM Writings, 7:220–21.

3. Adams, Lives.

4. Gilman, James Monroe; Morgan, Life; Cresson, James Monroe; Ammon, James Monroe.

5. Onuf, Mind; Burstein, Jefferson's Secrets; Appleby, Thomas Jefferson; Gordon-Reed, Hemingses; Meacham, Thomas Jefferson; Ellis, American Sphinx; for Madison see Bilder, Madison's Hand; Wills, James Madison. The interest in Madison may be seeping into the general public through the writing of more popular biographies like the one written by Lynne Cheney, former vice president Dick Cheney's wife. See Cheney, James Madison.

6. Forbes, Missouri Compromise; Sexton, Monroe Doctrine; Leibiger, Companion; Unger, Last Founding Father.

7. Monroe, Papers of James Monroe, ed. Preston.

8. JM Writings; see also Poston, review of Papers.

9. John Quincy Adams, Nov. 26, 1822, JQA Memoirs, 6:107. In discussing Monroe's message with John C., Calhoun Adams told the secretary of war this concerning the president's prose: "The message was very long, owing to the President's style of writing, as he was apt to dwell upon details. The whole substance of this message for example might be compressed into less than half the words in which he had clothed it."

10. James Monroe to Daniel Parker, Apr. 25, 1818, Quotations of James Monroe, ed. Preston and Stello, 35. "I send you my decision in the case of Major Hall which, if you can read it, you will have copied and carried into immediate effect."

11. Cogliano, *Thomas Jefferson*.

12. John Quincy Adams, Mar. 20, 1821, JQA Memoirs, 6:334. Interestingly, Adams thought he spent too much time on his diary. He thought it might have been more useful to spend the time with something else. But it seems clear that for his historical legacy the hours Adams spent writing in his diary were time well spent.

13. Found in Furstenberg, *Name*, 32.

14. Monroe, *Autobiography*, 24.

15. James Monroe to George Hay, May 2, 1819, *Papers of James Monroe*, ed. Preston, 1:619.

16. Monroe told the City of Charleston that he had long witnessed Jefferson's tireless "devotion to the liberties and happiness of his country." He knew that the country would feel forever grateful to Jefferson for all his efforts. See James Monroe to the Intendant and Council of the City of Charleston, Apr. 27, 1819, *Papers of James Monroe*, ed. Preston, 1:601.

17. James Monroe, *Columbia Centinel*, July 5, 1817, *Papers of James Monroe*, ed. Preston, 1:196.

18. Mitt Romney, "Transcript of Mitt Romney's Speech on Donald Trump," *New York Times*, Mar. 3, 2016, http://www.nytimes.com/2016/03/04/us/politics/mitt-romney-speech.html.

19. Winthrop, "Model," 7:31–48.

20. George Washington, "Farewell Address to the People of the United States," Sep. 19, 1796, *Something*, ed. Dunn, 80–93.

21. Thomas Jefferson, "First Inaugural Address," Mar. 4, 1801, in *Something*, ed. Dunn, 301–5.

22. James Monroe to Thomas Jefferson, June 2, 1823, JM Writings, 6:310; Cunningham, *Presidency*, 61.

23. Tucker and Hendrickson, *Empire*, x.

24. Smith, *Keeping*, 4.

25. Russell, *John Quincy Adams*, 8, 270.

26. Tocqueville, *Democracy*.

27. Sexton, *Monroe Doctrine*, 82–83.

28. Sexton, *Monroe Doctrine*, 97–110. Sexton claims that Polk essentially hijacked the Monroe Doctrine as a vehicle for imperialism.

29. James Monroe to James Madison, June 28, 1804, *Papers of James Monroe*, ed. Preston, 5:234–38; Albert Beveridge, "Speech in the Senate," Jan. 9, 1900, Congressional Record, 56 Congress, 1st sess., 704–12, in *Ideas*, ed. Graebner, 370–73.

30. Sexton, *Monroe Doctrine*, 97–110; Woodrow Wilson, "War Message," Apr. 2, 1917, in *Ideas*, ed. Graebner, 445–49.

31. Harry Truman, "Speech to Congress," Mar. 12, 1947, In *Ideas*, ed. Graebner,

729–31; see also Norman Graebner, "The Strategy of Containment," in *Ideas*, 711–21.

32. James Monroe to John Randolph, Nov. 12, 1806, *Papers of James Monroe*, ed. Preston, 5:546–47.

33. James Monroe, "Memo," 1801–2, *Papers of James Monroe*, ed. Preston, 4:557–59.

# SELECTED BIBLIOGRAPHY

**PRIMARY**

Adams, John. *The Diary and Autobiography of John Adams*. Ed. L. H. Butterfield. 4 vols. Cambridge, MA: Belknapp, 1961.

———. *John Adams: Revolutionary Writings*. Ed. Gordon Wood. New York: Library of America, 2011.

Adams, John, and Benjamin Rush. *The Spur of Fame: Dialogues of John Adams and Benjamin Rush*. Ed. John Aschutz and Douglass Adair. San Marino, CA: Huntington Library, 1966.

Adams, John Quincy. *The Lives of James Madison and James Monroe*. Buffalo, NY: George H. Darby, 1851.

———. *Memoirs of John Quincy Adams: Comprising Portions of his Diary from 1795–1848*. Ed. Charles Francis Adams. 12 vols. Philadelphia: J.B. Lippincott, 1875.

Adams, Samuel. *The Writings of Sam Adams*. Ed. Harry Cushing. New York: Octagon Books, 1968.

Aristotle. *Aristotle: On Man in the Universe*. Ed. Louise Loomis. Roslyn, NY: Walter J. Black, 1943.

Armstrong, John, Jr. *Exposition of the Motives for Opposing the Nomination of Mr. Monroe for the Office of President of the United States*. Washington, DC: Early American Imprints series 2, no. 37552.

Bland, Theodrick, Jr. *The Bland Papers*. 2 vols. Petersburg, VA: J.C. Ruffin, 1840.

Bush, George W. *Decision Points*. Large print ed. New York: Random House, 2010.

Butterfield, L. H., ed. *Adams Family Correspondence*. Cambridge, MA: Belknapp, 1973.

Calhoun, John C. *The Papers of John C. Calhoun*. Ed. W. Edwin Hemphill. 28 vols. Columbia, SC: University of South Carolina, 1963.

Cappon, Lester. *The Adams-Jefferson Letters: The Complete Correspondence between Thomas Jefferson and Abigail and John Adams*. Chapel Hill: University of North Carolina Press, 1959.

Cicero, Marcus Tullius. *Orations of Marcus Tullius Cicero*. Trans. Charles Yonge. New York: Colonial Press, 1900.

———. *Cicero*. Trans. Clinton Walker Keyes. New York: Putnam's Son's 1928.

Clinton, Bill. *My Life*. New York: Alfred Knopf, 2004.

Dunn, Susan, ed. *Something That Will Surprise the World*. New York: Perseus, 2006.

Ford, Paul Leicester, ed. *Pamphlets on the Constitution of the United States*. New York: Da Capo, 1968.

Franklin, Benjamin. *The Autobiography of Benjamin Franklin*. Philadelphia: J.B. Lippincott, 1868. Reprint, New York: Dover, 1996.

———. *The Complete Poor Richard's Almanacks*. Ed. Whitfield J. Bell. 2 vols. Barre, MA: Imprint Society, 1970.

———. *The Papers of Benjamin Franklin*. Ed. William Willcox. 43 vols. New Haven, CT: Yale University Press, 1984.

Hamilton, Alexander. *The Papers of Alexander Hamilton*. Ed. Harold Syrett. 26 vols. New York: Columbia University Press, 1961.

Hamilton, Alexander, John Jay, and James Madison. *The Federalist Papers by Alexander Hamilton, James Madison and John Jay*. Ed. Garry Wills. New York: Bantam Books, 1982.

Holland, Henry Richard. *Memoirs of the Whig Party during My Time*. Ed. Henry Edward Holland. 2 vols. London: Longman, Green, and Longmans, 1854.

Homer. *The Iliad*. Trans. Martin Hammond. New York: Penguin, 1987.

Hume, David. *Theory of Politics*. Ed. Frederick Watkins. Austin: University of Texas Press, 1953.

Jackson, Andrew. *The Papers of Andrew Jackson*. Ed. Harold Moser et al. 10 vols. Knoxville: University of Tennessee Press, 1991.

Jay, John. *The Correspondence and Public Papers of John Jay*. New York: Burt Franklin, 1890.

Jefferson, Thomas. *The Papers of Thomas Jefferson*. Ed. Julian Boyd. 28 vols. Princeton, NJ: Princeton University Press, 1950.

———. *The Papers of Thomas Jefferson*. Ed. Barbara Oberg. Princeton, NJ: Princeton University Press, 2010.

———. *The Papers of Thomas Jefferson: Retirement Series*. Ed. J. Jefferson Looney. 14 vols. Princeton, NJ: Princeton University Press, 2006.

———. *Thomas Jefferson: Writings*. Ed. Merrill Peterson. New York: Library of America, 1984.

———. *The Works of Thomas Jefferson*. Ed. Paul Leicester Ford. New York: G.P. Putnam's Sons, 1905.

———. *The Writings of Thomas Jefferson*. Ed. Andrew A. Lipscomb and Albert

Ellery Bergh. 20 vols. Washington, DC: Thomas Jefferson Memorial Association, 1904.

Jones, Joseph. *The Letters of Joseph Jones of Virginia, 1777–1787*. Ed. Worthington C. Ford. New York: New York Times, 1971.

Locke, John. *The Educational Writings of John Locke*. Ed. James Axtell. Cambridge, MA: University Press of Cambridge, 1968.

Lowrie, Walter, and Mathew St. Clair, eds. *American State Papers: Foreign Relations*. 6 vols. Washington, DC: 1832–59.

Madison, James. *James Madison: Writings*. Ed. Jack Rakove. New York: Library of America, 1999.

———. *The Papers of James Madison*. Ed. J.C.A. Stagg. 5 vols. Charlottesville: University of Virginia Press., 1984.

———. *The Papers of James Madison: Secretary of State Series*. Ed. Mary Hackett. 11 vols. Charlottesville: University Press of Virginia, 1998–.

Monroe, James. *The Autobiography of James Monroe*. Ed. Stuart Gerry Brown. Syracuse: Syracuse University Press, 1959.

———. *A Comprehensive Catalogue of the Correspondence and Papers of James Monroe*. Ed. Daniel Preston. 2 vols. Westport, CT: Greenwood, 2001.

———. *The Papers of James Monroe: Selected Correspondence and Papers*. Ed. Daniel Preston. 6 vols. Westport, CT: Greenwood, 2003.

———. *The People the Sovereigns: Being a Comparison of the Government of the United States with Those Republics Which Have Existed before with the Causes of Their Decline and Fall*. Ed. Samuel L. Gouverneur. Philadelphia: J.B. Lippincott, 1867.

———. *The Writings of James Monroe*. Ed. Stanislaus Murray Hamilton. 7 vols. New York: AMS, 1969.

Paine, Thomas. *The American Revolution: Writings from the War of Independence*. New York: Literary Classics of America, 2001.

———. *Common Sense*. Ed. Isaac Kramnick. New York: Penguin Books, 1986.

———. *The Complete Writings of Thomas Paine*. Ed. Phil Foner. New York: Citadel, 1945.

———. *Thomas Paine: Collected Writings*. Ed. Eric Foner. New York: Library of America, 1995.

Plato. *Plato*. Trans. B. Jowett, ed. Louise Ropes Loomis. Roslyn, NY: Walter J. Black, 1942.

Preston, Dan, and Heidi Stello, eds. *Quotations of James Monroe*. Charlottesville, VA: Ashlawn-Highland, 2010.

Richardson, James, ed. *A Compilation of the Messages and Papers of the Presidents*. 11 vols. Washington, DC: Government Printing Office, 1896.

Smith, James Morton, ed. *The Republic of Letters: The Correspondence between Thomas Jefferson and James Madison, 1776–1826.* New York: Norton, 1995.

Tocqueville, Alexis de. *Democracy in America.* Ed. J. P. Mayer and Max Lerner, trans. George Lawrence. Norwalk, CT: Easton, 1966.

Washington, George. *George Washington: Writings.* Ed. John Rhodehamel. New York: Library of America, 1997.

———. *Papers of George Washington: Presidential Series.* Ed. W. W. Abbot and Dorothy Twohig. Charlottesville: University Press of Virginia, 1993.

———. *The Writings of George Washington.* Ed. John C. Fitzpatrick. 39 vols. Washington: U.S. Government Printing Office, 1938.

Wilkinson, James. *Memoirs of My Own Times.* New York: AMS, 1816.

Wilson, James. *Selected Political Essays of James Wilson.* Ed. Randolph Adams. New York: Alfred A. Knopf, 1930.

### SECONDARY

Adair, Douglass. *Fame and the Founding Fathers: Essays by Douglass Adair.* Ed. Trevor Colburn. New York: Norton, 1974.

Ammon, Harry. *The Genet Mission.* New York: Norton, 1973.

———. *James Monroe: The Quest for National Identity.* New York: McGraw-Hill, 1971.

———. "James Monroe and the Election of 1808 in Virginia." *William and Mary Quarterly,* 3rd ser., 20 ( Jan. 1963): 33–56.

———. "The Richmond Junto, 1800–1824." *Virginia Magazine* 61 (Oct. 1953): 395–418.

Appleby, Joyce. *Capitalism and the New Social Order.* New York: New York University Press, 1984.

———. *Liberalism and Republicanism in the Historical Imagination.* Cambridge, MA: Harvard University Press, 1992.

———, ed. *Recollections of the Early Republic: Selected Autobiographies.* Boston: Northeastern University Press, 1997.

———. "Republicanism in Old and New Contexts." *William and Mary Quarterly,* 3rd ser., 43 (1986): 20–34.

———. *Thomas Jefferson.* New York: Times Books, 2003.

Bailyn, Bernard. *The Ideological Origins of the American Revolution.* Cambridge, MA: Belknap, 1965.

Banning, Lance. *Conceived in Liberty.* New York: Rowman and Littlefield, 2004.

———. "Jeffersonian Ideology Revisited: Liberal and Classical Ideas in the New American Republic." *William and Mary Quarterly,* 3rd ser., 43 (1986): 4–19.

Beard, Charles. *An Economic Interpretation of the Constitution of the United States.* New York: Macmillan, 1913.

Becker, Carl. *The Declaration of Independence: A Study in the History of Ideas.* New York: Vintage, 1922.

Bemis, Samuel Flagg. *John Quincy Adams and the Foundations of American Foreign Policy.* New York: Knopf, 1949.

Bilder, Mary. *Madison's Hand: Revising the Constitutional Convention.* Cambridge, MA: Harvard University Press, 2015.

Blanning, T.C.W. *The Short Oxford History of Europe: Nineteenth Century.* Oxford: Oxford University Press, 2000.

Boller, Paul F. "George Washington and Civilian Supremacy." *Southwest Review* 39 (Winter 1954).

———. *Presidential Anecdotes.* New York: Penguin Books, 1981.

Bond, Beverly. *The Monroe Mission to France.* Baltimore: Johns Hopkins Press, 1907.

Boorstin, Daniel. *The Image: A Guide to Pseudo-Events in America.* New York: Harper and Row, 1964.

Brant, Irving. *The Fourth President: A Life of James Madison.* Indianapolis: Bobbs-Merrill, 1970.

Braudy, Leo. *The Frenzy of Renown: Fame and Its History.* New York: Oxford University Press, 1986.

Brecher, Frank. *Negotiating the Louisiana Purchase: Robert Livingston's Mission to France, 1801–1804.* London: McFarland, 2006.

Brown, Ed Everett. *The Missouri Compromise: Letters of William Plumer.* New York: Da Capo, 1970.

Burstein, Andrew. *Jefferson's Secrets: Death and Desire at Monticello.* New York: Basic Books, 2005.

Chambers, William Nisbet. *Political Parties in a New Nation: The American Experience, 1776–1809.* New York: Oxford University Press, 1963.

Cheney, Lynne. *James Madison: A Life Reconsidered.* New York: Viking, 2014.

Cogliano, Francis. *Thomas Jefferson: Reputation and Legacy.* Charlottesville: University of Virginia, 2006.

Cohen, Bernard. *Science and the Founding Fathers: Science in the Political Thought of Jefferson, Franklin, Adams, and Madison.* New York: W.W. Norton, 1995.

Colburn, Trevor. *The Lamp of Experience: Whig History and the Intellectual Origins of the American Revolution.* Chapel Hill: University of North Carolina, 1965.

Combs, Jerald. "The Origins of the Monroe Doctrine: A Survey of Interpretations by United States Historians." *Australian Journal of Politics and History* 27, no. 2 (1981): 186–96.

Craven, Wesley Frank. *The Legend of the Founding Fathers.* New York: New York University, 1956.

Cresson, William. *James Monroe.* Chapel Hill: University of North Carolina, 1946.

Cunliffe, Marcus. *George Washington: Man and Monument*. Boston: Little, Brown, 1958.

Cunningham, Noble. *Jefferson and Monroe: Constant Friendship and Respect*. Chapel Hill: University of North Carolina Press, 2003.

———. *The Jeffersonian Republicans: The Formation of Party Organization, 1789–1801*. Chapel Hill: University of North Carolina Press.

———. *Jefferson vs. Hamilton: Confrontations That Shaped a Nation*. Boston: Bedford, 2000.

———. *The Presidency of James Monroe*. Lawrence: University Press of Kansas, 1996.

———. *In Pursuit of Reason: The Life of Thomas Jefferson*. Baton Rouge: Louisiana State University Press, 1987.

Dangerfield, George. *Chancellor Robert R. Livingston of New York*. New York: Harcourt, Brace, 1960.

———. *The Era of Good Feelings*. New York: Harcourt, Brace, 1952.

Davies, Norman. *Europe: A History*. New York: Harper Perennial, 1996.

DeConde, Alexander. *Entangling Alliance*. Durham: Duke University Press, 1958.

Diggins, John Patrick. *The Lost Soul of American Politics: Virtue, Self Interest, and the Foundations of Liberalism*. New York: Basic Books, 1984.

Dixon, Peter. *George Canning: Politician and Statesman*. New York: Mason/Charter, 1976.

Donovan, Frank. *Mr. Lincoln's Proclamation*. New York: Dodd, Mead, 1964.

Dunn, Susan. *Dominion of Memories: Jefferson, Madison, and the Decline of Virginia*. New York: Basic Books, 2007.

Durant, Will. *The Story of Philosophy: The Lives and Opinions of the Great Philosophers of the Western World*. New York: Simon and Schuster, 2005.

Eaton, David. *Historical Atlas of Westmoreland County*. Richmond: Dietz, 1942.

Elkins, Stanley, and Eric McKitrick. *The Age of Federalism*. New York: Oxford University Press, 1993.

Ellis, Joseph. *American Sphinx: The Character of Thomas Jefferson*. New York: Vintage Books, 1997.

———. *His Excellency: George Washington*. New York: Alfred A. Knopf, 2004.

Erikson, Erik. *Dimensions of a New Identity: The 1972 Jefferson Lectures in the Humanities*. New York: W.W. Norton, 1974.

Fenessy, R. R. *Burke, Paine, and the Rights of Man: A Difference of Political Opinion*. The Hague: Martins Nijhoff, 1963.

Ferling, John E. *The First of Men: A Life of George Washington*. Knoxville: University of Tennessee Press, 1988.

Fischer, David Hackett. *Washington's Crossing*. Oxford: Oxford University Press, 2004.

Fiske, John. *The Critical Period of American History, 1783–1789.* Boston: Houghton, Mifflin, 1889.

Forbes, Robert. *The Missouri Compromise and Its Aftermath.* Chapel Hill: University of North Carolina Press, 2007.

Formisano, Ronald. "Deferential Participant Politics: The Early Republic's Political Culture, 1789–1840." *American Political Science Review* 68, no. 2 (1974): 473–87.

Freeman, Joanne B. *Affairs of Honor: National Politics in the New Republic.* New Haven, CT: Yale University Press, 2001.

Fritz, Caitlin. *Our Sister Republics: The U.S. in an Age of American Revolutions.* New York: Norton, 2016.

Furet, Francois. *The French Revolution.* Cambridge, MA: Blackwell, 1988.

Furstenberg, Francois. *In the Name of the Father: Washington's Legacy, Slavery, and the Making of a Nation.* New York, Penguin, 2006.

Gay, Peter. *The Enlightenment: An Interpretation.* 2 vols. New York: Knopf, 1966.

Gilman, Daniel. *James Monroe.* New York: Houghton Mifflin, 1898.

Gordon-Reed, Annette. *The Hemingses of Monticello.* New York: Norton, 2008.

Graebner, Norman, ed. *Ideas and Diplomacy: Readings in the Intellectual Tradition of American Foreign Policy.* New York: Oxford University Press, 1964.

Gummere, Richard. *The American Colonial Mind and the Classical Tradition.* Cambridge, MA: Harvard University Press, 1963.

Hall, Kermit. *The Oxford Guide to the Supreme Court of the United States.* Oxford: Oxford University Press, 2005.

Hartz, L. *The Liberal Tradition in America.* New York: Harcourt, Brace and Jovanovich, 1955.

Heidler, David S., and Jeanne T. Heidler. *Henry Clay: The Essential American.* New York: Random House, 2011.

———. *Old Hickory's War: Andrew Jackson and the Quest for Empire.* Mechanicksburg, PA: Stackpole, 1996.

Hickey, Donald R. "The Monroe-Pinkney Treaty of 1806: A Reappraisal." *William and Mary Quarterly,* 3rd ser., 44 (Jan. 1987): 65–88.

Hofstadter, Richard. *The Idea of a Party System: The Rise of Legitimate Opposition in the United States, 1780–1840.* Berkeley: University of California Press, 1969.

Howland, Edward Tatum. *The United States and Europe, 1815–1823: A Study in the Background of the Monroe Doctrine.* New York: Russell & Russell, 1936.

Kaminski, John P., ed. *Founders on the Founders.* Charlottesville: University of Virginia Press, 2008.

Ketcham, Ralph. *James Madison: A Biography.* New York: Macmillan, 1971.

———. *Presidents above Party: The First American Presidency, 1789–1829.* Williamsburg: University of North Carolina Press, 1984.

Kirk, Russell. *John Randolph of Roanoke.* Indianapolis: Liberty, 1951.

Knott, Stephen. *Alexander Hamilton and the Persistence of Myth*. Lawrence: University Press of Kansas, 2002.

Koch, Adrienne. *Power, Morals, and the Founding Fathers*. Ithaca, NY: Cornell University Press, 1961.

Kohn, Richard H. "The Inside History of the Newburgh Conspiracy: America and the Coup-de-tat." *William and Mary Quarterly*, 3rd ser., 27 (1970): 187–220.

Leibiger, Stuart. ed. *A Companion to James Madison and James Monroe*. Malden, MA: Wiley Blackwell, 2013.

Lewis, James, Jr. *The American Union and the Problem of Neighborhood: The United States and the Collapse of the Spanish Empire, 1783–1829*. Chapel Hill: University of North Carolina Press, 1998.

———. *The Louisiana Purchase: Jefferson's Noble Bargain*. Chapel Hill: University of North Carolina Press, 2003.

Lewis, Jon E. *The Mammoth Book of Eyewitness Ancient Rome*. New York: Carroll and Graf, 2003.

Liell, Scott. *46 Pages: Thomas Paine, Common Sense, and the Turning Point to Independence*. Philadelphia: Running Press, 2003.

Longmore, Paul. *The Invention of George Washington*. Berkeley: University of California Press, 1988.

MacMullen, Ramsay. *Christianizing the Roman Empire*. New Haven, CT: Yale University Press, 1984.

May, Ernest. *The Making of the Monroe Doctrine*. London: Harvard University Press, 1975.

Mayer, David. *The Constitutional Thought of Thomas Jefferson*. Charlottesville: University Press of Virginia, 1994.

McColley, Robert. *Federalists, Republicans, and Foreign Entanglements*. New Jersey: Prentice Hall, 1969.

McDonald, Forrest. *The Presidency of George Washington*. Lawrence: University of Kansas Press, 1974.

McNamara, Peter. *The Noblest Minds: Fame, Honor, and the American Founding*. New York: Rowan and Littlefield, 1999.

McPhee, Peter. *Robespierre: A Revolutionary Life*. New Haven: Yale University Press, 2012.

Meacham, Jon. *Thomas Jefferson: The Art of Power*. New York: Random House, 2012.

Middlekauff, Robert. *The Glorious Cause: The American Revolution, 1763–1789*. Oxford: Oxford University Press, 1982.

Moore, Glover. *The Missouri Controversy, 1819–1821*. Lexington: University of Kentucky Press, 1966.

Morgan, George. *The Life of James Monroe*. Boston: Small Maynard, 1921.

O'Brien, Conner Cruise. *The Long Affair*. Chicago: University of Chicago Press, 1996.

Onuf, Peter. *The Mind of Thomas Jefferson*. Charlottesville, VA: University of Virginia Press, 2007.

Owsley, Frank, Jr. *The Creek War and the Battle of New Orleans, 1812–1815*. Tuscaloosa: University of Alabama Press, 2000.

Owsley, Frank, Jr., and Gene A. Smith. *Filibusters and Expansionists: Jeffersonian Manifest Destiny, 1800–1821*. Tuscaloosa: Alabama University Press, 1997.

Pancake, John S. "The Invisibles: A Chapter in the Opposition to Madison." *Journal of Southern History* 21, no. 1 (1955): 17–37.

Pangle, Thomas. *The Spirit of Modern Republicanism: The Moral Vision of the American Founders and the Philosophy of John Locke*. Chicago: University of Chicago Press, 1988.

Pasley, Jeffrey L., Andrew W. Robertson, and David Waldstreicher, eds. *Beyond the Founders: New Approaches to the Political History of the Early American Republic*. Chapel Hill: University of North Carolina Press, 2004.

Perkins, Bradford. *The First Rapprochement: England and the United States, 1795–1805*. Philadelphia: University of Pennsylvania Press, 1955.

Perkins, Dexter. *The Monroe Doctrine: 1823–1826*. London: Oxford University Press, 1932.

Peterson, Merrill D. *The Jefferson Image in the American Mind*. New York: Oxford University Press, 1960.

———. *Thomas Jefferson and the New Nation*. New York: Oxford University Press, 1970.

Pocock, J.G.A. *The Machiavellian Moment*. Princeton, NJ: Princeton University Press, 1975.

Poston, Brook. "Bolder Attitude: James Monroe, the French Revolution, and the Making of the Monroe Doctrine." *Virginia Magazine of History and Biography* 124, no. 4 (2016): 282–315.

———. Review of *The Papers of James Monroe: Selected Correspondence and Papers*. Vol. 4, *1796–1802*; Vol. 5, *1802–1811*, by Daniel Preston. *Journal of the Early Republic* 36, no. 3 (2016): 567–73.

Pratt, Julius W. "James Monroe." In *American Secretaries of State and Their Diplomacy*, ed. Samuel Flagg Bemis, 201–81. New York: Alfred Knopf, 1927.

Rahe, Paul. *Republics: Ancient and Modern*. Vol. 1, *The Ancien Regime in Classical Greece*. Chapel Hill: University Press of North Carolina, 1994.

Rappaport, Armin, ed. *The Monroe Doctrine*. New York: Holt, Reinhart and Winston, 1964.

Reinhold, Meyer. *The Classick Pages: Classical Reading of Eighteenth-Century Americans*. University Park: Penn State University, 1975.

Remini, Robert. *Andrew Jackson & His Indian Wars*. New York: Viking Penguin, 2001.

Richard, Carl. *The Founders and the Classics: Greece, Rome, and the American Enlightenment*. London: Harvard University Press, 1994.

———. *Greeks and Romans Bearing Gifts: How the Ancients Inspired the Founding Fathers*. New York: Rowman and Littlefield, 2009.

Risjord, Norman. *The Old Republicans: Southern Conservatism in the Age of Jefferson*. New York: Columbia University Press, 1965.

Robbins, Caroline. *The Eighteenth-Century Commonwealthman*. Cambridge, MA: Harvard University Press, 1959.

Rossiter, Clinton. *Seedtime of the Republic*. New York: Harcourt, Brace, 1953.

Russell, Greg. *John Quincy Adams and the Public Virtues of Diplomacy*. Columbia: University of Missouri Press, 1995.

Scarry, Robert J. *Millard Fillmore*. London: McFarland, 2001.

Scherr, Arthur. "James Monroe's Political Thought: *The People the Sovereigns*." In *Companion to James Madison*, ed. Leibiger, 324–42.

———. "The Limits of Republican Ideology: James Monroe in Thermidorian Paris, 1794–1796." *Mid-America* 79, no. 1 (1997): 5–45.

Seavy, Ormond. *Becoming Benjamin Franklin: The Autobiography and the Life*. University Park: Pennsylvania State University Press, 1988.

Selby, John. *The Revolution in Virginia, 1775–1783*. Williamsburg, VA: Colonial Williamsburg Foundation, 1988.

Sexton, Jay. *The Monroe Doctrine: Empire and Nation in Nineteenth-Century America*. New York: Hill and Wang, 2011.

Shalev, Eran. *Rome Reborn on Western Shores: Historical Imagination and the Creation of the American Republic*. Charlottesville: University of Virginia Press, 2009.

Sharp, James Rogers. *American Politics in the Early Republic: The New Nation in Crisis*. New Haven, CT: Yale University Press, 1993.

Sheldon, Garrett Ward, and C. William Hull. *The Liberal Republicanism of John Taylor of Caroline*. Madison, NJ: Fairleigh Dickinson University Press, 2008.

Skeen, Carl Edward. *John Armstrong Jr*. Syracuse: Syracuse University Press, 1981.

———. "Monroe and Armstrong: A Study in Political Rivalry." *New York Historical Society Quarterly* 57 (Apr. 1973): 121–47.

———. "Mr. Madison's Secretary of War." *Pennsylvania Magazine* 100 (July 1976): 336–55.

Smith, Robert W. *Keeping the Republic: Ideology and Early American Diplomacy*. Dekalb: Northern Illinois University Press, 2004.

Smith, William Raymond. *History as Argument: Three Patriot Historians of the American Revolution*. Paris: Mouton, 1966.

Spurlin, Paul Merrill, ed. *The French Enlightenment in America: Essays on the Times of the Founding Fathers*. Athens: University of Georgia Press, 1984.

Stagg, J.C.A. *Mr. Madison's War: Politics, Diplomacy, and Warfare in the Early American Republic 1783–1830*. Princeton, NJ: Princeton University Press, 1983.

Strauss, Leo. *On Tyranny*. Ed. Victor Gourevitch and Michael S. Roth. Chicago: University of Chicago Press, 2000.

Stryker, William. *Battles of Trenton and Princeton*. Boston: Houghton Mifflin, 1898.

Tucker, Robert, and David Hendrickson. *Empire of Liberty: The Statecraft of Thomas Jefferson*. Oxford: Oxford University Press, 1990.

Unger, Harlow. *The Last Founding Father: James Monroe and a Nation's Call to Greatness*. Cambridge, MA: Da Capo, 2009.

Walsh, James. *Education of the Founding Fathers of the Republic: Scholasticism in the Colonial Colleges; A Neglected Chapter in the History of American Education*. New York: Fordham University Press, 1935.

Walters, Raymond. *Albert Gallatin: Jeffersonian Financier and Diplomat*. New York: Macmillan, 1957.

Ward, Harry M. *The American Revolution: Nationhood Achieved*. New York: St. Martin's, 1995.

Weber, Max. *The Protestant Ethic and the Spirit of Capitalism*. Ed. Richard Swedberg. New York: Norton, 2009.

Weeks, William Earl. *John Quincy Adams and American Global Empire*. Lexington: University Press of Kentucky, 1992.

Whitaker, A. P. *The United States and the Independence of Latin America, 1800–1830*. Baltimore: Johns Hopkins Press, 1941.

Wills, Gary. *Inventing America: Jefferson's Declaration of Independence*. Garden City, NJ: Doubleday, 1978.

———. *James Madison*. New York: Times Books, 2002.

Wilmerding, Lucius. *James Monroe: Public Claimant*. New Jersey: Rutgers University Press, 1960.

Winterer, Caroline. *The Culture of Classicism: Ancient Greece and Rome in American Intellectual Life, 1780–1910*. Baltimore: Johns Hopkins University Press, 2004.

Winthrop, John. "A Model of Christian Charity." 1630. Published 1838, *Collections of the Massachusetts Historical Society*, 3rd ser., 7, 31–48. Published online 1996, Hanover Historical Texts Collection, Hanover College website, https://history.hanover.edu/texts/winthmod.html.

Wood, Gordon. *The Creation of the American Republic*. Chapel Hill: University of North Carolina Press, 1969.

———. *Empire of Liberty*. Oxford: Oxford University Press, 2009.

———. *The Radicalism of the American Revolution*. New York: Knopf, 1991.

# INDEX

BROOK POSTON is associate professor of early American history at Stephen F. Austin State University. He is the author of several journal articles, including "'Bolder Attitude': James Monroe, the French Revolution, and the Creation of the Monroe Doctrine" in the *Virginia Magazine of History and Biography*.

CPSIA information can be obtained
at www.ICGtesting.com
Printed in the USA
LVHW090101291218
602082LV00004B/13/P